Dynamics of Media Editing

For my mom, Lynn, who always would tell me,
"Go look it up. You have a dictionary in there,"
instead of telling me how something should be spelled, and my father,
Frank, who taught me how to hustle while I waited; for my wife,
Amy, who gives me the time, space, love and support to write all this stuff, and
my daughter, Zoe, who always wants to know,
"Did you put me in your new book?" Always, sweet pea. Always.

Dynamics of Media Editing

Vincent F. Filak

University of Wisconsin–Oshkosh

Los Angeles | London | New Delhi
Singapore | Washington DC | Melbourne

FOR INFORMATION:

CQ Press

An imprint of SAGE Publications, Inc.

2455 Teller Road

Thousand Oaks, California 91320

E-mail: order@sagepub.com

SAGE Publications Ltd.

1 Oliver's Yard

55 City Road

London, EC1Y 1SP

United Kingdom

SAGE Publications India Pvt. Ltd.

B 1/I 1 Mohan Cooperative Industrial Area

Mathura Road, New Delhi 110 044

India

SAGE Publications Asia-Pacific Pte. Ltd

18 Cross Street #10-10/11/12

China Square Central

Singapore 048423

Printed in the United States of America.

ISBN: 9781506379135

Acquisitions Editor: Lily Norton

Content Development Editor: Anna Villarruel

Editorial Assistant: Sarah Wilson

Production Editor: Bennie Clark Allen

Copy Editor: Jim Kelly

Typesetter: Hurix Digital

Proofreader: Jen Grubba

Indexer: Jeanne Busemeyer

Cover Designer: Janet Kiesel

Marketing Manager: Staci Wittek

This book is printed on acid-free paper.

Certified Chain of Custody
Promoting Sustainable Forestry
www.sfiprogram.org
SFI-01268

SFI label applies to text stock

19 20 21 22 10 9 8 7 6 5 4 3 2 1

BRIEF CONTENTS

DETAILED CONTENTS

PREFACE

Nearly 20 years ago, I was in a parking structure in downtown Las Vegas when I realized why editing can't just be "a newspaper thing." As I plugged coins into the meter, I saw a sign telling me that if the machine "failes to operate," I should call a certain number to get my money back.

As the years went on, I collected a number of examples of what happens when people fail to edit properly. I have a picture of a South Bend, Indiana, billboard that trumpets the area's "Pubic Schools." I have a tweet noting that a man "shit and killed himself." I have a press release that touts the opening of a "pubic library."

Beyond such simple, gut-wrenching errors, other problems germane to editing also emerged in these forms of media. News releases promoted events without explaining where they would take place. Advertisements used such awful images and design that it looked like a grenade hit a paint store. Websites had links that went nowhere or everywhere. The premise that someone should be careful, double-check information and provide clean content seemed antiquated at best.

The goal of this book is a simple one, mirroring the goal "Dynamics of Media Writing" had for writers: Provide a set of transferrable, universal editing skills to all media practitioners and then show how those skills apply to the practitioners' specific areas of interest. The outcome of approaching editing in this way should make content clearer, stronger and better for all media consumers.

THE AUDIENCE-CENTRIC APPROACH

Beyond making copy cleaner and content clearer, the purpose of this text is to shift the focus of editors toward taking an audience-centric approach to their work. Readers have more media competing for their attention than ever before. To really reach their audiences, media practitioners must spend less time writing and editing for themselves and more time finding ways to serve the readers. This book espouses an audience-centric philosophy, which clearly places the readers at the forefront of its actions and suggestions. That said, the book does not require that you pander to the basest interests of your readers to grab as many eyeballs as you can. Instead, it proposes a simple philosophy: You're not working for yourself. You're working for your readers. Work accordingly.

CONTENT AND ORGANIZATION

Much like "Dynamics of Media Writing," this book looks to serve a broader array of students than those who hope to work as copy editors. The first four chapters of the book provide the broad strokes of life as a media editor, including how best to reach an audience, how to work as a manager and how to apply legal and ethical standards to your work. The next four chapters provide you with the basics of editing that will matter to anyone who enters any aspect of editing. These chapters focus on punctuation, grammar, style, structure, content development and headlines. The third set of chapters involves the use of visual elements to augment your publication, regardless of which area of the field you enter. We discuss graphics, photography and design from a variety of perspectives and an inclusive point of view. Finally, the last four chapters take a chapter-by-chapter approach to outline editing issues pertaining to specific areas of the media: news, social media, public relations and marketing. These chapters use the prior sections of the book as a lens through which to view these topics and should give you a sense as to where the bedrock principles apply and how each media area requires variations of these rules.

FEATURES

You should notice a few features that repeat throughout the book. The goal of these elements is to draw attention to key aspects of each chapter, simplify important concepts and provide you with additional material where you need it most. Here are the main features you will see in the text:

Helpful Hints

Each chapter features at least one "breakout box" that provides key information on a topic that will matter to you as you move forward. In some cases, these boxes include a series of crucial definitions, while in other cases they outline some broader concepts to help clarify topics of interest. It's easy to skip these when told to read a chapter, figuring those ideas won't ever end up on a test. However, I'd ask you to take a look at them for your own benefit and see what's in there. They're called "helpful" for a reason.

View From a Pro

The inclusion of professional thoughts in this book is meant to help you see some of the areas in which editing applies to a wide array of careers and fields. Each professional provides key information about a topic of interest within the chapter as well as some sage words of advice to students as they look to apply this text to their career goals.

The Big Three

By the time you get to the end of a chapter, it can feel like you were just fed information with a steam shovel. Questions about what you just read abound: How much of this should I memorize? How much will matter for future chapters? What really matters?

To help simplify things, I crunched down each chapter into The Big Three, a highlight reel of the main points that matter most for each chapter. This should make it easier to know what you need to know most and help you recall key concepts as you move forward.

Review, Discuss and Practice

Each chapter closes with a collection of review questions and exercises to help you put the information you just read into practice. The goal here is to give you a chance to take a deeper look at the ideas the chapter raised and to help you apply your new skills in a writing or an editing exercise.

ACKNOWLEDGMENTS

This book would not be what it is today without Kenneth L. Rosenauer, who brought me in on a textbook project nearly a decade ago. His willingness to work with me over the years on that book helped create this one. I am grateful for his contributions to this text, especially the chapters on punctuation and word choice. The book you see here would be seriously diminished without his work in those areas.

I also owe Tim Gleason of UW Oshkosh a huge debt of gratitude for taking the time to help me understand the nuances of photography and assisting me in building the photo chapter. There is no way I could have done it without him.

Special thanks to Brody Karmenzind, Penny Fisher, Frank LoMonte, Allison Hantschel Sansone, Brian Cleveland, Chris Drosner, Reed Fischer, Lindsay Powers, Will Vragovic, Kori Rumore, Kyle Ellis, Amy Fiscus, Kelli Bloomquist, Elizabeth Connor and Eve Peyton for providing great professional perspectives on the key tenets of this book.

Thanks also to Fred Vultee for allowing me to use his fantastic "5-Minute AP Style Guide" (again), to Patrick Garvin and the Boston Globe for the use of their graphics and to the Advance-Titan staff for its provision of design elements.

I am constantly indebted to SAGE, especially Terri Accomazzo and Anna Villarruel for their constant willingness to work through whatever problems arise in my books, and there have been plenty. I also owe a major debt of gratitude to Jim Kelly, whose copy editing has kept me from looking like an idiot in multiple texts (including this one).

I always feel like I forgot someone when I write these things, and I'm sure that 10 seconds after it presses, I'll remember something I should have written. For this I apologize in advance, so please know I'm always so very grateful for everything people have done for me on a daily basis that makes it possible for me to do this work. My forgetfulness seeks only to reinforce the two important maxims I learned along the way from the great journalism teachers and pros I have known:

1. Everybody needs an editor, or maybe two or three of them.

2. Journalism is never done. It's just due.

SAGE Publishing gratefully acknowledges the following reviewers for their kind assistance:

Sandra Earley, *Savannah State University*
Sara Kelly, *National University*
Chandra K. Massner, *University of Pikeville*
Gary H. Mayer, *Stephen F. Austin State University*
Dr. Emmanuel U. Onyedike, *Virginia Union University*

ABOUT THE AUTHOR

Vincent F. Filak, PhD, is an award-winning teacher, scholar and college media adviser who serves as a professor of journalism at the University of Wisconsin Oshkosh, where he primarily teaches courses on media writing and reporting. Prior to his arrival at UWO, he served on the faculty at Ball State University and also taught courses at the University of Missouri and the University of Wisconsin–Madison. He also previously worked for the Wisconsin State Journal and the Columbia Missourian newspapers.

Filak has earned the Distinguished Four-Year Newspaper Adviser award from the College Media Association for his work with the Advance-Titan, UWO's student newspaper. CMA previously honored him as an Honor Roll Recipient for his work as the adviser of the Daily News at Ball State. The National Scholastic Press Association presented him with its highest honor, the Pioneer Award, "in recognition of significant contributions to high school publications and journalism programs."

As a scholar, Filak has received more than a dozen top conference paper awards, including those from the Association for Education in Journalism and Mass Communication, the Broadcast Education Association and the International Public Relations Society of America. He has published more than 30 scholarly, peer-reviewed articles in top-tier journals, including Journalism and Mass Communication Quarterly, Journalism and Mass Communication Educator, Newspaper Research Journal, the Atlantic Journal of Communication, Journalism: Theory, Practice and Criticism, the Howard Journal of Communication, Educational Psychology and the British Journal of Social Psychology. He is also the winner of CMA's Nordin Research Award, which goes to the best research paper completed on a topic pertaining to media advisers within a given year.

He has published several textbooks in the field of journalism, including "Dynamics of Media Writing" (SAGE), "Dynamics of News Reporting and Writing" (SAGE), "Convergent Journalism" (Focal) and "The Journalist's Handbook to Online Editing" (with Kenneth L. Rosenauer; Pearson).

He lives in Omro, Wisconsin, with his wife, Amy, and their daughter, Zoe.

1 AUDIENCE-CENTRIC EDITING

The one thing all media professionals have in common is the need to reach an audience. News journalists, public relations practitioners, advertising professionals, marketers and social media managers all know that without an audience, nothing they do will matter. The goal of this book is to approach each area of the media field through the lens of **audience centricity**, so we can come to a shared understanding of how to define an audience. We also need to determine what media content appeals to readers and what editors can do to help their media outlets connect with them.

Editors need to keep the audience in mind when assigning work, editing content and disseminating their products to consumers. An audience-centric piece is one that puts the focus on the people reading the content, not on the writer, the editor or the organization. Above all else, it should tell a story of some kind that engages the readers, makes them care about what they have seen and then connects them to future content from the author or the outlet. To that end, when we discuss the idea of "storytelling" in this book, it isn't a "newspaper thing" but rather a broader understanding of how best to reach the audience in a clear, valuable and meaningful way.

If you don't keep the audience in mind when editing, you will drive people away from your media outlet. As you read through any written piece, ask a few of the following audience-centric questions:

LEARNING OBJECTIVES

After completing this chapter, you should be able to:

- Understand why media professionals need to value the audience now more than ever.

- Know the key questions editors must ask of themselves to better understand and serve their audience.

- Understand what makes media users different today than in previous generations and how to use that knowledge to best serve your readers.

- Define an audience through demographic, geographic and psychographic elements.

- Apply the five elements of interest that attract readers: fame, oddity, conflict, immediacy and impact.

- Who cares about this story?

- Why should they care?

- Can I complete the sentence "This matters because . . ." as it relates to this story?

- Do the readers have everything they need to know about this story?

- Has the story kept the attention of the readers?

- Has the story been written at the appropriate level for this audience?

- Does the story tell the readers something new and/or different?

Unfortunately, this level of analysis has been undercut through the reduction of media staffs and the 24/7 pressures of getting content out on all platforms. In other cases, a sense of tradition and heavy reliance on news-writing staples have sapped copy of an audience-centric focus. Good editors will find a way to balance the pressure to perform for an organization and the needs of a readership to shape valuable content in a way that satisfies key interests of both sides.

For example, if you receive a report on a city council's decision to use a plot of land for a park instead of a set of condominiums, you need to know who is in your audience and what will most interest them. An editor for a newspaper might place the focus on the **5W's and 1H** elements of this issue. The editor will have a reporter dutifully explain the outcome of the vote, provide quotes from both sides of the vote and get reaction from people this decision most directly affects. This editor understands that the paper's audience is large, heterogeneous and likely to care about this issue in a variety of ways.

On the other hand, a public relations professional might edit this piece to accentuate one side of the topic, as it reaches an audience with a narrower interest. If that professional worked for a parents group, the focus might be more on the "win" for the park and what it means for families in that area. If that professional worked for the construction firm that lost the condominium project, the focus would shift to the "loss" at the council meeting and what the firm planned to do next. In each instance, the vocabulary, the emphasis and the approach will change on the basis of the people these editors wanted to reach with their content.

EDITING FOR AN AUDIENCE

When it comes to editing, we can easily get lost in the minutiae. "Farther" versus "further," "that" versus "which" and "who" versus "whom" can pull us deeply into the forest and have us staring at those particular trees. The idea of **microediting** is important, and we will discuss that at length later in the text, but if you spend all your time picking at the bark on the tree and ignoring the fact that you're in a forest, nothing you do will matter. Understanding the big picture starts with understanding your readers and what they demand of you. Here are a few things to keep in mind when you start picking through copy:

Don't Edit for Yourself

This applies to all media professionals, from newspaper and broadcast reporters to public relations practitioners and social media professionals, and editors serve as both the first and last lines of defense against this problem. When you assign something to a writer, it pays to spend some time discussing what you each think is important in the piece. At this point, you can emphasize your understanding of the audience's needs and see what the writer has to say on this issue. If you apply this lens early for your writers, they can more easily focus on specific elements of the story they want to tell and understand what to do and why.

When a writer turns in a draft of a piece, you can see how well the audience's needs are reflected in it and if it needs some fine-tuning. Depending on how much time you have to work on the piece and the availability of the writer, you can dig into the piece and tweak it to best emphasize those audience-centric elements of it. Before publishing the piece, you should work through the questions listed above and see how well the story addresses them. This will give you the chance to make any final corrections you see as necessary or important.

Determine How Your Readers Consume Your Work

Editors have to consider more than just what the content will be, but how it will be consumed. In previous generations, each branch of the media had clear and simple rules for each type of piece it produced. Newspaper stories published content in column inches on a printed page, with briefs usually being about 4 inches each and standard news stories sitting between 12 and 14 inches. Press releases ran one to two typed pages, depending on the topic. Advertisements mirrored these needs, with 30-second TV spots and quarter-page print ads.

Today, each of these media disciplines must reach readers on multiple platforms in various forms. Newspaper editors have to consider how a story will read in print, online and on mobile devices. Public relations practitioners now must reach people who are too lazy to scroll past the first screen of an email, while advertisers need to consider everything from sponsored tweets to native advertising. The choices of platforms and approaches can be dizzying and lead editors to revert to the tried and true standards of their old platforms, thus leaving readers disappointed.

The best way to address these problems is to figure out how your readers want the content you provide. Do they read you primarily on mobile devices, thus forcing you to improve your focus and tighten your writing in hopes of enticing them to click for more content? Do they read you in the "dead-tree edition," culling through paper press releases or turning broadsheet pages of news, thus placing more emphasis on headlines, structure and layout? Do they seek you as a force of habit, showing up at your website or picking up your paper every day? Conversely, do they only read things "pushed" to them through opt-in functions they clicked at some point in time or via social media connections they trust?

Also, when and where do they consume your content? Is it in a rushed fashion as they head into work, hoping to use what you have to say to spark conversations during the day, or is it on leisurely weekends when they want to plan projects, be entertained or simply decompress? Your goal as an editor is to shape content that works for the readers and gives them what they want from you. If you can do this, you will have a much larger and more engaged audience.

Cater, Don't Pander, to Your Readers

One of the worst slippery-slope arguments associated with audience centricity is the idea that if we give people what they want, all media outlets will be reduced to showing videos of cats that can play the piano. A clear line exists between audience centricity and pandering to the lowest common denominator, and it is an editor's job to keep the content on the right side of it.

Pandering media outlets slather clickbait headlines on stories that have nothing to do with the actual content of the piece, solely to gain website traffic. These outlets also feed readers "junk food" like cat videos and ideologically reinforced memes to support the readers' point of view, regardless of the accuracy of it. The goal here is like a version of an old "me generation" slogan: "The person who dies with the most clicks wins."

Audience centricity looks at what readers want and need to find a middle ground for the development and transmission of content. This means avoiding press releases that always start with "Company XYZ announces . . ." or news stories that tell readers, "The city council held a meeting . . . ." It means digging into what is already there that matters and refocusing it to best serve the audience members in a way they will accept and understand. It means breaking away from tradition that exists simply because it is traditional while still adhering to time-honored values because they matter. You want to develop a relationship with your readers in an honest, valuable and meaningful way. Editing to emphasize the simple philosophy of "We know you and we think you might need this information" will make your content audience-centric without forcing you to rely on hyperbolic headlines and vapid videos.

VIEW FROM A PRO
BRODY KARMENZIND

Courtesy of Brody Karmenzind

Brody Karmenzind is a partner manager at Facebook, where he serves as the main point of contact for a group of key advertising agency partners. As such, he understands the importance of researching, developing and understanding an audience.

"Facebook as a company is mission driven and all decisions are made through the lens of fostering community and bringing people together," he said.

Karmenzind graduated with a degree in journalism before heading off to Pandora Radio, where he started as an entry-level account development specialist on the sales team in Oakland, California. After working at Pandora for a number of years and moving into the more senior role of account representative, he was recruited by Facebook.

In working with these innovative companies, Karmenzind said he found a common thread of learning how to adapt the organizational approach to fit what readers, viewers and listeners wanted.

"Facebook's philosophy is to use bottom-up feedback to inform product development," he said. "One example of this is the Facebook marketplace. Research teams noticed that folks were selling products on groups and they decided to create the marketplace. After six months, the marketplace had hundreds of millions of products being sold because they followed user behavior using bottom-up feedback versus top-down strategy. Listening to key audiences to inform decisions and being able to pivot quickly is crucial in the digital age."

Karmenzind said his time as a journalism major helped him understand not only how to listen to the audience members but also how to deliver content to them.

"The two advantages I carry with me after going through a journalism program are the ability to concisely deliver a high-impact message to an audience and the ability to move fast," he said. "Due to my ability to write in a concise way, I have been able to effectively communicate with both internal and external stakeholders. In addition, the ability to move fast, be scrappy and knowing that things are never done, they are just due has served me extremely well and has set me apart in the workplace."

In looking at where media is going, he said he has seen some shifts currently that will likely continue as readers and viewers evolve their consumption habits.

"I think there's been a pivot to less objective stories to drive clicks to fuel revenue," he said. "I think this is a mega trend in the wrong direction and more objective news sources will be the winners over the next few years as people lose trust in extremely subjective news organizations."

With digital media continually evolving and audiences continuing to fragment, Karmenzind said nobody truly knows what media companies will need to do in the future to remain audience-centric. That said, Karmenzind said he had a few "best guesses" as to how things would unfold over the next several years.

"If I had to predict where the industry is going I would predict a few things," he said. "The formats will change in the short term into two spectrums: 1. A vertical story format that is very casual, fast paced and not polished is going to explode and will replace newsfeeds. . . . 2. Extremely digestible text formats that will exist in messenger-based platforms will also become popular that folks can digest while engaging with news-based messenger bots."

MEDIA USERS TODAY

To begin understanding media users, you need to know how people use the media. News organizations no longer have the luxury of serving as gatekeepers for all content. Advertisers are no longer at the mercy of one newspaper or three networks to disseminate a message to a large audience. Public relations practitioners are no longer restricted to sending out press packets and hoping for the best. The democratization of media production and consumption created through the internet and other digital media tools means the playing field is much wider than it once was. This provides all media professionals with exciting opportunities and dangerous pitfalls, as they ply their trade in unfamiliar ways to reach an audience they might not fully understand.

Today, digital media has become the dominant force in the field of news, with new platforms and new sources supplanting traditional journalists. According to a 2017 study from the Pew

Research Center and the Knight Foundation, roughly 93 percent of adults get some of their news online via computers or portable devices. News consumers use both "legacy" media outlets, such as traditional print or broadcast sources, and digital-only products. The study also revealed that 43 percent of people frequently get their news from digital sources, which puts this category only 7 percentage points behind television.[1] In the 2016 version of the study, that gap was 19 points, thus demonstrating how digital media is gaining ground quickly. It's also worth noting that the study revealed that advertisers continue to increase spending online, moving from 33 percent of all advertising placed in 2015 to 37 percent in 2016.

The shift from a mass medium to a series of niche sites to serve fractured audiences can be a concern to those media outlets that don't embrace this change. To better assist you as an editor for an outlet that seeks to reach this new generation of readers, consider these things that make this generation of audience members different from those of the mass-media era:

Unlimited Access to Information

Journalists may continue to hold medium-based biases, but consumers have no use for these demarcations. The audiences aren't tied to specific platforms or outlets as much as journalists, who saw themselves as being "newspaper reporters" or "broadcasters," might be. They want information that is stimulating and valuable to them on whatever platform they have available whenever they feel the need for it. In short, they see media content as a buffet of information, and they have many choices as to how, when and where they will consume it.

Editors have to adjust their approach to planning content and providing it to the audience members. A study by the Media Insight Project revealed that audience members of all generations are essentially platform neutral when it comes to how they consume information. Readers tend to select media they see as important to them and then adopt a "my media" attitude when comparing it with the less trustworthy category of "the media."[2] As far as how people want content, this study showed that advertising developed specifically for mobile devices was more successful than pieces built for other forms of media and merely transferred over.

Today's readers also have a heightened **surveillance need**, meaning they constantly want to be aware of anything happening that might be relevant, useful or interesting. This concept is captured in the "fear of missing out," or "FOMO," phenomenon that emerged in the digital era. If publications aren't providing information as quickly as the audience members want, the readers will likely go elsewhere.

This study and others like it demonstrate an uncomfortable point for all media professionals: The audience members are calling the shots now, and we need to adapt to their consumption habits. Media professionals can't hope that what we think matters will serve our readers. We have to adjust our way of thinking to address content and delivery systems to meet the needs of the audience. Editors are crucial in this aspect of audience outreach, as they traditionally determine what gets done, how it is delivered and when readers get to see it.

The Fake News Phenomenon

Hoaxes, falsehoods and flat-out lies have populated the media landscape for generations. Everything from ongoing coverage in the Weekly World News of "Bat Boy" to the "shocking" tales of the National Enquirer have kept people entertained and amused as they pondered the ridiculous nature of these stories. What makes today's **"fake news"** more concerning is the massive amount of it and the degree to which people believe it.

Thanks to digital media, lies really can outpace the truth and dig deeper into the minds of the readers. A 2018 study from the Massachusetts Institute of Technology found that falsehoods posted on social media are six times faster in their spread and deeper in their penetration than true stories. Although truth tellers had more Twitter followers, posted more often and had stronger overall networks, people who passed along blatantly fake news saw their content shared and liked at an exponentially faster pace.[3]

As an editor, you must work diligently to push past this glut of fake news and demonstrate your importance as a media outlet and a truth teller. As everyone else is crying out for attention, you need to showcase the value of accurate, quality information. That means spending more time carefully editing your copy, fact-checking your information and providing the best possible version of reality to your readers. Don't give people a reason to think you lie to them.

Short-Attention-Span Syndrome

The days when people sat down and thoughtfully consumed every word of a daily newspaper or a monthly magazine are long gone. When it comes to today's media, people are more easily distracted than a cat chasing a laser pointer. A recent study by Microsoft revealed that people have an attention span of 8 seconds, which is 1 second less than that of a goldfish.[4] That means we need to work harder to trim out excess content, eliminate boring verbiage and focus our audience on the things that matter most.

The content we provide must demonstrate value and must constantly prod the audience to read on. If we fail to grab and keep their attention, we have failed to do our job as media professionals. Although a great amount of that rests in the hands of the writers and reporters, editors have to work more diligently than ever to assure the readers that all the weakest elements of a piece have been eliminated and that only the valuable content remains.

Loss of Gatekeeping

Editors used to be the primary "gate" through which information had to pass in order for content to see the light of day. A study by David Manning White in the 1950s helped coin the term "**gatekeeping**," which referred to the process by which editors would select or reject content for publication. In his work, he found that news values and the editor's personal preferences tended to inform what made the cut.[5]

In that day and age, whatever content the gatekeeper deemed unworthy would not reach the readers. However, today, with the explosion of media outlets, the reduction of barriers to entering the media universe and the ability to reach well beyond physical and geographic borders, editors are no longer the tail that wags the dog. Therefore, the goal of good editors is to stay ahead of the curve when it comes to providing content to readers while also feeding them important content.

You might feel conflicted between trying to make your audience happy by providing "junk food" stories and trying to tell a diminishingly interested group of people things you think they should know. You can't force people to value content the way you want them to, but you can work to understand your audience members so that you can reach them in ways they find acceptable. If you apply the interest elements outlined in this chapter to the premise of audience centricity, you can serve more as a tour guide than a gatekeeper, a role that will make your readers appreciate you and your publication.

HOW TO DEFINE YOUR AUDIENCE

If you want to reach your audience, you first have to understand who is in your audience and what they want from you. Media professionals often make the mistake of writing things they want to tell people instead of writing things readers would want to hear. This approach creates a disconnect between readers and content providers, leaving both sides unsatisfied. Consider the following ways in which you can analyze and organize your audience:

Demographic Information

Demographics include "check-box items" like age, gender, race and education and allow you to create population segments that share specific interests. These simple but useful categories can help you obtain a rough sketch of the people you want to serve and thus allow you to better understand what they want from you. For example, if the readership of your company newsletter is primarily men in their 60s who have worked at your company for at least 25 years, the topics of that publication would likely include stories on aging and retirement. If the publication's audience were men and women, ages 22 to 30, with less than two years at the company, topics such as childcare, health benefits and job training might matter more. As an editor, understanding these demographic trends will allow you to better select content for your media outlet.

HELPFUL HINTS
HOW TO FIGURE OUT WHO IS IN YOUR AUDIENCE

Knowing the demographic, psychographic and geographic demarcations of your audience can help you determine how best to serve the people in it. Consider these ways to help you gather that information:

Readership surveys: The benefit of a readership survey is to allow you to determine who is paying attention to your media outlet, what they like about it and what they want you to change. This is a nice way to check in and see if you fully understand who is in your audience and what it is they value about your publication. Association Media and Publishing[6] states that readership surveys allow you to see if the needs of your readers have changed over time and where you stand in terms of readership value and to determine if the content you are providing still draws people to your publication. Most organizations see these as something worth doing every year or two, especially in this rapidly changing media environment.

Focus groups: If the surveys give you the broad answers to the "who," "what," "when" and "where" of your readership, focus groups can help you better understand "why" and "how" your readers consume your content. Marketing and advertising professionals frequently use these groups to figure out the rationale behind an audience's behavior. This kind of research has great value to news editors as well, given that the raw data provided by a survey can provide only the broad strokes when it comes to audience analysis. A focus group gives you the chance to delve more deeply into specifics, and the thoughts of one participant can spark ideas in others, giving you a robust understanding of their needs.

Website analytics: The use of analytics online provides website owners with the opportunity to fine-tune their operations in many key ways. Media providers have the opportunity to understand what draws people to their site, what the people do when they are there and what pieces are the most popular. A survey of the American Society of News Editors found that nearly 97 percent of newsrooms monitor web traffic in this fashion, examining the number of visitors, visits, pageviews and more.[7] The benefit of this type of analysis is that it can give you a clear sense of how people behave when not being directly asked to explain themselves. In addition, studying these data can help you better craft questions for your surveys and your focus groups.

Psychographic Information

Although demographic information has value, it doesn't fully define who your readers are from an intrinsic point of view. **Psychographics** help you assess an audience on the basis of personality traits, personal values and strength of attitudes on given topics. These data can help you tap into social ideologies and determine how important specific things are to your readers. For example, some areas of the country rely heavily on agriculture while others tilt toward technology. Some segments of the population have extremely deep faith in a particular religion while others see it as a tangential part of their lives. Certain universities place a great deal of value on the success of their sports teams while others are less interested in athletic conquests. If you understand these values your readers espouse, you can tailor your content to entice them.

Geographic Information

Digital media has removed the geographic tethers from us in terms of being able to get information from a variety of places, regardless of where we are or from where that information comes. That said, people still care greatly about things happening near them, which is why **geographic information** remains a valuable way to examine your audience. People will care if their local gas station gets robbed or if their area school district is raising funds for building repair. Newspapers keep track of how far their circulation reaches and how many readers they have in a given area, and website managers can use analytics to locate the source of their most frequent visitors. As an editor, knowing where your readers are will help you determine how to allocate resources and coverage to give the audience information about things happening near them.

WHAT ATTRACTS AN AUDIENCE?

Editors have power over content selection, and that is a powerful opportunity to reach an audience. However, to connect with those readers effectively, editors need to understand what draws an audience to content and then accentuate those elements in their daily work.

The book "Dynamics of Media Writing" outlines a series of **interest elements** that can help you attract an audience.[8] To remember them, you can use the mnemonic FOCII, like the plural of focus, but with two I's. Here is a brief examination of those elements:

Fame

People always have an interest in what celebrities are doing at any point in time. This is why the president of the United States has 53 million followers, but Kim Kardashian West has almost 60 million. Still, both of them pale in comparison to singer Katy Perry, who boasts 106 million followers. **Fame** is a powerful force, and it draws people's attention, so it is worth your time as an editor to find ways to emphasize this interest element.

Fame tends to fall into two basic categories: long-term and short-term fame. The people who are long-term famous tend to be heads of state, actors and singers. In addition, they can be infamous people like serial killers Charles Manson and Jeffrey Dahmer. The short-term famous are living out their "15 minutes" of fame, such as lottery winners, Instagram celebrities and news oddities.

Oddity

Speaking of odd things, people like to see things they've never seen before. The rarities in society get attention, which is why people will stand in line to see the "Mona Lisa" or the original copy of the Declaration of Independence. It's also why people will head to Mike Carmichael's house in

Alexandria, Indiana, to see "The World's Largest Ball of Paint."[9] When a story contains a rarity, a special item or something that's just plain weird, you should accentuate that **oddity**. Any time you can clearly show that something is the largest or the smallest or the longest or the shortest, you can use special elements to attract readers and keep them hooked.

Conflict

When two or more people or groups of people have mutually exclusive goals, conflict will result. **Conflict** can be as large as two countries that each want to win a war or as small as two people vying for the same seat on a bus. As an editor, you can find conflict in most of your stories, but you shouldn't become myopic about it. Just because you have a reporter who has "both sides" of a story, it doesn't necessarily follow that the story is complete. Make sure that all participants within a conflict dynamic are represented and that all of the "sides" get their say when explaining a situation. If a writer has only a two-dimensional story, you should send that person back into the field to seek a more nuanced approach to this interest element.

Immediacy

The concept of "FOMO" or "fear of missing out" isn't a recent trend. People have had a basic survival need for surveillance since the first humans walked the Earth. Things have changed since those early days, when inattentive behavior could turn a person into an animal's lunch or a rival clan's victim, but this primal need still exists, and media professionals can take advantage of it. Digital outlets provide media professionals with a 24/7 window to reach interested audience members with important information. These ever-present platforms will give you the opportunity to keep people in the loop as events unfold. Editors must weigh the value of the content against the issue of **immediacy**. Accuracy and audience centricity remain at the core of all we do in media, so if you are an editor, you have to keep these concepts front and center so you don't deluge your audience with a glut of unengaging or erroneous content.

Impact

The concept of audience centricity is central to this interest element. People will always want to know "Why should I care?" when they encounter information via the media. Good editors will find a way to answer that question and demonstrate a particular story's effect on the readers. You can show people how content will have an **impact** on them in a variety of ways. Quantitative impact will showcase the range of the impact, such as how many people were displaced during a hurricane, while qualitative impact shows the severity of an impact, such as the death of one student at your college.

THE BIG THREE

Here are the three key things you should take away from this chapter:

1. **Pay attention to your readers:** Editors can no longer take the audience for granted. They must adjust to the needs, interests and whims of readers when it comes to content, format and platform. The loss of gatekeeping functions, the rise of alternative outlets and the presence of social media mean that editors have to define and serve the audience first and foremost.

2. **Emphasize interest elements:** As you work with writers to develop content, focus on the FOCII of each piece of copy, and place additional emphasis on these interest elements. Fame, oddity, conflict, immediacy and impact have demonstrated the ability to draw audience members to stories and engage the content, so use them to your advantage.

3. **Make people care:** If the story doesn't tell people why they should care about something, they probably won't. In most cases, an editor's job is to help a writer craft a message that reaches the readers, so focus on the people in your audience and give them a reason to think your stories matter to them. If you can't complete the sentence "This matters because . . ." the readers probably won't understand why it does.

KEY TERMS

5W's and 1H 2
audience centricity 1
column inches 3
conflict 9
demographics 7
fake news 5

fame 8
FOCII 8
gatekeeping 6
geographic information 8
immediacy 9
impact 9

interest elements 8
microediting 2
oddity 9
opt-in 3
psychographics 8
surveillance need 5

DISCUSSION QUESTIONS

1. In examining the media you consume, how well do these media outlets do in terms of creating audience-centric content? Do you feel the media outlets cater to you or pander to you? What drives you to continually use these outlets?

2. In your opinion, how problematic is the "fake news" phenomenon in the media world today? How do you think this will affect your ability to reach an audience as an editor of any type of media?

3. Of the five interest elements outlined in this chapter (fame, oddity, conflict, immediacy and impact), which ones do you see most frequently highlighted in the media outlets you use? Which ones are least prevalent? Compare your answers with those of your classmates and see if any trends emerge.

WRITE NOW!

1. Explore the demographic aspects of your school in terms of age, gender, race and the in-state/out-of-state gap. Look for specific details you think define your school. Then review the campus publication that serves students. This could be a school website, a student newspaper or another media outlet. On the basis of the demographic aspects of your school, how well do you think this outlet is doing at serving its audience? What makes it good or bad? What could be improved? Write a short essay that outlines your findings about your school as well as your thoughts on the student publication you analyzed.

2. Define the concept of gatekeeping and explain how it had strength in previous generations, when traditional media dominated information dissemination. Then, explain why gatekeeping has eroded over time and how this will affect you as a media editor. How do you see your job as an editor in today's media environment? Do you see it as being easier or harder than the work of editors who operated in the glory days of gatekeeping? Explain your answers in a short essay.

3. Select a copy of a local or student media outlet and analyze its use of the five interest elements. How many stories contain one or more of these interest elements? How well did the authors and editors do at accentuating the elements within the stories? What would you do differently and what would you leave the same? Explain your thoughts in a short essay.

Visit **edge.sagepub.com/filakediting** to help you accomplish your coursework goals in an easy-to-use learning environment.

2 EDITORS AS LEADERS AND MANAGERS

When you become an editor, you likely will be both excited and frightened. If you find yourself afraid about what you will do or how well you will do it, don't feel bad. Fear is a natural and normal response to taking on this important position in your organization.

Fear comes from a lot of places, but you need to find ways to deal with that fear. If you can do that, your anxiety will become a mild bit of trepidation that you can use to your advantage.

In this chapter, we will review the ways in which you can prepare to be an editor and the jobs associated with the editor position. We will discuss the various aspects of the job as well as how to identify your managerial style. Although the whole book will discuss the various aspects of line-level editing, this chapter will spend the most time on the managerial and oversight aspects of the job.

PREPARING TO BE AN EDITOR

The key to becoming a good editor is to feel like you have a handle on what is about to happen to you. Just like you prepared as a writer to go get a story or as a photographer to shoot an event, you need to prepare as a leader.

You want to find out from previous and current editors what was expected of them. What did they do? What didn't they do? What do they wish they had done? What should they have never done?

You should talk to the people who will now work for you. Find out from them what they think the previous editor did well and what they think that editor did poorly. Some people will be less than honest, while others will tell you exactly what they think. In either case, start with what they tell you and see to what degree you can meet their needs. (We will talk more about working with people later in the chapter.)

Look through editorial policy manuals, the position's job description and any other documents related to your position as editor. If you find that these items don't exist, see if people who hold positions similar to yours at other organizations have something they'd be willing to share. Then, use those materials to build your version, on the basis of the parameters of your position and the way in which your organization operates.

> ## LEARNING OBJECTIVES
>
> After completing this chapter, you should be able to:
>
> - Understand crucial elements of preparation necessary to be an editor.
>
> - Assess various leadership approaches and identify the one that best fits your approach to management as an editor.
>
> - Identify the various jobs associated with an editor position and determine ways in which they can be done properly.
>
> - Understand ways in which you can coach writers to improve their overall work.
>
> - Apply a basic editing process to a piece of copy as you work with a colleague to improve a story.

In short, dig through filing cabinets, read like crazy, shake more hands than a politician and get a full lay of the land. This preparation will help you feel more confident as you move into your editorial position. Beyond that, here are some simple tips to help you ease into your leadership role:

Know What You Know and What You Don't Know

The first myth of editing is that you know everything. You'd be more likely to find someone who walked on the moon than you are to find an editor who knows everything. Fortunately, it's not a key requirement of the job.

You need to know a lot, but being a good editor requires more than using your head as a repository for useless knowledge. You don't have to know which way every city council representative voted on every issue for the past 10 years. You don't have to know which streets have seen the most car accidents after each snowfall. You don't have to know what the average daily rainfall in Nigeria was in 2017.

What you do need to know is where to find these types of things when they come up in your job. For example, while most editors have a working knowledge of the Associated Press Stylebook and the organization's local stylebook, they don't have these books memorized backward and forward. Instead, they know the kinds of things that are in the books and how to look them up.

Deal With Your Mistakes Honestly

The best way to deal with a mistake is not to make it in the first place. That being said, you probably will err from time to time, and you will need to deal with the fallout from those errors.

You might make an error, or someone working for you might have made it. Errors can be sins of omission or commission. They can be things that affect the public or create problems internally for you and your staff.

You need to recognize when you have made a mistake and then talk to the people who need to know about it. You should explain what happened and what steps you will take to rectify the situation.

Editors who fail to admit mistakes or blame mistakes on others tend to be bad leaders. They come across as arrogant and self-important, two traits that don't endear them to staff members. Mistakes are part of life, so take responsibility for them and move on.

Be a Problem Solver

The ability to solve problems is one of the most important skills you can have as an editor. You need to be able to assess the situation, determine what has gone wrong, seek out solutions and keep applying them until something works.

Bad leaders react to problems in a number of counterproductive ways. Some fly into a rage or complain bitterly about the problem. Others are defeatists, who self-flagellate and wonder why the problem has occurred. Still others sit idly by and hope the problem will go away somehow. No matter which approach that bad leader takes, the problem will remain.

As an editor, you want to make sure that you're looking for solutions, not complaining about the problem. Keep your head level and start working through the problem.

THE JOB OF AN EDITOR

An editor is required to do more than parse the difference between "farther" and "further" or "that" and "which." An editor is a leader, a colleague and a servant. A good editor is also a coach, a traffic cop and even a junior psychologist.

The job comes with a set of tasks that remain consistent from organization to organization. Beyond those basics is a long list of things you might be expected to do. Just like editing itself, management is part art and part science. It will take time and experience to determine what you should and shouldn't do.

Below are the rudimentary tasks you will perform as an editor. The list is by no means exhaustive and can vary on the basis of the specific editorial role you have, but it should give you an idea of what you are getting into.

Assign Content

An editor can shape the content of a publication through the assignment process. On the basis of the size of your staff and the scope of your publication, you can cover everything from speeches and meetings to investigations and features. In public relations, internal and external newsletters can provide readers with an intimate sense of how an organization or a client operates.

Organizations will have meetings to determine what content should be in a publication, on a website or part of a campaign. This is where editorial oversight comes into play and your role as a manager becomes vital. For example, many newsrooms have a daily editorial meeting to determine how they will approach each day's news. The staff members determine which stories will matter most to the audience, which stories will get the most coverage and what format that coverage will take. In the end, it's often up to the editor to make the final decision as to what needs to be covered and how that will be done.

Let's say you receive a press release regarding a carnival that a town in your coverage area is hosting. If you think this story is of little interest to your audience, you would have a reporter write a small piece based on the information in that release. If you think the story would be important to your readers, you would assign a reporter to cover the event.

Once you decide to cover the event more fully, you need to figure out how best to tell the story. You have multiple storytelling options to cover this event, including video, audio, text and still photography. Whether you use all or some of these tools will depend greatly on which ones you think will be most effective and which tools your audience members tend to embrace. With a story like a town carnival, chances are that photography and video will tell the story in a vibrant manner. A text story can support this material, but a standard feature story on this topic will be less engaging than the visuals.

Learning how to decide what needs to be covered and how best to cover it will be an important component of your job as an editor.

Edit and Write Copy

Much of this book will teach you specific ways to edit copy. It covers aspects of grammar, style and punctuation as well as issues of clarity, audience centricity and accuracy. It also discusses ways to effectively write teases, headlines and keywords.

HELPFUL HINTS
CHECKLIST OF IMPORTANT SKILLS

Basic Writing

- Have a firm grasp of grammar
- Understand style
- Know how to spell and what words actually mean
- Understand effective sentence structure
- Know how to use transitions to improve flow

Basic Marketing

- Know how to pitch a story to your audience
- Understand your audience
- Love data analysis
- Engage in search engine optimization

Basic Leadership

- Be firm yet flexible
- Understand various personality types and how to work with people who have them

- Be patient
- Know how to do multiple things at the same time
- Realize that you don't have to do everything better than everyone who works for you
- Show how you value the skills of others

Basic Computer Skills

- Don't fear technology
- Garner enough experience with programs to be proficient; expertise comes later
- Practice your skills when you are not on a deadline
- Learn the value behind a piece of software before trying to learn it
- Learn software for all of your storytelling approaches, including photo, video and audio
- Embrace social media

Each subsequent chapter will build on those specific ideas, but it's important to note here that going through the copy will be one of the most important things you do. Whether this editing process is easy or hard will be determined by how well you train your reporters and what you know about your audience.

Manage Staff

If you want to keep your organization operating smoothly, you must communicate effectively with your staff members. You want to know who is working on a piece, if it has problems, when it will be finished and what it will say. You also need to know what platforms the staff member will use to disseminate that content.

You can then communicate this information to other members of the staff and give them a sense of what will be forthcoming from your department that day. In addition, it will help you figure out if you will be able to promote your work to your audience members. If you promise part one of a three-part series for Monday, your readers will expect to see that story. If you promise a three-part series over three days, you want to make sure that the reporter isn't missing key information for the second part of the series.

Understanding what people are doing is important. This is where you serve as a traffic cop for your organization. The more organized you are, the better your content will be.

Work With Other Departments

Your role as an editor will vary on the basis of the size of your media organization and how far up the food chain you sit. Some editors oversee all the content for an organization's publications, including specialty publications for niche audiences as well as internal newsletters. Some editors oversee a platform, like a website, but leave the technical aspects of assignments and content dissemination to people below them. In some cases, a publication is composed of section editors who oversee specific parts of the publication, like news or sports. In other cases, editors are managers overseeing specific aspects of content, like photography or graphics. With that in mind, you will need to work across departments to incorporate text, visuals and design elements of storytelling as you work to create content.

You need to communicate effectively with the people who are providing you with content. If a photographer is accustomed to gathering only a few images for a magazine, you will need to explain how many you will need for an effective slideshow. If a writer is used to working for a traditional print publication, you will need to suggest ways to incorporate other storytelling tools, such as social media.

Understanding what content you need to make your publication work effectively will aid you in reaching out to other departments and helping them help you.

Update Information

One of the larger responsibilities you have is to update information as it continues to evolve. Readers want their information fast, and they won't wait for you to be ready to get it to them. If you don't keep things current, you can fall behind the curve and lose your audience in the process. Your job is to make sure they get the best and most up-to-date information possible. For example, if your organization is doing public relations for a charity fundraiser, people will want to know how well things are going. The use of social media and a strong web presence can help you let people know the minute you reached your goal.

You must make quicker decisions better if you want to survive as an editor in the digital age. In the days before the web became a powerful media outlet, print or broadcast reporters might have gotten away with sitting on a story for a day without losing the scoop. Now, if you sit on a story for an hour, your website might go from being first with the news to being last. Organizations that hoped they could dodge bad news by ignoring it or failing to respond to a single reporter's calls now have to deal with citizen journalists and bloggers who will break news on the basis of leaked information and inside sources.

Establish Guidelines for Publishing

A good editor understands when something should and shouldn't be published. Sometimes, it's a matter of the law; in other cases, ethics and taste dictate your course of action.

The editor feels pulled in two directions: the desire to publish content before others can and the desire to produce accurate and fair material. This isn't a new conundrum, as editors have always dealt with this dichotomy, but with the speed of the web, you are forced to make tougher decisions faster.

VIEW FROM A PRO
PENNY FISHER

Courtesy of Penny Fisher

Penny Fisher has spent the past decade in a variety of managerial roles, and at each stop, she has found herself balancing the needs of the big picture with the day-to-day grind of the office.

"Focusing on the big picture and small stuff at the same time is one of the biggest challenges I face," she said. "I get lost in pings and dings of emails, tweets, posts, voicemails, letters and more. I'm obsessed with responding to anyone who reaches out to me. I read every single email, and I can't go to sleep with unread emails. Throughout my career I have struggled with delegation. It's one of the hardest things to do as a manager and a leader. I've had to force myself to do it to find time to strategize and look at the big picture."

Fisher began her career in Florida working as a presentation editor for The Banner in Bonita Springs. She moved up to associate editor after a year, before becoming the managing editor of community publications for the Naples Daily News. She then took on the job of associate editor at the Daily News before being named the interim editor at the paper. In November 2016, the "interim" tag was removed, and she took over as the publication's editor.

The Naples Daily News serves as a primary news source for citizens of the area. Of the Naples primary market area, 67 percent of adults read a copy of the paper or visit the publication's website each week. The site, naplesnews.com, ranks No. 1 among adults in the area visiting local internet sites each month, with more than 7 million page views and more than 800,000 unique visitors each month.

With a staff of 55 that has to serve an actively engaged audience, Fisher said the biggest key to keeping the Daily News running on her end is communication.

"Communication is an extremely vital component of my leadership style," she said. "The editor team meets every morning at 9:30 a.m. for a digital huddle. We discuss digital wins from the day before and what's trending today. I ask about missed opportunities, and we determine ways to avoid them in the future. I ask them the same question every morning, 'What is Naples talking about today?'"

She said she also meets with the publication's planners each day, the management team once a week and the entire staff every other month.

"These meetings and emails can be a time suck for me, but I consider them to be valuable for the newsroom," she said. "These constant interactions help me keep the newsroom on the same page and keep us all moving forward in the same direction. I also think it's important to share a newsroom vision and goals at the beginning of the year. I have the highlights on the dry eraser board behind my desk as a constant reminder of where we want to be."

Aside from keeping the publication humming, Fisher said it is important to recognize good work and to show her staff members that she appreciates them.

"I find time to write letters of encouragement for staff members each month," Fisher said. "If someone is nailing a new initiative or putting in long hours on an investigation project or offered to help a colleague, I leave them a note on their desk. It's easy to get wrapped up in what we can do better and to constantly push and challenge everyone to be better. But, when someone is doing an excellent job, it's important to recognize that, too."

When it comes to taking on the role of an editor, Fisher said a lot of people get thrown into the role with little to no training. She said she entered management early in her career and didn't get a chance to take part in a professional training program for about seven or eight years. In the meantime, she said she relied on a lot of on-the-job training and good advice from valuable mentors.

"I have had some great mentors in my career," she said, "ones that talked with me about my goals and aspirations and helped me pave the path to get there. Each of them invested in my success. I also try to surround myself with people who are extremely intelligent and look at things differently than me. I like to have conversations and a development of ideas vs. yes men and women."

People who want to become successful editors and managers should learn to roll with the punches and embrace change, Fisher said.

"My best advice for journalists wanting to elevate their career is to look for opportunities to grow and to challenge yourself," she said. "Find some mentors inside and outside of the media industry. Learn from them and give back to others who look to you as a mentor."

If you publish information that is inaccurate or has ethical problems, you will damage your reputation and your relationship with your readers. If they feel you are not trustworthy, they can go to another source and establish a relationship with those journalists. If you establish a good set of publishing guidelines, you can make sure your readers get the best information as soon as it is ready to be consumed.

THE EDITOR AS A MANAGER

People are said to be "born leaders," but that's a bit of truth surrounded by a shroud of hyperbole. You aren't a born leader any more than you are a born basketball player, a born cellist or a born politician. You may possess leadership instincts that you can shape and hone through work and experience, but those gifts alone aren't enough to make you a good leader.

Editors are at a disadvantage when it comes to management because they aren't selected for the job the same way managers are in other fields. At most other jobs, good people are plucked from the rank and file and given a lot of training. The organization provides them with formal training, and bosses and coworkers help them fit into their new role.

In many media fields, the joke is that editors are staff members who have hung around the longest. When an editing job becomes available, someone in the chain of command says, "Hey, you're doing a great job in your position. We should promote you to this editor position." That promotion moves you to a job that requires a different set of skills, a different mindset and a different approach to journalism. Many places don't offer editors a set of management classes or even broader formal training. New editors get to "shadow" for a few days the person they are going to replace, and then they are on their own. It becomes sink or swim.

HELPFUL HINTS
DEFINE YOUR LEADERSHIP STYLE

Some editors view their position as a job. It beats wearing a hairnet in the cafeteria, and the pay is slightly better. Others view it as a responsibility that was handed to them by someone they trusted. Still others have a passion for the craft and want to excel at editing.

How you view your job can influence how you lead your staff. Although the list below isn't exhaustive, it covers a broad range of leadership styles. See which one fits you best:

Servant: These leaders believe they are there to help others at all costs. They work for their staff, provide a lot of support, seek contributions from many people and try to team-build as much as they can. The goal of a **servant leader** is to have a happy staff and good teammates who can work together to provide the best possible product.

Curator: These leaders are akin to museum curators. **Curators** know they don't own the organization, but they want to use their position for the betterment of the general public. They put on a display of talent and craft, using the pieces in the best way they know how.

Curators seek input but know they are ultimately in charge. They also know that when their turn as curator is over, they lock up the place and hand over the keys to the next person. When they are done, they know they did the best they could for all concerned but also know they were rewarded for their efforts.

Owner: These leaders believe they are in charge. They've got the keys to the bus, and they're driving it. They know people might not like their methods, but they get things done. They often are respected though not necessarily liked. **Owners** understand that a time will come when they are no longer in charge, but they don't like thinking about that. They have a vision as to how things need to be, and they have no problem changing things to make the place reflect their vision.

Teammate: These leaders view themselves as the first among peers and act accordingly. The goal of these managers is to be a part of the mix when decisions are made, but to make sure that they're not deciding everything for everyone. They jump in when a crisis occurs or a situation demands additional work. The **teammate** approach can win you the admiration of your staff, but it also has drawbacks if your staff requires more direction than collaboration. Some staff members will also take advantage of this "flatter" approach to leadership and ignore you or force you to exert your authority to rein them in.

As a leader, you will find positive and negative aspects of each of these leadership types. You will also find that few people fit neatly into one of these three categories.

The key to leading is to be yourself. If you're not a harsh taskmaster, don't try to be one because you think you should be. If you're not a warm person who gives a lot of hugs and pats on the back, don't try to be that way. You likely will come off seeming insincere.

Identify what type of leader you are and understand the ups and downs of that style. This will make things easier on you as an editor.

One of the biggest challenges in moving from a staff member to an editor is finding ways to work with others. Your job is no longer to be responsible only for you but for others as well. Even if you never edited a day in your life, you probably worked with a number of bosses, and they always seemed to be like snowflakes: No two are exactly alike.

Some bosses want to hear from you every single minute of the day. Others never want to hear from you. Some bosses are extremely detail oriented, and others are sloppy and careless. Some bosses feel the need to critique you constantly, and others never give you any feedback. The list of polar opposites and points along the spectrum can go on and on.

If you look back on those experiences honestly, you likely will find some managerial traits that were helpful and others that were annoying. You should take these traits as a starting point as you develop your approach to leadership.

If you hated a boss who never trusted you when you said you restocked a shelf or filed a form, be trustful of your employees. If you enjoyed hearing positive and negative, but constructive, feedback when you did a job, be someone who gives a lot of feedback to your writers.

This is not a perfect system, and you need to adjust your approach to management as situations arise. You might determine that after trusting a writer several times, that person doesn't deserve your trust. You might decide to give less feedback to all your writers than you initially wanted to because you don't have the time to do it for every staff member all the time. As you become acclimated to your job, you will figure out how to best meet the needs of your staff and your organization. If you change your approach to leadership, it doesn't make you a hypocrite. It makes you someone who is willing to adapt to your surroundings.

COACHING WRITERS

If you played any kind of sport, you know what a coach does. The coach yells, praises, argues, laughs and more, but the coach isn't playing. It's up to the players to play. The coach's job is to make them play better.

Good editors help their writers in the same ways coaches work with their players. Below you will find a few coaching tips for your writer-editor relationships.

Use Teamwork

Editors and writers work together as a team, just like coaches and players do. A good coach will prepare the players for the task at hand. A good coach will help players get ready for what they should expect from their assignments and offer suggestions as to how to work through any problems that might come up. Good coaches prepare their players.

When you prepare your writers for their assignments, you should follow the same tenets outlined above. You can help them get ready for their assignments, offer suggestions on how to complete their assignments and tell them what to expect when they get back from their assignments. This preparation can improve the quality of the product and the relationship between you and your writers.

Demonstrate Trust

A good coach trusts the players to make smart decisions. The coach also understands that sometimes things aren't as easy as they seem from the bench. If the players trust the coach and the coach trusts the players, a strong bond can form as they work for the betterment of the team.

Editors also have to rely on trust when they assign content to their staffers. Although you might have a sense of what you expect, it remains up to your staff members to create the content and serve the readers. For example, if you assign a writer to work with a client to launch a new publicity campaign, you might believe a serious tone will fit best for this content. However, if a writer meets with the client and finds that humor would work better, it is in your best interest to at least hear out that staffer. Good editors will allow some discussion and provide some level of trust in the staff members who work for them.

Ask Questions

Editors who have spent much of their careers as reporters have been trained to ask tough questions that poke at the credibility and veracity of the material they are receiving. Writers don't mind asking questions like these when they confront sources, but they hate when they have to respond to such questions. In other words, what's good for the goose is not good for the gander in their mind.

So, when you ask, "How good is this source?" or "Are you sure these figures are right?" your writer will likely become defensive. He might be sarcastic, indignant, angry or dismissive, but he is clearly not happy that you aren't seeing what he wrote as pure and inspired.

The way you phrase a question means a lot in how it is received. You want to make it clear to your writers that you are an advocate for them. The better you understand the piece of content, the better case you can make to better promote it or get it some visual elements. Also, you want to make sure that errors don't get into their copy, which will look bad for both of you. Writers will know more about their content than you do, so it is natural that you will have some questions. Make sure they understand what you want to know and why you want to know it.

THE BIG THREE

Here are the three key things you should take away from this chapter:

1. **Editing requires collaboration:** As an editor, you are in a position of authority, but nothing will work out well without the help of others. You need to have people working for you who trust you and other editors who want to help you. If you don't build an environment of teamwork, you will likely fail at your job.

2. **You don't have to be perfect:** As a leader, you will make mistakes, and others working for you will err as well. The best thing you can do is learn from those mistakes, fix them and move on. As Penny Fisher said, it helps to surround yourself with smart people who can provide you with insight and assistance. Don't think you must have all the answers to be successful.

3. **Edit on multiple levels:** Editing requires more than adhering to style and structure. You have to help writers improve their work, build stories that showcase the bigger picture and meet the audience's needs. Look for ways to incorporate the big picture and the small stuff at the same time as you look to reach your readers in an effective and valuable way.

KEY TERMS

curator 17

owner 17

servant leader 17

teammate 17

DISCUSSION QUESTIONS

1. In looking at the various aspects of an editor's job, which one do you feel most comfortable doing? Which one scares you the most? What makes you feel these ways about these particular aspects?

2. Reread the Helpful Hints box on the four types of basic but important skills necessary to be a good editor. How many of those skills did you check off? Which of the four areas did you have the most skills covered, and which area did you have the least? How do you see yourself improving on the area where you had the weakest level of proficiency?

3. What is it about you that makes you think you would be a good editor? What do you think would be your biggest weakness in terms of the requirements of the job, the management function and the coaching element? What do you think it would take for you to improve enough to feel confident in that aspect?

WRITE NOW!

1. Of the four leadership types listed in the chapter, which one do you think most accurately defines your approach to leading? Of all of the people for whom you have worked, which of them had a leadership style you really liked, and which type was it? Did you ever have a boss who led in a way you really disliked? What type of leader was this person, and why was the person's leadership problematic for you? Outline your thoughts in a short paper.

2. Compare and contrast the explanation here regarding the editor as a coach to any experience you had with regard to being coached. This could be something like working with a coach in a sport or working with a director in a play. Think about the positive and negative aspects of that experience and then relate them to how you could see things improving if they were done differently. Then, write up an outline of things you would want to do as an editorial "coach" and things you would avoid, on the basis of these reflections.

3. In her thoughts in the "View From a Pro" feature, Penny Fisher said this about balancing her responsibilities as an editor: "Focusing on the big picture and small stuff at the same time is one of the biggest challenges I face. I get lost in pings and dings of emails, tweets, posts, voicemails, letters and more. I'm obsessed with responding to anyone who reaches out to me. I read every single email, and I can't go to sleep with unread emails. Throughout my career I have struggled with delegation. It's one of the hardest things to do as a manager and a leader. I've had to force myself to do it to find time to strategize and look at the big picture." In thinking about the short-term and long-term aspects of the job of an editor, how do you think you would balance those elements? What benefits and drawbacks do you see in putting too much or too little time into either of those aspects? Write a short essay on this topic.

3 LAW AND ETHICS

Online media has forced the law to move beyond traditionally accepted views on what the press is and who journalists are. Much of our press law is rooted in the 19th and 20th centuries and clings to norms set forth in newspapers and magazines. Because of this, the web and digital media have spawned numerous problems for journalists, legal scholars and the general public.

Certain rules transfer nicely from print products to the online realm, while other laws differ drastically between the two media. Some elements of the law provide more freedom to news organizations than they do to public relations firms or advertising agencies. As an editor, you need to know your legal rights and responsibilities.

In this chapter, we will review the aspects of law you will face as an editor. We will outline how the laws apply to various forms of media. In addition, we will explain the ways you can defend yourself and your organization against legal action. Better yet, we will show you how to avoid getting into trouble in the first place.

FREEDOM OF THE PRESS AND COMMON MISCONCEPTIONS OF IT

The **First Amendment** to the Constitution guarantees freedom of the press, along with freedom of speech, freedom of religion, freedom to petition the government and freedom to peaceably assemble. In singling out the freedom of the press, the Founding Fathers placed a high value on media and gave media outlets exceptional rights and responsibilities.

The law has grown and changed over time, applying the First Amendment to various forms of media in different ways. For example, in 1942's Supreme Court case Valentine v. Chrestensen, the court ruled that advertising was purely commercial and did not enjoy the same First Amendment protection as did newspapers or similar media outlets.[1] However, the Central Hudson Gas & Electric Corp. v. Public Service Commission ruling of 1980 found that banning advertising does represent a violation of the First and 14th Amendments.[2]

The underlying value of the First Amendment is that it outlines the right to publish content freely without fear of governmental intrusion. This right traditionally has been associated with newspapers and magazines. Television and radio broadcasts are regulated by the **Federal Communications Commission**, which puts the government in an oversight role for these media, because of the public's ownership of the airwaves and the scarcity of the frequencies available for broadcast. As these issues do not apply to the web, courts have viewed online media as being akin to print and have afforded publishers the protections outlined in the First Amendment.

Here are some common misconceptions related to the First Amendment:

No One Can Stop You From Publishing What You Want

The First Amendment only guarantees that government agents or agencies can't exercise prior restraint, which is to say they can't prevent you from publishing something. Even this guarantee comes with some exceptions, such as infringing on copyright or trademark, which we will discuss below. Issues involving national security and some court-imposed gag orders can also limit free press and free speech. If you ignore a court order, you will find yourself in a good deal of legal trouble. If your media outlet is privately owned, a publisher can prevent you from publishing something. Other higher ranking editors can also stop you. At the high school level, the case of Hazelwood v. Kuhlmeier determined that principals can censor school newspapers if they can demonstrate a legitimate educational interest in doing so.[3] Private universities also can exercise censorship of student media because they are not governmental agencies and thus not subject to First Amendment freedoms. Just because the government can't stop you from publishing doesn't mean you can publish anything you want.

Freedom of the Press Protects You From Legal Ramifications

As an editor, you are given only **editorial discretion**. This does not mean that people will not be upset with whatever you publish. It also doesn't mean that if you are wrong, you will be free from legal repercussions. What it does mean is that government can't stop you from publishing something. After you publish the material, you are held to the same legal standards as anyone else. Just because you *can* publish things doesn't mean you *should* publish them.

The First Amendment Applies Only to Professional Media

The rise of blogging, Twitter and other forms of citizen journalism has rankled traditional media outlets. Newspapers, magazines, television stations and other "legacy" media have attempted to create a demarcation between themselves as professionals and others as being a second tier of writers and reporters. However, the First Amendment doesn't offer the media or media professionals any special rights. In this country, we do not license journalists, nor do we state that only professionals are protected. Instead, the law guarantees the right to a free press, regardless of who is running it. Even more, the First Amendment serves as the bedrock of our democratic system. It wasn't set up to establish a media hierarchy or offer media professionals special rights. It was meant to protect all of us from an overreaching government.

The Rights Established in the First Amendment Are Absolute

In theory, yes. In practice, no. Laws have been established and struck down over the years that have sought to prevent people from saying or publishing things that other people didn't like. In the World War I era, Congress passed the Espionage Act and the Sedition Act, which made it a crime to interfere with the war effort and to obstruct military recruiting efforts. These laws also put a damper on expression, as they made it a crime to publish or say anything that was viewed as disloyal to the country. The Smith Act in the 1940s also made it a crime to advocate the violent overthrow of the government. Other laws and rules have limited the freedoms noted within the First Amendment. Time, place and manner restrictions have been imposed upon speech and assembly. The fighting words doctrine notes that speech can be curtailed when the words are meant to do nothing more than incite people to a "breach of the peace." Some court cases, such as ACLU v. Reno, have also demonstrated that online obscenity can be unprotected. In short, while the First Amendment protects many things, it is always open to interpretation.

LIBEL

Anyone who publishes content can run the risk of defaming someone on a daily basis. People steal, lie, cheat and commit other illegal or immoral acts, and reporters are responsible for conveying that information to the public. Public relations practitioners must pair content with advocacy to draw attention to important issues, which leads to concerns regarding potential defamation risks. Even political advertising, which some courts have ruled to be almost bulletproof when it comes to **libel**, can include prejudicial and harmful commentary about candidates, political parties and organizations. The field is rife with risks that someone somewhere will not like what someone else published about him or her and thus threaten to sue. Editors in every area of the field must balance the risk associated with libeling someone against the public's right to know something.

Libel is the primary form of defamation that you will need to understand as an online editor. A few key elements included in many definitions of libel are:

- The material must harm a party's reputation.

- The material must be published (distributed to someone other than the offended party).

- The material exposes the party to hatred, contempt or ridicule.

- The party claiming libel must be identifiable.

It has also been said that you can't libel the dead, as only living people are legally allowed to make a claim of libel. Yet courts have allowed a libel case to continue when the person making the claim dies in the middle of a trial. Some states have considered laws that allow the next of kin to sue for libel when they can demonstrate that their reputations were hurt through libelous claims levied against their dead relative. Given these changes as well as the fluidity of the law, it's best to keep up to date on this issue.

The Student Press Law Center (SPLC) in Arlington, Virginia, has outlined a good checklist for determining libel. In order for someone to establish that he or she has been defamed, that person must prove each of these four elements:

Publication

The material must be disseminated to someone other than the person who is claiming to be libeled. You can call a classmate all sorts of names to her face without risking libel. It is mean, and it might be stupid, but it is not libel. However, if you post those thoughts on a blog, you could be in trouble. **Publication** can also include content in a press release, as was the case when an energy company sued an attorney in Georgia. Infinite Energy argued that David Pardue defamed the organization by stating that it "engaged in deliberate misinformation and scare tactics" in its dealings with his client, the Korean Cleaners Association of Atlanta.[4] Although an appeals court in 2016 cleared Pardue, the saga dragged on for years, going through several levels of litigation.[5]

Publication includes the republication of libelous statements other people make. When you are quoting neighbors in a dispute, for example, and one neighbor libels another, you can find yourself in hot water for republishing those statements. The defense of "Well, I just accurately repeated what they said, so I'm not responsible" isn't a defense at all.

Identification

The material must be "of and concerning" the person suing for libel. In many cases, the material names the person and thus establishes **identification**. For example, a story that says, "Mike Malinowitz, a junior at Smithville University, has been arrested on suspicion of stealing computers," makes it clear who is being accused of theft.

If your media outlet does not include a name in a story, it does not mean you didn't identify a person. Other identifying features within the material must disguise the identity of the person enough that he or she can't be reasonably identified. In addition, the material must not libel an uninvolved third party. If you were editing a story about a school with 100 teachers, you could hide an identity fairly easily: "A teacher at Smithville High School has been suspended after the school received a complaint that she punched a student." However, the more specific you get, the riskier it is: "A 35-year-old female music teacher, whose husband serves as the school's principal, has been suspended. . . ."

Large groups cannot be defamed, but courts have ruled that smaller groups (often viewed as having fewer than 25 members) can claim libel. Corporations and other private entities can also assert a libel claim under this standard.

Harm

The person suing must demonstrate that the published material does serious damage to his or her reputation. The standard for establishing harm varies on the basis of the context, the person, the community and other issues. If you published that a 27-year-old woman had sexual relations with a 28-year-old man, that material could be benign or defamatory. If the woman and man are married, the likelihood of harm coming from that publication is pretty low. However, if the woman is a Catholic nun and the man is a Catholic priest, the likelihood of harm is pretty high.

Some areas in which harm can occur include:

- Accusing someone of committing a crime

- Making sexual references, including intimations regarding sexual activities, sexual proclivities and sexual orientation

- Producing claims of unethical or unscrupulous behavior

- Associating someone with a contagious disease or unsavory actions

- Using statements that allege racism or other forms of bigotry

Fault

The person alleging libel must demonstrate that the reporter created harm through an act of commission (did something wrong) or omission (failed to do something he or she should have). The standard for establishing fault differs on the basis of the plaintiff in the case. Private individuals must only show that the defendant acted with **negligence**. Public figures must demonstrate that **actual malice** was present.

To establish negligence, courts use a reasonability standard, which questions whether the defendant was reasonably prudent or careful in reporting and publishing the material. In many cases, the courts will attempt to determine how much effort the defendant went through to avoid making a mistake.

For example, if your student paper publishes a story stating that a candidate for student body president was arrested on suspicion of stealing items from people in his residence hall, that candidate could sue for libel. If the reporter found a police report stating that charges were filed, talked to several students who noted that the candidate was around several rooms when the thefts occurred and found out from the school that the student was under investigation, this would put the paper on a strong footing. If the reporter talked to the candidate himself, and the candidate refused to comment on the situation, this would also help. However, if the

VIEW FROM A PRO
FRANK LOMONTE

Courtesy of Frank LoMonte

As an attorney with a strong interest in media law, Frank LoMonte finds himself working to help young journalists better understand their rights and responsibilities. One of the biggest issues he has seen in recent years, he said, is the concerns journalists have shown regarding student privacy.

"The biggest single issue has been the resistance in many high schools to using names and faces on the web," he said. "There is a powerful phobia that posting students' identifying information on a news web site will lead to liability suits against schools in the event that some harm comes to a student. While it's understandable to be conservative where student safety is involved, this really misconceives the level of information that is already in widespread public distribution."

LoMonte serves as the director of the University of Florida's Brechner Center for Freedom of Information. Prior to taking his position in Florida, he spent nine years as the executive director of the Student Press Law Center, where he worked to defend the rights of student journalists.

LoMonte said the Family Educational Rights and Privacy Act requires that schools safeguard confidential information that comes from student records. However, he noted, the information can be published, depending on how journalists get the information.

"The information in student news outlets does not come out of student records," LoMonte said. "Typically, it is volunteered by the students themselves, and people are always free to give out their own information."

The wide reach of the web has made journalists more aware of issues concerning privacy and libel, but LoMonte said many of the traditional media norms remain an editor's best guide.

"The best 'libel insurance' you can buy is simply to activate your internal fairness meter," he said. "If someone is being accused of behavior that you would personally find hurtful to your reputation, ask yourself whether you've really provided them ample opportunity for rebuttal."

Even with the advent of easily searchable archives and viral web stories, LoMonte said journalists still enjoy clear legal protections against libel claims.

"The courts are pretty protective of the media against stale libel claims, and the archiving of previously distributed content should be protected under the 'single publication rule,' which basically says that your time clock to file a defamation suit begins the first time that the material appears," he said. "If you wait 10 years until the material starts showing up in Google searches of your name, you've waited too long."

Conversely, he said, journalists shouldn't view the web as the place to publish material they wouldn't print in traditional media.

"As a general matter, it would be a very hazardous practice to relax one's libel standards because material is 'only' going online," LoMonte said. "There may be a false sense of comfort that errors are less permanent and more readily correctable online, but cached versions of erroneous material can live on, and even briefly publishing something false is still 'publication.'"

reporter had only one source for the story, failed to check with additional people, didn't contact the police or the university and published the material without offering the candidate a chance to comment, the paper would be on shaky ground.

In this case, the courts would need to establish if this person were a public figure or a private individual. Public figures who allege libel must demonstrate actual malice. Public figures include public officials who have some semblance of responsibility over public affairs and celebrities or others who have gained public notoriety. People who have involuntarily entered the public lexicon through the commission of crimes and people who have voluntarily entered the public eye through leadership roles in issues of public interest are also viewed as public figures. People in that last group are called "limited purpose" public figures and thus are subject to actual malice standards only as they pertain to their public actions.

If a public figure sues for libel, that person must establish that the publication either knew the material was false and published it anyway or had a reckless disregard for the truth, and this standard is often difficult to demonstrate. For example, in 2014, an Iowa state senator lost his defamation suit upon appeal to the state's supreme court because of this issue.[6] A lower court's decision stated that Rick Bertrand was libeled by a 2010 political advertisement that implied he sold deadly drugs to children while working for a pharmaceutical company. During that case, Bertrand demonstrated that he never sold the drug or owned the company, and he had presented evidence to that end to his opponent. However, Rick Mullin's campaign continued to run the ad. Despite this, Mullin's appeal to the Supreme Court was successful because the judges ruled that none of this rose to the level of "actual malice," the standard necessary for public figures.

SPLC recommends that you worry less about whether a person is a public figure and instead hold your work to the negligence standard. That more restrictive standard will help you avoid this distinction, and it will also lead to an overall stronger position in your defense.

TECHNIQUES TO AVOID LIBEL CONCERNS

Think of your editor's job as being similar to that of a hockey goalie: You are the last line of defense between what's coming at you and a negative outcome. While spelling and grammar errors can injure your organization's reputation, a libelous statement can do far worse things.

Here are some tips to help improve your libel-proofing skills:

Don't Buy the Brooklyn Bridge

If something seems too good to be true, chances are it is. If your weakest reporter returns from a mundane meeting with a fantastical story regarding corruption and money laundering, it is a pretty safe bet the story has a problem. However, situations are not always that clear cut. A source might tell a good reporter that a city official with a shady past is once again engaging in shady activity.

As a PR professional, a client might push you to use language in a press release that goes beyond what you feel accurately reflects the outcome of a lawsuit. If you feel pressured or uncertain about material that has the potential to libel someone, give it a second or third look. It is always better to be late on a story than it is to be wrong.

Remove Dangerous Modifiers

Adjectives and adverbs can add value, texture and richness to your copy. They can also put you into hot water if you are using them incorrectly. Some modifiers are vague and present few problems, such as referring to a child as "large" or "small." However, other terms can be problematic. When you include words like "fat" or "shrimpy" to modify your nouns, you are in trouble.

If your writers believe these words are accurate descriptors, have them provide information in their stories that supports these claims. Instead of having them write, "The corrupt senator testified at a hearing on Capitol Hill on bribery," have them rework the sentence to support the claim. "The senator, who faces six counts of receiving bribes, testified at a hearing on Capitol Hill." In short, don't tell your readers how to feel or what to believe. Give them the information available to you and let the readers figure out how they feel or what they believe on their own.

Be Careful With Crime

Anyone who publishes information regarding criminal acts must take care with legal terms. A person who has admitted to killing someone is not necessarily a murderer. That term is reserved for people found guilty of that charge in a court of law, and it requires that the person acted with cool deliberation or depraved indifference to human life. "Murder," "homicide," "manslaughter," "self-defense" and other terms can blur into one ridiculous mess. Make sure you know what the terms mean.

In addition, people in the United States are innocent until proven guilty. To that end, make sure writers don't say that people are arrested "for" something. They can be arrested on suspicion of something, and the city, county or state can then charge them with a crime. However, saying someone was arrested for murder or for burglary includes an implicit notion of guilt.

"Allegedly" Isn't Enough

Writers incorrectly believe the word "allegedly" will save them from libel suits. The word "allegedly" is a libel lawyer's dream because it provides no legal protection to the person who uses it. A story that calls someone "an alleged thief" or "an alleged rapist" is no different than one that calls the person a thief or a rapist. All "allegedly" does is indicate that someone has made an accusation. At this very moment, with no proof and no rationale, your professor can accuse you of cheating in your editing class. Now, you are "the alleged cheater." How does that feel?

Instead of relying on thinly veiled accusations, strengthen the writing and the reporting. Rely on attributions to help you here. Instead of writing, "Smith allegedly cheated on his taxes" or "Jones, the alleged killer, testified in court today," attribute the information to an official source or rely on provable facts. "According to IRS documents, Smith cheated on his taxes" works well, as does "Jones, who is charged with two counts of murder, testified in court today."

Don't Assume Anything

An adage in reporting states, "If your mother says she loves you, check it out." The same thing applies in editing when it comes to libel concerns. Make sure every fact is verified. Make sure every opinion is attributed. Make sure the story is strong, accurate and fair.

Edit Small Pieces of Copy Carefully

A grizzled veteran of many copy desks was fond of saying that you can drown just as easily in two inches of water as you can in the Pacific Ocean. His point was that a poorly written press release on a local pancake breakfast is just as likely to cause a problem as a giant story covering the seediest details of corruption.

Just because something is small, short or uncontroversial doesn't mean it is immune to libeling someone. Look carefully at headlines, captions, briefs and other mundane pieces of copy for potential libel. Mistakes can slip by easily in these areas. In addition, media professionals often cut corners when trying to fit all the relevant information into a 280-character tweet, thus leading to potentially erroneous claims. Always edit every piece of copy with care.

Ask for Help

If you don't understand something or are concerned about something, ask for help. Ask coworkers for their thoughts regarding the risks associated with a piece of copy. If you can't reach a consensus or the risks are too great, seek legal counsel. Once the material is published, you can't get it back.

DEFENSES AGAINST LIBEL

Even the most careful and diligent media professional can be sued for libel. If you find yourself or your organization in the midst of a suit, here are the primary ways you can defend yourself:

Truth

Truth wasn't always a defense against libel. The 1735 jury verdict in the case of John Peter Zenger helped establish that while material can be damaging to a person's reputation, if it is factually accurate, the publisher cannot be held liable. Today, truth remains your best defense against libel suits.

Most courts review the material in question to determine if it is substantially true as opposed to absolutely true. In other words, if the plaintiff finds spelling or minor factual errors in the material, it doesn't mean that person will win a libel suit. The standard of substantial truth requires that the material's main elements were factually accurate.

To win a libel suit, a plaintiff must show not only that the material published harmed his reputation or exposed him or her to hatred, contempt or ridicule but also that the material is factually inaccurate. If you publish a story that says your mayor has stolen city funds and used them to buy a Corvette, you have obviously harmed the mayor's reputation. However, if the story is true, you have the best defense against a libel suit.

Privilege

This defense is usually divided into **absolute privilege** and **qualified privilege**. Absolute privilege allows judges and government officials to say whatever they want while acting in their official roles. Statements made during meetings of public bodies and public meetings in which information of public concern is discussed falls under this area of privilege as well. This privilege also applies to statements and documents that arise in the course of legal proceedings, such as witness statements, police reports and attorney summations.

Media practitioners operate under qualified privilege, meaning they are allowed to accurately report on these statements, events and documents even if the material defames someone. This standard has been applied successfully in news stories, press releases and other forms of published material.

Journalists can also quote without fear officials who are acting in their official capacity. In some states, this applies to police officers who are making statements regarding criminal cases. In other states, the law draws a distinction between private statements a police officer makes to a reporter that go beyond the scope of the official report. As long as the material was reported in a fair and balanced manner, reporters who operate under qualified privilege are protected against libel actions.

HELPFUL HINTS
HOW TO DETERMINE IF SOMETHING IS OPINION

Courts that deal with libel cases must parse the differences between opinion and fact. When a U.S. court of appeals examined the case of Ollman v. Evans in 1984, it created a four-part process to help consider this issue. The **Ollman test** provides a good set of guidelines for editors to determine if material is opinion or not. The four elements are:

Can the statement be proven true or false? In order for a libel suit to be successful, the plaintiff must demonstrate that the material in question is false. If the material is pure opinion, it cannot be proved true or false and thus cannot be libelous.

What is the common meaning of the words? If you call someone an idiot, did you mean that person has a profound level of mental retardation with an inability to guard against common physical dangers? A long-gone mental classification system once used these growth markers to denote someone as an "idiot," but now this term is less specific. People understand that to call someone an "idiot" these days is to simply question how smart he or she is. If a column uses the term "idiot" to describe a coach or a politician, simply proving that the person knows enough not to run out into traffic won't demonstrate the statement to be factually false. The common meaning overrides the primary claim of factual distinctions.

What is the journalistic context of the remark? Stories that appear in the news section of a website, newspaper or magazine are expected to be factually based. Pieces marked as commentary or items run on blogs that specialize in commentary are expected to contain high levels of opinion. Press releases can be defended in either realm, depending on the source and the tone associated with the material. Comments a network anchor makes during the nightly newscast are different than comments a rock and roll DJ makes during the radio station's morning show. How and when comments were made will play a role in how seriously the courts will take them.

What is the social context of the remark? Certain forms of speech are given more latitude on the basis of their social context. A professor's lecture on quantum physics is expected to be primarily factual, while a debate between two politicians has the potential to be heated and opinionated. Statements made at political rallies are different than those made at a medical conference.

Fair Comment

The law has traditionally held that commentary should be shielded from libel suits. In providing this shield, the law allows media outlets to offer political criticism, perspectives on sports teams and reviews of restaurants. **Fair comment** also gives journalists protection as they write band, book and album reviews as well as editorials and opinion columns.

This defense does not allow unfettered libel under the guise of an opinion. Nor does it protect every defamatory statement that begins with the phrase, "In my opinion . . . ." The material underlying the commentary must be rooted in fact. You can publish a review of a local band's concert in which you state, "The drummer lacked focus and failed to keep up with the band." However, if you add "because he was high on drugs during the concert," you must have the facts to back that statement up.

Satire and Hyperbole

The courts have held that in some cases material is so farfetched that no reasonable person could assume it to be true. In those cases, courts have ruled that the publishers cannot be held liable for defamation. These types of material often fall into the area of satire and hyperbole.

Satire is a literary work that uses irony and wit to attack the human condition. Mad Magazine and Saturday Night Live often parody real life in an attempt to satirize everything from politicians to movies. While satire can offend some people, courts have consistently ruled that it is immune from libel laws.

For example, the 1988 Supreme Court decision in the case of Hustler Magazine, Inc. v. Falwell[7] stated that public figures were not due compensation for emotional distress in the case of parody. The publisher of Hustler was appealing a lower court ruling that awarded the Rev. Jerry Falwell $200,000 after a parody advertisement mocked him. The ad suggested that Falwell had intimate relations with his own mother while in an outhouse and that he often drank heavily before preaching. The Supreme Court held that reasonable people would not have viewed the ad as making statements of fact and thus vacated the lower court's ruling.

Rhetorical **hyperbole**, which includes the use of excessively outlandish statements, falls along the same lines. A restaurant review that says, "The service was so bad that it made me wish I had died as a child, never to have seen such horror" obviously has a level of outlandishness to it. In addition, no reasonable person could consider this to be true. However, statements of this nature can be libelous if they don't reach a high enough level of outrageousness. It is best to avoid reaching for this as a defense.

COMMUNICATIONS DECENCY ACT

Many websites have provided open forums for readers to discuss issues of importance. Some sites offer a comment function at the end of each story so readers can leave feedback for the writer or offer opinions on the story's topic. Anyone who has seen these comment boards knows that the material posted here can quickly devolve into name-calling and other behavior best reserved for ill-mannered first-graders. If the material posted here were published in a newspaper or broadcast over the airwaves, the media outlets would likely face serious legal repercussions. However, in an attempt to keep the web a free and open space for discussion, cybershield laws have emerged to protect publishers from harm arising from content like this.

Section 230 of the **Communications Decency Act** states that internet providers and other media platforms are not liable for content posted to their sites by people who are not directly connected with the organizations. Prior to the passage of this act, the law viewed providers who monitored message boards as making publication choices, which made them responsible for the content. They were held to the publisher's liability standard, which made them fully liable for all defamation claims because they were "creatively involved" in the process of publishing it. However, sites that allowed the comments to turn into a venomous free-for-all without acting were viewed as distributors, much like a bookstore or a newsstand owner, in that they were not expected to examine the material before distribution. The law held these sites to a lower standard and viewed them as not liable for the content.

This approach to the law meant several things, none of which was good for journalists or the furthering of democracy. The law was actively encouraging publishers to leave libelous comments online for fear of being held responsible for all of the comments if they touched one of them. Publishers were also likely to decide that these boards were more trouble than they were worth, thus eliminating them and limiting speech.

To fix this problem, Congress provided Section 230 as a shield for providers who wanted to monitor discussion forums and remove offensive content. While the earliest court cases involved internet service providers, such as America Online, courts have broadly applied the protections under this section. They have immunized social networking sites like Facebook and sales sites such as Amazon for comments users made on their sites. Site operators run a risk of losing that immunity if they actively encourage people to post illegal material. Beyond that exception, however, the courts have generally favored publishers.

As an editor, this gives you a valuable tool in monitoring material users post to your site. If you determine the comments to be defamatory or in other ways inappropriate, you have legal protection to screen and filter them.

However, the more you are actively involved in the process of creating or altering the content, the less protected you are. Courts have ruled that people who made minor edits to content did not lose immunity, but they have not determined at what specific point altering user-generated material changes the content's status. If you make substantive changes to this type of content, you run a risk of being liable for it.

INVASION OF PRIVACY

While privacy is not a right explicitly stated in the First Amendment or elsewhere in the Constitution, courts have ruled consistently that people have a right to be left alone. Balancing this right against the rights of journalists to publish newsworthy information has been a struggle. The law has delineated four areas of privacy, all of which are important to journalists: public disclosure, false light, intrusion and misappropriation.

Public Disclosure

Courts have held that certain facts about private citizens are off limits to the press because of their sensitive nature or potential for embarrassment. Medical records are viewed as private, as are educational records. Therefore, the student newspaper at your school can't get access to the transcripts of everyone on campus and run a story titled "Who's the DUMBEST Kid on Campus?" Other private details of private citizens that might be viewed as intimate and highly offensive to a reasonable person are not subject to **public disclosure**.

Individuals who wish to publish facts like these can offer a defense that the material is newsworthy and thus not private. Any information about celebrities and well-known public officials will likely meet this standard, as well as any coverage of criminal activity. Health and sexual issues remain difficult topics to cover unless the publishers can demonstrate that sharing this information is vital to the public.

False Light

A claim of **false light** means that a person is portrayed as something he or she is not. For a successful false-light claim, the plaintiff must demonstrate that the publisher's actions were reckless or done deliberately and that the material must be highly offensive to a reasonable person.

Attorney Larry Stecco filed a false-light suit against filmmaker Michael Moore for his portrayal in Moore's film "Roger & Me." According to Emily Schultz's biography on Moore, he interviewed Stecco at a high-society party where Stecco said that Flint, Michigan, is a "great place to live." Moore then juxtaposed this piece of film against one of a sheriff's deputy gutting an abandoned house. Stecco said these comments and this editing cast him in a false light as a fat-cat lawyer who was unaware of the poor conditions in the city. The jury agreed and awarded Stecco $6,250.[8]

This also applies to photographs with "funny" captions. A photo of a large person on the street with the caption "Am I pregnant?" can lead to legal action. As was the case with Stecco's false-light claim, photo captions like this can be offensive and misleading.

Intrusion

This applies more to the reporting of material than editing, but as a manager, you need to be aware of this standard. **Intrusion** upon seclusion prevents journalists from entering a private area to gather material for a story. In addition, it prohibits journalists from gathering information about a person in a place where that person has an expectation of privacy.

Journalists generally are allowed to enter private spaces that are open to anyone, such as a mall or a business. However, they are also expected to leave when asked by those in charge of that area. Most often, this standard applies to the act of trespassing or entering private property without an owner's consent. If you hear a rumor that a local hog farmer is violating environmental protection standards, you can send a reporter out there to investigate. However, that reporter must get permission to enter the farm before doing so. Failure to do so can result in an arrested reporter and an embarrassed media outlet.

This standard also prohibits surveillance or the use of hidden cameras in areas where people would expect privacy. While a government-owned highway rest stop is a public area, people have a reasonable expectation of privacy in the bathrooms there. Using a recorder to gather sound or taking pictures of people in there would likely meet the intrusion standard.

Misappropriation

Courts have supported the notion that individuals have the right to determine when their likenesses, voices and other items associated with them can be used to promote something. In news, this is rarely an issue, as the claim to newsworthiness allows reporters to write, record and photograph individuals participating in actions of public interest. However, if that material is used for a commercial purpose, such as advertising or marketing, an individual can claim **misappropriation**.

If your website runs an image your photographer took of Tom Brady holding the Super Bowl trophy as part of your sports coverage, that's acceptable. If you repurpose that photo for an ad for your website, stating something like "SportsIcon.com: Where winners get their sports news!" you have misappropriated that image and could be liable for damages.

The best defense against any of these claims is consent. Make sure you get this permission from someone who is capable of giving it, such as the owner of a building you want to enter or the owner of the likeness you want to use. Also, try to get this permission in writing, especially in the case of promotional or advertising use.

COPYRIGHT

The purpose of copyright law is simple: If people could take your work and use it as their own without providing credit or compensation, why would you bother creating the work? If you feel like being altruistic and giving away your work, that's fine under **copyright** law. However, it should be up to you to give it away, sell it or do neither. To that end, copyright isn't always about making money, but it is about controlling how your work is used.

For example, let's say you created a cartoon for your website, and a group on campus put it on T-shirts to promote their cause. The underlying assumption is that your work is some way tied to this group or that you are providing support to this group. You might oppose everything this group stands for. You might never want to be associated with this group. Without copyright law, you would be unable to prevent the group from using your work.

People who violate copyright can face serious consequences. Because copyright attaches itself upon the creation of a creative work, the author has all the rights associated with that work. This includes the rights to sell, make copies, make derivative works and display the work publicly. Anyone else who does any of these things can be subject to statutory damages of between $750 and $30,000 per infringement, plus any other actual losses and attorney's fees. In some cases, courts can levy additional criminal punishment.

While copyright has always been a big issue for journalists, in the digital realm it becomes the primary legal concern for editors. The ability to easily copy images, use music or transfer text has left many people with the erroneous assumption that they aren't breaking any laws.

Fair use is a provision in copyright law that allows a balance between an individual's or organization's desire to control how material is used and the public's interest in having access to that material. This doctrine allows people to use copyrighted material to enhance news coverage, inform the public and provide commentary. Fair use is not an impenetrable shield against copyright suits, nor is it a clear-cut area of law. Below is a list of things courts consider when they look at whether an organization has overstepped the fair-use provisions in the law:

How Is It Being Used?

Noncommercial uses, such as efforts to further news coverage, tend to receive more protection than commercial uses, such as advertising or marketing. Thus, a small bit of a song or a movie star's marketing headshot could be used fairly within news coverage of that band or star. However, if you attempted to sell ads using those same pieces of material, fair use would likely not protect you.

How Much Did You Take?

The law has not defined a strict number of words, portion of a performance or percentage of the overall work as being fair use. However, a rule of thumb has emerged that you can copy 10 percent of a published work or use 30 seconds of a song without fear. The law does not consider this amount the exact breaking point between fair use and copyright infringement, but the more material you use, the bigger the risk that you are violating copyright. In addition, the doctrine offers protection for the "heart" of the work, which means that if you take what is essential to this work and use it for your own, you might be in violation, regardless of the quantity of the material you took.

Do You Create a Financial Detriment to the Owner?

The purpose of copyright is to allow the copyright holders to maintain control over their content and profit from it as they see fit. If your use of their material infringes upon these rights, courts will likely rule that you violated the law. When you decide to use material that isn't yours, ask yourself if your actions create a secondary market for the material. If you do a review of a movie and run a small image of the movie poster, you aren't undercutting the poster business. However, if you upload the whole movie to a website and tell your readers to watch it for themselves to see if they agree with your review, you are clearly in violation. The tipping point for this discussion isn't clearly outlined, so it is best to err on the side of caution.

ONLINE LIMITS TO LIABILITY

Just as the law has recognized that content providers cannot be held liable for every potentially libelous action its users take, it has also recognized this problem with regard to copyright infringement. In opening their sites to user-generated content, providers ran the risk of letting users post material that violated copyright.

To help address this issue, lawmakers struck a balance between protecting copyright and indemnifying websites against harm. The **Online Copyright Infringement Liability Limitation Act (OCILLA)** provides a process for all parties involved to work through issues associated with illegally posted material.

As an editor, you might need to participate in this process, so understanding the steps you must take will be important (see the Helpful Hints box for a step-by-step examination). If your organization designates you as the agent who is to receive these notices for copyright infringement, the organization should register you with the Register of Copyrights. This will establish you as the main conduit for these cases.

If your organization decides to use someone else, you still have responsibilities as the online editor. You need to post contact information for your organization's agent on the site in an obvious place so people know whom to contact. You also need to include a general explanation of OCILLA and how your organization will process claims of copyright infringement.

Beyond that, you will want to establish a policy for dealing with people who repeatedly break the law on your site. This should include ways in which you establish patterns of bad behavior and how you will contact these people regarding their actions. It should be clear and fair, with a listing of what users should not do and the consequences if they violate your rules. It would also be worth your time to discuss these issues with your technical support staff to see if anything can be done to limit copyright issues from a technology standpoint. This could include the creation of an online consent form that requires users to attest to their rights as copyright holders or filtering software that limits users from posting certain types of material.

The more proactive you are and the more closely you follow the steps outlined in OCILLA, the more protected you will be against legal action.

HELPFUL HINTS
THE STEPS UNDER OCILLA

If a user illegally posts a piece of copyrighted material, such as a photo or drawing, to your website, here is the process for working through this problem:

- If the copyright owner contacts your organization regarding the infringement, he is expected to provide the following information:
  - His contact information
  - Information that identifies the photo or drawing
  - The internet address of the photo or drawing
  - A statement that demonstrates a good-faith belief that copyright has been infringed upon
  - A statement that, under penalty of perjury, he is the legal copyright holder or has been empowered to act on behalf of the copyright holder
  - His signature
- After being made aware of the infringement (either via this contact or through an independent discovery), your organization is expected to "expeditiously" remove the content and notify the person who posted it of your actions.
- If that person believes the content was unfairly removed, she can send a counter-notice that

includes much of the same information noted in the first step, but argues that the organization was incorrect in removing the material. She should then state she would be willing to have the case heard in a court of law to determine the outcome of the posting.

- Your organization would then notify the person who asked that the material be removed, informing him of the counter-notice. At that point, he can file suit against the person who posted the content, and the courts will sort things out. If he does not file suit, your organization can put the material back online between 10 and 14 business days from the time you notify the original complainant.

If either of these people files suit after that, OCILLA states that your organization should be immune from damages associated with those actions. However, these "take down" and "put back" provisions are general guidelines, and you need to be aware of more specific language within the law. When you are in doubt as to this process, seek advice from your boss and/or legal counsel.

CREATIVE COMMONS

In traditional copyright protection, the phrase "all rights reserved" has provided copyright owners full control over how their products will be used. When copyright expires, however, the protections disappear, and the material enters the public domain. Very little middle ground existed or needed to exist prior to the internet. However, many people want some level of control over their work but would prefer that others can use it and forward it in an attempt to broaden the overall reach of their messages.

Creative Commons licensing has attempted to find a way in which some rights can be reserved while still furthering the free exchange of material. CC licenses allow content to grow and flourish beyond the original owner's intent through copying and distribution without the express written consent of the creator. The licenses are built on copyright principles but also allow the creators to set specific limits for their work and how it is to be used. Creators can determine if the work can be used for commercial and/or noncommercial uses, if the material can be altered or if it needs to be disseminated as it was created or a variety of other guidelines.

You can use material marked with a Creative Commons license provided you abide by the restrictions the creators set. This approach to sharing material can allow you to substantially augment your website without being bogged down in protracted problems trying to secure copyright. However, you should always make sure you are using the material properly. You should also make a strong effort to create the material yourself or have someone on your staff create it for you.

WAYS TO AVOID COPYRIGHT CONCERNS

The issues of law are sticky and difficult to wade through. Once you find yourself running afoul of the law, it takes a lot of time, effort and money to get things resolved. The best way to avoid problems with regard to copyright is often to avoid making the mistake in the first place. Here are some key things to do in order to make life easier on you and your website:

Ask Permission

The best way to avoid copyright infringement is to get the right to publish the material from the copyright's owner. If you want to republish an article, post a photo or attach some video that you don't own, ask the person who does own it if he or she would grant you reprint rights. Many times, people are happy to share their material if they know it will be used for the betterment of others or in a way that is similar to their original vision for it. Some places have a universal policy that needs to be followed or a specific form that needs to be filled out, so keep that in mind when you are running against a deadline and you need to use something. However, usually a phone call or an email can get the job done. Keep a written record of that authorization, in the form of the email or letter you received. If you get approval over the phone, note the name of the person with whom you spoke, the time and date of the conversation and any other pertinent information. You might need that information later.

Use Your Own Previous Work

Many media organizations create content for their own uses, and much of that material is archived for historical purposes and later use. If the organization owns the copyright and it has the material, it can, in many cases, reuse the material as it sees fit. For example, if your PR agency created a logo for a campaign on physical fitness, and you now want to create a new "be healthy" campaign, you could reuse that logo if you saw fit. The same idea applies when an organization creates a "mascot" or standing figure that represents its organization. The visual representation is often transferred from campaign to campaign with a few aesthetic alterations.

Don't Be Lazy

It is always easier to use something you can find on Google than doing your own work. However, laziness is not an excuse for violating copyright. If you want a photo of an event to go with the story on that event, have someone go out and get it. If you need a logo or an icon or something to match up with some copy, don't take someone else's stuff. Have someone on your staff make it for you or make it yourself.

Look for Material That Lacks Copyright

Some things can't be copyrighted, such as color schemes or phrases. Others were placed into the public domain via Creative Commons licensing, mentioned above. Images in the Library of Congress can be used without fear, as can material for which copyright has expired. Works that were originally created after Jan. 1, 1978, have copyright protection that lasts for 70 years after the death of creator. Work created prior to this date has varying levels of protection, depending on how it was registered, if it was published or how old it is. Using material that has either no copyright or an expired copyright can keep you out of trouble.

Don't Steal

When stealing something tangible, such as a candy bar from a store or money from someone's purse, the morality and legality are pretty clear. However, the digital sharing phenomenon has made this concept seem more acceptable. It's not. If you don't own it and you can't get permission to use it, don't steal it. It makes people less likely to cooperate with you in the future, it casts your organization in a bad light and someone will likely sue you. In most cases, what you are taking isn't worth the hassle you will face for violating the copyright. Keep your hands off other people's things.

THE BIG THREE

Here are the three key things you should take away from this chapter:

1. **The law isn't simple:** In most cases, legal opinions do not provide an ironclad answer to every question. This means it's often hard to come up with a simple understanding of what you can and cannot do with content. You should take care and rely on the basic tenets outlined here with regard to libel, invasion of privacy and copyright infringement before you publish content. If you aren't sure, seek help from coworkers or legal experts before you disseminate material that could land you in hot water.

2. **Be skeptical:** Whether you are questioning a new reporter about a story that seems too good to be true or working with a staffer who is trying to "jazz up" a press release, use skepticism to keep both of you out of trouble. Editing is often about clarifying and improving content, but it is also about pushing back on fantastical claims. Be firm in your responses and make sure everyone who works with you can back up their claims before publication.

3. **Don't steal:** Copyright infringement is one of the more common concerns in media practices today. Digital content can appear to be free because it is so easy to take and repurpose. However, that doesn't mean you aren't violating the law. Contact copyright holders and get the rights to the material before you use it. Also, consider creating your own content or repurposing something you already own before you take the easy way out and grab something that doesn't belong to you.

KEY TERMS

absolute privilege 28
actual malice 25
Communications Decency Act 30
copyright 32
Creative Commons 35
editorial discretion 22
fair comment 29
fair use 33
false light 31

Federal Communications
    Commission 22
First Amendment 21
hyperbole 30
identification 24
intrusion 32
libel 23
misappropriation 32
negligence 25

Ollman test 29
Online Copyright Infringement
    Liability Limitation Act
    (OCILLA) 34
publication 23
public disclosure 31
qualified privilege 28
satire 29

DISCUSSION QUESTIONS

1. Of the four misconceptions about the First Amendment, which one surprised you the most? Which one or ones did you already know? How confident are you in the freedoms afforded you under the First Amendment as a citizen and a journalist?

2. One of the key aspects of libel law is "publication," which means disseminating the content to people other than the person who was identified in the potentially libelous material. How often do you think about the issue of libel when you use social media like Twitter or Facebook to share information about people you know? Knowing what you now know about social media as "publication" as far as a libel suit goes, how concerned are you about things you have published in the past?

3. What are your feelings on the concept of copyright, especially in the digital age? Do you think it is too restrictive or that it doesn't go far enough to protect content? Or are you somewhere in the middle on this issue? Do you think your position would change if you were put in charge of a publication as an editor? Why or why not?

WRITE NOW!

1. Below is a list of scenarios in which there is potential to invade someone's privacy. First, note if you think each constitutes an invasion of privacy. Then, if you determine it to be invasion of privacy, list which of the four types of invasion best applies:

   a. Carl is doing laundry next to the equipment manager for the university's cheerleading team. When the manager walks away, Carl sneaks a peek at the team's list of clothing, which includes all of the sizes of their underpants. He then publishes a column in the student paper about who has the biggest butt on the team, citing that list.

   b. The president of the university and his wife are having a screaming fight in their home when the president runs outside, followed by his wife, who is chasing him with a shotgun, all in full view of a public street. Jamie takes several photos of this from her position on a public sidewalk and posts them to her blog.

   c. The kicker on your football team is deeply religious, and he always gets down on one knee to pray after each game. Elsa takes a picture of him in the kneeling position and runs the photo with her column on how un-American it is that football players are taking a knee during the national anthem as a form of protest.

2. Review your social media feeds and examine them for potentially libelous statements you or your friends made. Select several posts you think could meet the definition of libel, and then walk through the standards required for a successful libel suit. Explain how each standard applies to the content you selected in a short written piece on each post.

3. Select a piece of content you feel has the potential for libel and apply the Ollman test to it. Walk through each of the four questions associated with the test and explain how it supports or does not support the concept that the material is opinion based.

Visit **edge.sagepub.com/filakediting** to help you accomplish your coursework goals in an easy-to-use learning environment.

4 ETHICS

Journalism is a trust-based system. Writers trust that sources will be honest and forthright with them during the information-gathering process. Editors trust that their staff members have gathered information fairly and properly. The audience trusts that the material the media outlet publishes will be as close as possible to the truth and that the outlet will atone for and correct any errors that slip through. If trust is forsaken, the system can come crashing down.

Unfortunately for journalists, recent studies show that media users lack faith in most of the content they consume. A 2018 Gallup/Knight Foundation report revealed that only 44 percent of the country can name a source they view as unbiased. In addition, 73 percent of the participants in the poll said the spread of inaccurate information on the internet is a major problem. Only half of the respondents said they could cut through bias to get to the facts, and only one-third of the people said they are very confident in being able to distinguish fact from commentary in the news.[1]

The state of journalism ethics is not pretty, as allegations of "fake news" abound in political and other discourse. Politico reported that nearly half of voters believe the news media made up stories intentionally to skew people's views of the president.[2] Other sources also report that people are generally unsure whom they can trust and which sources are the most honest.

Ethics help journalists and their audience members reach a common understanding about what is and is not acceptable behavior. In most cases, ethics involve balancing the rights of some people against the needs of others. As an editor, you will have a number of opportunities to form, shape and develop your ethics. The purpose of this chapter is to help you define ethics, allow you to examine some ethical issues and help you understand how best to deal with ethical dilemmas.

In this chapter, we will examine the overall concept of ethics as well as some of the key tenets that exist among the many disciplines of media. We will also assess the ways in which media editors can work to gain and retain the public trust while dealing with difficult issues that matter to audience members.

ETHICS DEFINED

The underlying concept of **ethics** is simple: Think of it as dealing with things that aren't illegal but can cause problems for you. Some scholars have used phrases like "right and wrong," "morality play" and "good and evil" to help explain ethics. Authors of ethics texts have also discussed issues of fairness, objectivity and social dignity when it comes to examining ethics.

In some of your earlier classes, you have likely talked about ethical issues, such as printing the names and addresses of people accused of crimes or even those of crime victims. If you took courses in news reporting or public relations, you likely came across the idea of payola, which is the provision of free items as part of sponsored events. Public relations practitioners and news reporters often view these freebies with varying levels of ethical standards, with some seeing the practice as merely providing a hospitable environment and others considering it bribery.

Editors, however, have an even harder job, because not only are they responsible for maintaining their ethical standards, but also they need to keep an eye on everyone else's. Editors often craft ethical policies for the media outlet, so they have to figure out what they feel is ethical and why they espouse those beliefs. The "why" part is especially important because they must justify those policies to others, who will be required to abide by them.

Think about it this way: When you were in high school, did you ever want to do something your parents weren't keen on? You explained why you thought you should be allowed to do it, and your parents kept saying no. When you asked why, one of them said, "Because I'm the PARENT, that's why!"

I'm certain that wasn't a satisfactory answer for you. You likely didn't say, "Oh, well, that clears that up. Sorry to bug you." Similarly, you will want to have a rationale behind what you are doing and what you expect your staff members to do so your answer doesn't become "Because I'm the BOSS, that's why!"

MODELS OF ETHICS

In their book on media ethics, authors Philip Patterson and Lee Wilkins outline several ethical philosophies.[3] In reviewing the great philosophers and ethicists throughout time, the authors list a wide array of approaches that will be worth considering as you craft your own ethical paradigm.

Aristotle's Golden Mean

The ancient philosopher believed people could exercise solid reasoning. To that end, society should judge a person on the basis of his or her actions, for they would be representative of that person's moral base. In explaining this ideal further, Aristotle established the **golden mean** as a way to judge the actions of an individual and thus determine that person's ethical approach.

The golden mean assumes that virtue is found between the extremes of a situation. The best decisions, Aristotle would argue, are found in the middle ground. For example, the decision to run or not run a story might create tension between what your writer (run everything exactly the way I wrote it) wants and what the person's sources want (don't run the story and never speak of it again). As an editor, you could find a way to work out a compromise in which you embrace a middle ground and thus provide the most benefit without giving either side exactly what it wants.

Kant's Categorical Imperative

The authors note that Immanuel Kant's philosophy of ethics rests on the assumption that every decision you make could become a law for all people. Actions should therefore be logically based, but every situation should be treated the same. Thus, Kant's philosophy has often been compared to the Bible's "golden rule": Do unto others as you would have them do unto you.

The underlying philosophy of the **categorical imperative** states that it is the act, not the outcome or the person engaging in the act, that is to be judged as ethical or unethical. The test of each act is whether the act can apply to everyone equally.

If it is OK for a journalist to lie to get some information, it is equally acceptable for a source to lie to a journalist for a similar reason. Although some have taken Kant's philosophy to the extreme, in which the only thing that matters is the act, Patterson and Wilkins argue that consequences are relevant under Kant's philosophy. In either case, Kant's approach requires you to examine your actions as opposed to what comes out of them.

John Stuart Mill and Utilitarianism

Although Mill and philosopher Jeremy Bentham are credited with the introduction of **utilitarianism** into the discussion of ethics, you have probably heard the underlying aspects of it in many other places. Although often ascribed to great philosophers from ancient times, the well-worn phrase "The needs of the many outweigh the needs of the few" is utilitarian and relatively recent. Mr. Spock spoke it to James T. Kirk during "Star Trek II: The Wrath of Khan."

The utilitarian approach argues that an action's consequences are important in determining the ethics of that action. For example, an editor may decide to put out a press release that alerts car owners that the manufacturer is conducting a major recall because of safety issues. The decision probably will damage the reputation of the company in the short term, and it might cost a few people their jobs. The choice will also demonstrate long-term values and give car owners a reason to have faith in the company, thus leading to additional growth down the road.

This approach shifts the focus from Kant's argument about examining actions toward examining the outcomes of those actions. Utilitarianism, Patterson and Wilkins note, can be determined in terms of individual actions (act utilitarianism) and a broader overall construct (rule utilitarianism).

Again, this philosophy can be taken too far in the case of "bean counting." If you were to add up the pluses and the minuses of a situation and see which had more weight, you would abide by the letter, but not the spirit, of utilitarianism. The ethical philosophy requires you to weigh the outcomes and assess which actions will create the most and least desirable ends.

Pluralistic Theory of Value

William David Ross argued in the 1930s that more than one ethical value exists at any point, and those values compete for dominance in the decision-making process. Ross lists several duties, including those based on fidelity, gratitude, justice, beneficence and self-improvement. In this philosophy, the importance of one act can outweigh another act.

Patterson and Wilkins give the example of a reporter who was supposed to attend a meeting with a mayor but came across a major car accident. In stopping to help the victims of the wreck, the reporter broke a promise to meet the mayor. In this case, the authors argue, the action was ethical because the postponing of the minor commitment allowed the reporter to serve a greater good. Had the crash been less severe or the meeting been more important, the reporter might have changed the way in which he weighed the choices.

Pluralism explains why we often feel awkward when we choose between ethically challenging options. Ross's argument is that the tension between these duties keeps us out of balance.

Although many other ethical philosophies exist, the important thing for you as an editor is to understand what makes a choice ethical or unethical in your mind. Although you don't have to subscribe to a specific ethical philosophy, understanding ethics and the ways in which you will approach ethical situations can matter a great deal.

Media professionals build and refine their ethical codes over the course of their careers. In some cases, people hold true to absolute rights and absolute wrongs. In other cases, they allow the facts of the situation to guide them. Experience is a great teacher when it comes to outlining ethical choices and shaping the way in which you determine your approach to ethics-driven situations.

AUDIENCE STANDARDS AND THE BREAKFAST TEST

As with most of the things we have discussed to this point, your audience will determine in large part how you approach your ethical paradigm. Some websites embrace obscene and vulgar language, whereas others eliminate every "heck" or "darn." The expectations of your audience will help guide you in this regard.

The same can be said for what can and can't be shown. Some publications apply the "**breakfast test**" when it comes to graphic images. In using the test to determine whether to run bloody accident photos or images of animals that hunters have killed, the editor has to ask whether these pictures are suitable for viewing at the breakfast table.

Other publications have a laxer standard when it comes to visuals. Niche publications and public relations outlets with nature-based clients often run full galleries of people proudly posing with their quarry. Some websites will even run autopsy photos or crime-scene images with the idea of either providing the most unvarnished version of reality or just trying to push the envelope. Different places, different audiences, different standards. This is one reason understanding your audience is crucial to being a good editor.

ESTABLISHING RULES AND GUIDELINES

Before you send your staff members into the field, you want to have a clear and shared understanding of what is and what is not acceptable ethical behavior. In most cases, newsrooms will have a policy manual that deals with what reporters should and shouldn't do. However, given the changes to the media landscape over the past several years, it never hurts to go back through that manual and assess its standards. Even if the policy is up to date and covers web-based situations, you want to discuss your expectations with the reporters.

Journalists are often required to make snap decisions when it comes to getting important information. In that brief moment, they might be willing to agree to things that go against your ethics policies in the desperate hope of getting a nugget of news or a client to agree to a plan. Editors have the broader view of a situation, understanding that allowing a reporter to make a deal for a short-term gain can have long-term negative impacts. This is particularly true when it comes to shielding a source.

It is important to seek out and review any long-standing policies at your media outlet. What has the outlet's policy been on anonymous sources? Is there a rule or a specific response for

HELPFUL HINTS

DEFINING TYPES OF INFORMATION AND SOURCES

Journalists will have to decide how to handle reticent sources and inside information. Here is a common set of terms associated with source protection, quoting people and what they mean.

On the record: This is the most common form of interview standard. When a writer and a source engage in a series of questions and answers regarding a topic, the interview is said to be on the record. This means the source can be quoted and information provided can be used and attributed to the source. When journalists identify themselves as such and begin asking questions, convention dictates the material obtained at this point is on the record.

Off the record: This term is often misunderstood and has caused a great deal of consternation for journalists and sources alike. In the most basic sense, deciding to go **off the record** is an agreement between a source and a journalist to discuss something that will not be attributed in a way that on-the-record information will be. What will be used and how it will be used needs to be clarified.

In some cases, the people will agree that the material is "not for direct attribution," meaning the material can be used but not attributed to the source by name. In other cases, the material is said to be "not for attribution," meaning the material can't be attributed to the source, but can be used. Finally, the term "deep background" is used to describe material that is only to be used to foster further reporting. This is more of a news tip than information that may or may not be attributed.

The interviewer and source should agree upon the rules and the way in which the information is to be used before the interview. They must also agree what is on and off the record. A source cannot unilaterally decide to go

off the record, and journalists should remind a source of this. A clear understanding of how the interview and the material that is discussed will be handled can prevent bruised egos and hurt feelings.

Unnamed source: Journalists often converse with people who do not want to have their names used. The reasons can vary, but it is up to the journalist to determine whether the information the source will provide is worth keeping that person's name a secret. When someone has important and unique information, you might agree to use that person as an **unnamed source**. When the person is talking about whether he or she is enjoying the county fair and yet doesn't want to give his or her name, make sure the reporter knows enough to find another source.

Anonymous source: This term has tended to blanket unnamed and unknown sources, but in its purest definition, it skews more toward the latter. An unnamed source is someone the writer knows but who has received anonymity from that writer. In other words, the writer wants to use the information from the source and has agreed to do so without naming that source.

An **anonymous source** is often someone who is unknown to the writer. An email tip or a phone call from someone who will not give his or her name fits this definition. Although using unnamed sources can be risky, using anonymous sources can be dangerous. When discussing the situation with your staff members, make sure you understand if the source is anonymous or just unnamed. In addition, you need to determine the truthfulness of the information and value behind it. Finally, you will want to have the reporter get on-the-record information to verify and support the information from the unnamed or anonymous source.

dealing with someone who asks for special treatment? Who picks up the check at a restaurant or a bar? All of these things need to be fleshed out ahead of time to establish a clear sense of what is allowed and what is not. It's the job of the staff member to abide by the rules, but it's the job of the editor to make sure the rules are clear to everyone involved.

MANAGEMENT AND ETHICS

Sometimes, the rules aren't clear or they are violated, which leads you to a bigger problem: now what? This is where editors demonstrate their skills as managers.

For example, during an investigation of a particularly heinous crime, a reporter legally obtained the name of the suspect. Being a good reporter, she called the jail to see if there was either a criminal record for that person, a mug shot or both. It turned out the suspect had been jailed before, and the jailer, not knowing anything about the crime that had just been committed, gladly handed over a copy of the record and the mug shot.

For the police, this became a huge problem: If the suspect's picture appeared in the paper before the victims of the crime, who were incapacitated but alive, could identify their attacker, that would be bad. The defense would likely argue that the victims saw the suspect's picture in the paper, and the visual cue influenced their identification. If the paper published this photograph, it could inadvertently damage the police's investigation.

The reporter argued that it was a legitimate news story and the picture had value. Other journalists argued that the mug shot didn't add anything to the story and that the story could run without it. Others argued that other media outlets likely had or could get the mug shot, so it would look bad for the paper not to publish it.

VIEW FROM A PRO
ALLISON HANTSCHEL SANSONE

Courtesy of Allison Hantschel Sansone

Allison Hantschel Sansone has worked in multiple media fields with varying ethical codes and approaches to producing and editing content. She spent 10 years in newspaper journalism in the Chicago area, served as the executive director of the Ernest Hemingway Foundation of Oak Park and helped launch the American Writers Museum, where she now serves as the organization's program director.

She also authored or edited five books, writes about politics for DAME magazine and operates First-Draft, a journalism and political blog that was founded in 2004.

The one thing she said remains at her core is the concept of ethical behavior and how working in media has codified those tenets for her.

"One of the best things a background in journalism gives you is a strong sense of right," Sansone said. "If you train in the craft of reporting and writing you are always observing the human condition, searching for an untold story, a loose thread, an unheard voice. What animates you in that job animates you to find ways of doing things that other people don't think about, and that's a skill that benefits you wherever you go and whatever you do."

Although some people view ethics as a leash that restricts how journalists operate, Sansone said she sees a strong ethical code as an inspiration to produce amazing content.

"This is about wanting to do great work," she said. "Great work comes from a place of fearlessness. It means opening up to questions of, 'Am I doing this in a way that hurts someone unnecessarily?' and 'Is this the hill I really want to die on?' It also means willingness to learn and correct. That's critical. When you get called on something, instead of throwing a defensive hissy on social media and talking about how you're not really a racist/sexist/bigot or your heart is really pure and everybody who's upset is just too dumb to understand you, shut up and listen. If you made a mistake, correct it. If you did something wrong, apologize. Learn and move on."

Sansone said ethical codes tend to be things "most people only pay attention to when they're writing an employee manual nobody's going to read" or when a disaster strikes. The problem with this approach, she said, is that it prevents the code from becoming more of an organizational mindset.

"Look, this stuff isn't that difficult," Sansone said. "Leaders in your organization need to be mindful of power, theirs and others', in all aspects of their work. That's all ethics is, using power and privilege mindfully, and protecting the people who have the most to lose and the least ability to risk. If you're the boss, you stand between your people and the problem and make sure when the shit hits the fan it's pointed at you. Do that in the boss's office, and your people will very quickly get the message that that's how it should work all the way down."

She also said media operations tend to work best when people think broadly about ethics and how they connect an audience with the organization.

"Most people think of ethics as 'Do I name the crime victim?' or 'Do I use a clickbait headline?' instead of thinking of it as 'How do I serve my audience well?'" she said. "Most of the time you serve your audience well by imagining you are them. What would you want to know? And how would you want someone to tell it to you?"

In most cases, you won't face something like that, but minor situations can lead to big problems. A source might agree to speak with a reporter but only if the reporter doesn't include a certain piece of information in the story. As an editor, you might not agree if the reporter accepts that condition. Is it worth it to sell out the reporter and potentially burn a source? Is it better to stick to what the reporter agreed to do, even though it seems to have compromised the story and undermined the news outlet's integrity?

What you decide and how you decide to handle ethical situations like this will determine in large part how your staff will work with you and what outside organizations will think about your organization. The big thing to remember is that you are establishing a precedent as to how your group will behave and what you value. The editor always has to look at both the short-term impact and the long-term outcome of a choice.

WORKING WITH STAFF MEMBERS

You will rely on your writers to do their jobs well, and in most cases, that's a safe bet. From time to time, you will find yourself at odds with staffers who are less skittish than you are about certain things. Writers often see important details where you see landmines. They see protected statements where you see libelous accusations. Here is a list of the protestations you will likely hear as you work through your writers' copy and some ways in which you can address them:

"But It's a Fact!"

When is it OK to point out a fact about someone? Sounds like a silly question. Facts are facts, right? But when you don't use facts fairly, sometimes they become an issue of ethics.

If a person is African-American, a staffer might include a line in a press release stating, "Bill Smith, the African-American congressman from Maryland, said he opposes the bill." The person who put it in there is likely to argue that it's a fact and shouldn't be removed. It isn't as if Smith is going to call up your media outlet and argue that he's not an African-American.

In describing his race, the person points out something about the source in a way he or she probably wouldn't for someone white. You probably can't name the last time you saw a sentence like this: "Bill Smith, the white congressman from Maryland, said he opposes the bill."

In his book "Ball Four," author and former professional baseball player Jim Bouton recalled talking with a teammate who was black about the issue of race. The man noted he wouldn't mind it if the newspaper would say he was the black first baseman if they would call his replacement "the white first baseman."

The same standards apply with age, gender and social background. In some cases, these things tie into the story. You can't craft an advertising campaign that uses the story of Jackie Robinson, the first man to integrate baseball, without addressing the issue of race. That's germane to your approach. If you are going to publish a feature on a woman who was born into a very poor family but became a multibillionaire, you can't avoid focusing on the poor upbringing and the eventual wealth. That's journalism.

When it comes to details that add nothing but can be used to bias the readers in some way, you need to be careful. If you are editing a piece of copy about a vote at the statehouse, is it important to point out that someone who voted against a measure is divorced? Maybe if it is a bill dealing with marriage, but in most cases, probably not. Is it a good idea to mention that the person is a recovering drug addict or alcoholic? If the bill deals with those issues or if the person has made no secret about how these issues influence his or her votes, you might consider it.

The big take-away here is that you should make sure you aren't including "facts" in a piece of copy in a way that can bias a reader.

"But It's Something We All Say!"

One of the bigger changes in media organizations from the 1970s through today is the effort toward improving diversity. The reason behind this is that diversity in terms of race, gender and social background allows readers to better understand a broader array of perspectives. In addition, people find out that some things "everybody says" aren't necessarily things people outside of their small group of like-minded people say.

If you let a writer call an older woman "a spry grandmother of three who wants to be your next mayor," you had better make the case that you would say the same thing for a "spry" grandfather of three. Better yet, what makes someone "spry"? Or "feisty"? Or "emotional"? Make sure these aren't code words for "elderly but not infirm" or "short and female" or "illogical wimp." Even in cases in which you don't think the writing is out of control, you need to make sure you are not using language that is out of bounds.

In some cases, it is the historical context of a word that makes it offensive, even if many people have forgotten the word's origins. In police vernacular, it is said that someone had to call in the "Paddy wagon" to take suspects to jail. That term doesn't sound bad until you realize its origin: "Paddy" is an offensive term aimed at the Irish. The term is said to have originated during the New York draft riots of 1863, in which Irish people protested and were hauled away en masse. Others have attributed it to a time when police were called out to bring large quantities of drunken Irishmen to jail. In either case, it's an offensive term despite its more generic usage today.

Keep an eye on words and phrases that draw attention to age, gender, race, religion, sexual orientation and other such characteristics. Ask whether those words and phrases have merit and are necessary to tell the story or if they're simply there because the writer put them there. If they detract from the story or introduce bias, delete them.

"But It's in a Quote!"

The purpose of a quote is to add flavor to a story, and good reporters should find engaging and provocative quotes on topics of interest. However, a line exists between provocative and out of bounds. Although Chapter 3 outlines issues of law regarding quotes, you also need to look at quotes from an ethics perspective.

Punchy quotes have always been part of the vernacular of journalism, particularly in sports, where athletes are often hyperbolic. Before Super Bowl XIII, Thomas "Hollywood" Henderson of the Dallas Cowboys ridiculed his opponent's quarterback, Terry Bradshaw. Henderson said the Steelers' signal caller was so dumb "He couldn't spell 'cat' if you spotted him the 'c-a.'"[4]

Another example came from former Michigan University basketball player Jalen Rose, who referred to Duke University's basketball program as recruiting "Uncle Toms." The "Uncle Tom" reference is one that goes back to Harriet Beecher Stowe's novel "Uncle Tom's Cabin" but in current vernacular is meant to describe African-Americans who are subservient to white people. Although Rose later clarified his statements, it was clear the quote had gone beyond simple rivalry.[5]

Although a quote can in some cases be protected legally, it won't matter much to readers who find the material offensive. Quotes aren't a shield against people thinking you and your media outlet are biased, crass or stupid.

THE BALANCING ACT

Sometimes, it's not going to be cutting something out that will be an ethical issue; it will be leaving something in. People will ask reporters to avoid publishing something because it is embarrassing or because publishing it could create some collateral damage.

Some media outlets have a rule about reporting on suicides, although those policies vary greatly. Some say it is never mentioned, citing an apocryphal story that people who commit suicide are doing it to seek attention, and running a story will encourage other people to kill themselves. Others say it is not a news story unless it happens in a public place. Some say you cover everything all the time, using the rationale of "the people's right to know everything about everybody."

In cases like these, you will find yourself trying to balance a number of interests, including those of your outlet, the sources and the public. In ethically reviewing your approach to topics like these, you will want to keep your audience at the forefront of your mind. Your job is to serve the audience.

VISUAL ETHICS

Although many of the editing decisions you will make will involve text, visual elements you publish also merit ethical considerations. Photographs and graphics can create problems on the basis of how they are framed, cropped, toned and altered. To keep your work fair and accurate, you need to understand how visuals can manipulate perception.

During the transition from film to digital photography in the 1990s, the question of what alterations were acceptable became an important topic. Traditional photojournalists argued that programs like Photoshop would cheapen their product while introducing visual falsehoods into their frames. During the time when chemical developing processes and digital photography competed equally, the ethical benchmark for computer manipulation was set at "nothing more or less than what you can do in a darkroom." As photo processing moved out of the wet lab and onto the computer monitor, this standard became more difficult to assess. Furthermore, crafty photographers have always been able to manipulate images via chemical and technical processes. The concept of the darkroom as being the standard for purity has always been a bit of a falsehood. (We will discuss photography and these issues further in Chapter 9.)

Understanding what makes for an ethical or unethical choice in terms of the use of visuals matters a great deal. Here are a few things to think about when determining what works and what doesn't:

Cropping

While in the field, a photographer selects a sliver of time and a slice of space to capture in a photograph. However, when the photographer returns with the image, some alterations might improve the focus or value of the frame. Cropping allows a photographer or an editor to remove unwanted outlying portions of a frame and shift the focus of the image. (This concept is discussed at length in Chapter 9.) Although cropping is a common practice, the issue of what is being removed or left behind can lead to an ethical problem. In 2015, more than 20 percent of the entries in the World Press Photo competition had been disqualified because of "significant addition or subtraction to the image content."[6]

In 2009, Newsweek used a heavy crop to focus on Vice President Dick Cheney to illustrate a quote he had given regarding torture conducted by the Central Intelligence Agency. The image was a full page of Cheney leaning over a cutting board as he prepared a bloody piece of meat. The photographer of that frame, David Hume Kennerly, was shocked when he saw what had been done to his image.

The image Kennerly sent to the magazine showed a family gathering at the home of Cheney's daughter, Liz. The original shot included Cheney's wife, his two daughters and one of their grandchildren, all of whom were gathered in the kitchen, preparing for a family dinner. By taking an aggressive crop of the shot, the editors of Newsweek changed the entire meaning of the image, Kennerly argued.[7] Newsweek issued a statement on the matter, stating that the photo was cropped and that cropping is an acceptable photographic practice. Even though the magazine said the image was used to make an editorial point, Newsweek stated that the photo had not been altered and that the staff had used "editorial judgment to show the most interesting part of it."

As an editor, cropping will likely be one of the more common edits you or others on your staff will make. Photos can be cropped to make them fit a specific area, to change the frame from a horizontal to a vertical or to show an interesting part of an image. However, keep in mind that a crop should not be used to alter the underlying meaning of a photo.

Color and Tone

The lightening or darkening of images has often been necessary because of the messy business of printing. An image can look great on a monitor, but it might become muddy and dark when the ink hits the page. To capture nuance, value or even clarity, editors have changed the brightness, saturation and hue of photos for years. Programs like Photoshop make it easier to do this, and they also allow editors to home in on a specific portion of a frame and increase or decrease some of its color and tone distinctions.

Lightening or darkening a photograph can have ethical implications. In 1994, former football great O.J. Simpson was arrested on suspicion of killing his ex-wife, Nicole Brown Simpson, and her friend Ronald Goldman. As is the case with most people who are arrested, Simpson had a mug shot taken at the time of his booking. The media frenzy surrounding Simpson's arrest led to his landing on the cover of Time and Newsweek.

Critics argued that Time had attempted to make Simpson look "blacker," thus connecting his race to the issue of crime. Time officials argued that they were attempting to show the "darkness" of the situation. In either case, when compared side by side, it is clear the covers are drastically different, leading to questions about each magazine's approach to this subject.[8]

Photo Illustrations

An editor with a solid grasp of Photoshop can make almost anything possible when it comes to image manipulation. People can be added or removed from images. Background colors can be changed. Events can be merged. Most photographers will tell you that doing any of these things constitutes a violation of a photographer's ethical code.

To get past that major issue, many organizations have taken to making a minor alteration to their images: They add the term "photo illustration." Although this term has a broad range of applications, the underlying premise is that the picture the publication is presenting is not a photograph, but rather an altered visual image.

In many cases, these photo illustrations are obviously manipulated shots, such as a picture of a dinosaur driving a car. However, in other cases, the term is used as a crutch to allow minor changes that would be ethically suspect if the image were considered a photo. Experts in psychology and media have noted that a visual representation of reality, even when it is not real, is enough to override other functions within the brain.[9] Thus, you need to make sure people really understand that something is a photo illustration and that the illustration is worth your choice to manipulate reality.

AN ETHICAL THOUGHT PROCESS

How you make an ethical decision is more important than the decision you make. In most cases, ethics aren't right or wrong, but simply better or worse. As an editor, you need to have a process you use to figure out what you should do in a situation and the best approach to take. Here are some important things to think about and some thought-provoking questions you might want to use to help your thought process along.

Why Do I Want to Do This?

Sometimes, it is easy to get caught up in the moment. Journalists get excited about a big opportunity, and sometimes the adrenaline kicks them into overdrive. That rush can be exhilarating, but it can be a bad place from which to make solid and measured decisions.

When you are faced with a situation that might have ethical ramifications, you should ask yourself why you want to proceed in a certain way. Try to determine whether you are satisfying your own interests or if you see value in the material. You want to ask yourself if you think the material will benefit your audience members or just shock them. Figure out if you want to do something because it's important or because it's cheap, easy and "everyone else will probably do it." If you can figure out why you want to do something, it can help ground you as you make your decisions. A bad decision made quickly can come back to haunt you.

Is the Juice Worth the Squeeze?

As an editor, you need to take a longer and broader view of a situation. Although a staff member might look at one piece on a chessboard, you are required to review the entire board. That is why you need to determine what you are giving up and what you are getting back. What is the trade-off in your decision?

If you decide to put out a hyperbolic press release this week, will it have people distrusting you for a long time after that? If you decide to burn a source for one story, will it cost you a strong source and several other important stories down the road? If you publish something that is derogatory or mean spirited, will you get attention, but not in the way you want it?

In some cases, you will try to find a middle ground that allows everyone to win. In other cases, you run the story because you know it is important, despite the backlash you will face. In many instances, discussion will be your ally as you work through the ethical dilemma. It's like haggling over the price of a used car or an item at a rummage sale: You get what you want for the most part, but you give up something as well, and neither side is completely happy.

What Is It Like on the Other Side of This?

If you can take the perspective of others into account, you can make a better decision. However, this can become a dangerous question, in that you can forgive a lot more than you should. In any case, it's worth at least cracking that door a little bit and taking a peek inside.

You can make an argument not to look at the other side. Criminals have mothers who will say, "He was such a good boy," and politicians who commit adultery have spouses who stand by them publicly. However, when someone dies through no fault of his or her own, it can be difficult for a survivor to be comfortable being interviewed by a reporter. A crime victim can be reluctant to speak, or even relatives of people who committed crimes might not want to share their thoughts on the matter.

If your sister or brother died or if your best friend did something reprehensible, how likely would you be to show calm, restraint and perfect grammar as a swarm of journalists descended upon you? As an editor, you want to make sure to give your writers the tools they need to succeed, which includes a reasonable dose of humanity. You should follow the same premise when conducting your edit.

Will I Be OK With This Choice Once I Make It?

You can never undo a deed that is done, so make sure you're confident in what you are about to attempt. You can retract a story, correct an error, apologize profusely and myriad other things, but the deed has been done. It's worth remembering that when you take a look at an ethical situation.

How are you going to feel about what you did? Are you going to be OK with it? Decisions with ethical ramifications aren't perfect, and you will likely feel slightly uncomfortable with what you did, regardless of which way you go. However, if you do something you know is dishonest or unethical, it can eat at you for a long time, so do your best to avoid taking those actions.

Sometimes you do what's best, but you will have trouble looking at yourself in the mirror or sleeping at night. That's fine, as it happens to almost everybody. However, you want to minimize the number of sleepless nights you will face.

THE BIG THREE

Here are the three key things you should take away from this chapter:

1. **Credibility isn't a boomerang:** As an editor, you have to take the long view when it comes to ethics. Just because something is simple or easy, it doesn't always make sense to do it and cause bigger problems down the road. The only currency you possess in the world of media is credibility, and once you throw it away, it's not coming back.

2. **Ethics help you make better decisions:** A good ethical policy and a strong set of personal convictions can help you determine what you should do and why you should do it in your job. The ethics to which you adhere will provide you a solid map for navigating the various interests of your publics as well as the choices you need to make as you serve them.

3. **You have to live with it:** Regardless of the choices you make or the philosophies to which you adhere, you will have difficult choices to make, and you need to learn to live with them. You could make the same decision 10 times and have 10 vastly different results. However, the goal is to learn to live with what you did and why you did it, and to learn something of value from each outcome.

KEY TERMS

anonymous source 43

breakfast test 42

categorical imperative 41

ethics 40

golden mean 40

off the record 43

pluralism 42

unnamed source 43

utilitarianism 41

DISCUSSION QUESTIONS

1. Of the four ethical paradigms listed in the chapter, which one do you see as fitting your approach to ethics the best? Which one do you find to be the most unlike you? What is it about these philosophies that attracts or repels you?

2. Allison Hantschel Sansone noted in her "View From a Pro" interview the following problem with how journalists approach ethics: "Most people think of ethics as 'Do I name the crime victim?' or 'Do I use a clickbait headline?' instead of thinking of it as 'How do I serve my audience well?'" Do you agree with her that serving an audience is an ethical issue? Why or why not?

3. How much faith do you have in information within a story or document that comes from a source that was not named? What makes you feel that you can or can't trust that information? What other aspects of the story would help make you feel more or less comfortable in trusting that information?

WRITE NOW!

1. Think back to a time when you dealt with an ethical dilemma in any part of your life, and write a short essay on your experience with that situation. Outline the situation in a few brief paragraphs, then explain what it was you did and how the situation resolved itself. Finally, walk through the four questions listed in the section "An Ethical Thought Process," and answer each one.

2. Look up an ethical code for any area of the media profession, such as the National Press Photographers Association, the Society of Professional Journalists or the Public Relations Society of America. After you review the code, select the specific aspects of it you feel are most important and explain why you believe this to be the case. Then explain the areas you find would be most difficult to uphold. What bothers you about those aspects of the code, and how difficult do you think it would be to explain this? Write a short essay on this topic.

3. On the basis of your understanding of the breakfast test, which of the following types of photos would you run in a local publication if you were its editor?

    a. A police officer taping off a homicide scene, where you can see a chalk outline of a dead body in the background.

    b. A local hunter skinning a deer he shot.

    c. An accident scene with two completely mangled vehicles.

    d. A person hanging from a tree after committing suicide in a public park.

    e. High school students crying after escaping from an active shooter in the building.

    f. A zipped-up body bag at the scene of an area death.

4. Consider the following ethical dilemmas and determine how you would resolve them.

    a. A client asks you to avoid mentioning a minor side effect of his new "miracle drug" in your promotional material, something that is not illegal in your state, but is often seen as bad practice.

    b. While running a political campaign, you discover that your candidate's opponent was arrested 30 years earlier as a high school student for a "senior prank" that involved spray painting the principal's car. The staff is divided on making this part of your latest advertisement against the opponent.

    c. The son of a longtime advertiser in your paper is arrested on suspicion of drinking and driving.

The advertiser calls the city desk and asks you not to mention this in the paper.

d. A photographer took several shots of a domestic violence reenactment that was part of a police officer training. A tighter crop on the photograph would improve its visual storytelling, but could also make people think the scene was a real incident.

e. A source revealed important details of an ongoing court case to your reporter, who has a great story ready for publication when the source calls you and asks you not to run the comments. He says he knows he shouldn't have said these things, and now he fears he might be fired if his name is attached to them publicly.

$SAGE edge™

Visit **edge.sagepub.com/filakediting** to help you accomplish your coursework goals in an easy-to-use learning environment.

5 PUNCTUATION

Without the various marks and symbols of punctuation, understanding and correct reading of printed passages would be challenging. Therefore, punctuation can be a minefield for the journalist with only a passing interest in these rules that aid clear writing.

While it is easy to locate critics who bemoan the poor use of punctuation among students, this chapter will avoid that temptation and instead provide a review of the basic rules all editors should know and follow. This involves the careful art of nitpicking, whose aim is to deliver well-edited copy that is as clear and correct as it is effective.

Some punctuation involves the precision of mathematics. The rest is somewhat subjective and open to interpretation of the rules. The fact is that you need to be as confident knowing that "Joplin, Missouri," is correctly punctuated as knowing that 3 + 5 = 8. Because dealing with punctuation can be tedious, this chapter may not be a fun read. Yet these guidelines are essential to your success as an editor.

The rules of punctuation for media writing are nearly identical to those for other types of writing, so what you find here is what you would find in most standard English handbooks. Another resource is the Associated Press Stylebook, which offers entries covering rules and examples of all punctuation, as well as AP's handy Guide to Punctuation.

In this chapter, you will review punctuation so that you can reinforce and build on what you already know and acquire some additional punctuation rules that are unique to media writing. Along the way we'll see how punctuation errors can lead to problems for readers and how to fix those. In the end, you should know that using punctuation correctly is not just a virtue; it is a necessity. Applying these long-held principles makes it easier and more effective for media writers to communicate with their audiences.

To simplify this review, we will consider three categories of punctuation: end marks that stop, internal marks that pause and specialty marks that explain.

END MARKS THAT STOP

In this category are periods, question marks and exclamation points. The first is the go-to mark to end most sentences, while the other two signal full stops for special sentences. These marks tend to be the clearest and easiest punctuation you will review.

Periods

Writers use lots of periods, and most of the time their use is straightforward. They bring readers to a full stop of one thought before proceeding with the next. Also, many abbreviations and most initials use periods. Finally, an ellipsis uses periods. Check your familiarity with the following rules.

a. Periods are the most common ending mark for a sentence, specifically what is called a declarative sentence, which makes a statement as opposed to issuing a command, exclaiming or asking a question:

   ○ *The Chicago Cubs won the 2016 World Series, their first series win since 1908.*

   ○ *Climate change has become a hotly contested issue.*

In addition to marking the ends of most sentences, periods have three other roles.

b. Use periods following many abbreviations. For complete information, see Chapter 6.

   ○ *New York Gov. Andrew Cuomo*

   ○ *Jan. 1*

   ○ *7 a.m.*

   ○ *P.S.*

c. Use periods with initials in names:

   ○ *Donald J. Trump*

   ○ *Janet K. Thompson*

When someone goes by initials and surname, such as *E.G. Marshall*, don't put a space between the *E.* and the *G.* AP recommends this so that the initials will stay together on the same line. Also, when using only initials for a person's name, as in *HRC* or *JFK*, do not use any periods.

d. An ellipsis is occasionally used to suggest an unfinished thought or to indicate missing words in a direct quote. The Stylebook recommends handling an ellipsis as though it were a three-letter word, by using three periods one space before and one space following.

   ○ *"I don't know what . . . I don't understand . . . I'm speechless," the surprised award recipient said.*

When writers remove words from a direct quote, they seek to improve the flow and to remove extraneous content. The ellipsis should never be used to change the original meaning, however. Here is an example of correct use:

   ○ Full quote: *The congressman said, "After much consideration and some passionate debate, which went on and on and on, we passed the bill."*

   ○ With ellipsis: *The congressman said, "After much consideration and some passionate debate . . . we passed the bill."*

e. Follow a period at the end of a sentence with a single space.

Question Marks

Using question marks is simple. They follow direct questions:

• *Is there any solution to the current economic woes facing the U.S.?*

• *"Are you ready to leave?" he asked.*

However, do not use a question mark after an indirect question:

- *She wondered if there were any solutions to the current economic woes facing the U.S.*

- *He asked if she was ready to leave.*

- *The question is whether the economy is actually growing as much as the numbers suggest.*

Exclamation Points

Even simpler to apply and less frequently used are exclamation points. They follow expressions of surprise, disbelief or strong emotion:

- *"Stop!" he shouted. "You can't go any farther."*

- *She cried, "Oh my goodness!"*

INTERNAL MARKS THAT PAUSE

This category has four marks: commas, semicolons, dashes and colons. Writers are most familiar with commas, of course, but they probably have much less understanding of and practice with the other three.

Commas

Because of their frequent and varied uses, commas may be the bane of many media writers and editors. Part of the problem is that too many writers drop commas into their sentences like flower girls dropping rose petals down a wedding aisle. A few here, a few there, with no sound reasoning behind their use.

Although some comma usage is discretionary, most follows long-held rules. It's not rocket science, just a little tedious, perhaps, and at times confusing. In addition, you may wish to check the Stylebook for additional explanations and examples.

a. Use a comma with a compound sentence, where a coordinating conjunction joins two complete sentences. Check the differences in each of the following examples.

   ○ Wrong: *President Donald Trump is the oldest man to be elected president at age 70 and former President Ronald Reagan is now the second oldest to be elected at age 69.*

   ○ Right: *President Donald Trump is the oldest man to be elected president at age 70, and former President Ronald Reagan is now the second oldest to be elected at age 69.*

   ○ Wrong: *The reporter waited three hours outside the mayor's office but she was unable to see her about the city's budget problems.*

   ○ Right: *The reporter waited three hours outside the mayor's office, but she was unable to see her about the city's budget problems.*

The following is also correct because removing the "she" in the second sentence means that the **coordinating conjunction** is now joining two phrases, not two sentences. Some editors would argue that this is the better version because it is tighter.

   ○ Right: *The reporter waited three hours outside the mayor's office but was unable to see her about the city's budget problems.*

   ○ Wrong: *The polls leading up to the presidential election favored Hillary Clinton yet she lost to Donald Trump in the Electoral College vote.*

○ Right: *The polls leading up to the presidential election favored Hillary Clinton, yet she lost to Donald Trump in the Electoral College vote.*

Do not confuse coordinating conjunctions with similar words, **conjunctive adverbs**. The latter cannot join two independent clauses with only a comma. Instead, use a semicolon or a period. Here are examples of conjunctive adverbs at work:

○ Wrong: *The reporter waited three hours outside the mayor's office, however, she was unable to see her about the city's budget problems.*

○ Right: *The reporter waited three hours outside the mayor's office; however, she was unable to see her about the city's budget problems.*

○ Wrong: *The summer heat became oppressive, therefore, the media advised residents to restrict their time outdoors.*

○ Right: *The summer heat became oppressive. Therefore, the media advised residents to restrict their time outdoors.*

b. Use commas to separate three or more elements in a series — whether they are nouns, adjectives, adverbs or phrases — but drop the comma preceding a conjunction in most series. Consider these examples:

○ Wrong: *The doctor asked for a scalpel, gauze, needle, and thread.* [Series of nouns.]

○ Right: *The doctor asked for a scalpel, gauze, needle and thread.*

○ Wrong: *The cottage was old, run-down, and altogether uninhabitable.* [Series of adjectives.]

○ Right: *The cottage was old, run-down and altogether uninhabitable.*

○ Wrong: *He strode quickly, purposefully, and directly to the front of the classroom.* [Series of adverbs.]

○ Right: *He strode quickly, purposefully and directly to the front of the classroom.*

○ Wrong: *She grasped her boyfriend by his collar, held him directly in front of her face, and planted a warm kiss on his lips.* [Series of phrases.]

○ Right: *She grasped her boyfriend by his collar, held him in front of her face and planted a warm kiss on his lips.*

c. Use commas to separate two or more coordinate adjectives in front of the noun they describe. The AP Stylebook calls these equal adjectives. In other words, adjectives are coordinate or equal if you can replace commas with "and" without changing the meaning of the sentence, as in these examples:

○ *Her piercing, critical gaze froze him midbite.* [Note that "and" makes sense here, as in "piercing and critical gaze."]

○ *He relished the brief, quiet moments before the shop opened at 9 a.m.* [Same here.]

However, adjectives that are cumulative do not take commas; inserting "and" or changing the order of presentation doesn't make sense, as in these examples:

○ *The former secret agent spoke to the gathering of students.* [Inserting "and" here makes no sense, as in "former and secret agent." Note, too, that flip-flopping the order also doesn't work, as in "secret former agent."]

○ *The bright red fire truck sparkled in the afternoon sun.* [Same here.]

d. Use commas to set off elements that introduce a sentence and are positioned in front of the subject. These include **adverb clauses**, **participial phrases**, **infinitive phrases**, long prepositional phrases and conjunctive adverbs. Consider the following examples:

   ○ *When the temperature drops below freezing, she begins to thrive.* [Introductory adverbial clause. Note that no commas are needed if the adverb clause follows the main clause, as in this example: *She begins to thrive when the temperature drops below freezing.*]

   ○ *Tired and worn out, the runner collapsed 120 yards from the finish line.* OR *Driving too slowly, the elderly woman caused a three-block traffic jam.* [Introductory participial phrases. However, when a present participle, such as driving, is used as a noun, no commas are needed, as in this sentence: *Driving is one of her great passions.*]

   ○ *To run for a city council seat, a candidate must complete an application at city hall.* [Introductory infinitive. Note that no comma is needed when an infinitive is working as a noun, as in this sentence: *To run a long race demands both physical and mental stamina.*]

   ○ *At the end of a long day, it's nice to be able to put one's feet up.* [Long introductory prepositional phrase. Usually, prepositional phrases should be more than four words to be considered long.]

   ○ *Unfortunately, the football team lost again.* OR *Nevertheless, the woman was unwilling to give up her seat.* [Introductory conjunctive adverbs.]

e. Commas set off **nonrestrictive clauses** and phrases from the rest of the sentence. The Stylebook calls these nonessential clauses and phrases. A clause or phrase is nonrestrictive when it can be deleted without losing the basic meaning of the sentence:

   ○ *Edwin Smith, who is an associate circuit judge, was a longtime resident and well known in the community.* [The clause "who is an associate circuit judge" is nonrestrictive; cutting it will not alter the sentence's meaning.]

   ○ *His brother, Steve, was a long-distance trucker.* [The name Steve is nonrestrictive — and set off by commas — if the writer has only one brother; however, if the writer has more than one brother, Steve is restrictive, as in this example: *His brother Steve was a long-distance trucker.* Without it readers cannot know which brother the writer is referring to.]

   ○ Wrong: *President, Donald Trump, is the seventh New Yorker to hold the highest office in the country.* [No comma needed because *Donald Trump* is restrictive. Also, as we'll see in Chapter 6, short titles go in front of names and don't use punctuation.]

   ○ Right: *President Donald Trump is the seventh New Yorker to hold the highest office in the country.*

   ○ Right: *Donald Trump, 45th president of the United States, is the seventh New Yorker to hold the highest office in the country.* [The phrase "45th president of the United States" is nonrestrictive. Removing it will not alter the meaning or understanding of the sentence.]

f. A comma sets off attribution, also called a speech tag, from most direct quotations, as in these examples:

   ○ Wrong: *She said "The winner of the pageant should be delighted with the cash prizes, gifts and awards."*

- Right: *She said, "The winner of the pageant should be delighted with the cash prizes, gifts and awards."*
- Wrong: *"The winner of the pageant should be delighted with the cash prizes, gifts and awards" she said.*
- Right: *"The winner of the pageant should be delighted with the cash prizes, gifts and awards," she said.*
- Wrong: *"The winner of the pageant" she said "should be delighted with the cash prizes, gifts and awards."*
- Right: *"The winner of the pageant," she said, "should be delighted with the cash prizes, gifts and awards."*

g. When the attribution precedes indirect quotations, also called paraphrases, do not use a comma, as in this sentence:

- Wrong: *She said, the pageant's winner should like the prizes, gifts and awards.*
- Right: *She said the pageant's winner should like the prizes, gifts and awards.*

However, use commas if the tag follows or is embedded within the paraphrase:

- *The pageant's winner should like the prizes, gifts and awards, she said.*
- *The pageant's winner, she said, should like the prizes, gifts and awards.*

h. Use commas to set off a person's age or hometown whether or not "of" is used, as in these examples:

- *Stan Smithton, 45, was charged with killing his wife.*
- *Smithton, of Boston, was unable to post the $1 million bond.*

i. Commas set off states and nations when presented with cities:

- *Lawrence, Kansas, is home to the University of Kansas Jayhawks.*
- *His sister in Tucson, Arizona, phoned him about local flooding.*
- *She was unable to sleep the night before leaving for Dublin, Ireland, for her family reunion.*

j. Commas set off years when presented with dates:

- *She was born on April 2, 1949, in Savannah, Missouri.*

k. A comma follows "yes" and "no":

- *No, Barack Obama is not the first Illinoisan elected president.*
- *Yes, both Abraham Lincoln and Ulysses Simpson Grant were Illinoisans when elected president.*

l. Set off elements of direct address with commas:

- *"Sir, are you prepared to defend yourself?" the judge asked.*
- *"I'm unsure, Mattie, if you should be driving home after drinking three beers," her sister said.*

m. Use commas with figures larger than 999:

- *Enrollment at the university is 5,950.*
- *More than 112,000 people in the state are jobless.* [Numbers larger than 999,999 usually are not written out, according to AP style. So, the number 2,325,000 would be written as 2.32 million.]

HELPFUL HINTS
DEFINING KEY TERMS

Even after reading rules of punctuation, you may have trouble applying them if you are unfamiliar with the terms used here. Take a quick look at these now, and refer back to them as needed.

Adjective: These words describe nouns and pronouns. **Coordinate adjectives**, also called paired adjectives, are two or more adjectives that precede and equally describe the same noun.

Adverb: These words describe verbs, adjectives and other adverbs. While conjunctions connect sentences, phrases and words, conjunctive adverbs connect ideas, describing the entire clause of which it is part. Many conjunctive adverbs go at the beginning of a clause, but they can appear anywhere within a sentence. An adverb clause is a subordinate, or dependent, clause that acts like an adverb within the main clause.

Clause: This is a related group of words that includes a subject and verb. **Independent clauses**, also commonly called sentences, communicate a complete thought. It may be in the form of a declaration, a question, a command or an exclamation. **Dependent clauses**, as you might guess, cannot stand alone and depend on an independent clause to make sense.

Compound sentence: These sentences contain two or more related independent clauses joined by a coordinating conjunction.

Conjunctions: These are words that connect clauses, phrases and other words. Coordinating conjunctions are only six words that join sentences or phrases and words within sentences. They are "and," "or," "nor," "but," "for," "yet" and "so." **Subordinating conjunctions** involve a much longer list of words that join unequal elements, such as independent and dependent clauses.

Phrase: These groups of two or more sequential and related words, which cannot include both a subject and a verb, enable greater detail and clarity as writers work to make meaning within sentences. The following six are common types of phrases: **appositive phrase**, **gerund phrase**, infinitive phrase, **noun phrase**, participial phrase and **prepositional phrase**.

Semicolons

Semicolons are simpler than commas to use correctly. The prevailing wisdom is that they are more of a pause than a comma but less than a period. Some writers never use semicolons, because they don't understand them. Fortunately, you need to know and apply only two simple rules.

a. First, use semicolons to connect two independent clauses (complete sentences) without a coordinating conjunction, as in these sentences:

   ○ Wrong: *The notion that college freshmen gain an average of 15 pounds is widespread, however, at least one recent study says otherwise.* [This is a common error. Although "however" helps connect the two ideas, it is not a coordinating conjunction. It is a conjunctive adverb.]

   ○ Right: *The notion that college freshmen gain an average of 15 pounds is widespread; however, at least one recent study says otherwise.* [Two independent clauses joined by a semicolon.]

   ○ Wrong: *Freshmen in the survey gained 2.7 pounds on average, that figure still is five times greater than the general population.* [The error here, of course, is using only a comma to join two independent clauses.]

   ○ Right: *Freshmen in the survey gained 2.7 pounds on average; that figure still is five times greater than the general population.* [The solution is a semicolon.]

b. Second, semicolons help clarify a series that includes one or more commas. These semicolons may seem curious or awkward, but the goal is to ensure that each element in the series is clear:

   ○ Wrong: *At the grocery store Eleanor bought six bananas, each with just a tinge of green, three oranges, which are her favorite fruit and five apples, including two Jonathans and three Golden Delicious.* [Even the most careful reader might have problems connecting related items in this series.]

- ○ Right: *At the grocery store Eleanor bought six bananas, each with just a tinge of green; three oranges, which are her favorite fruit; and five apples, including two Jonathans and three Golden Delicious.* [Two semicolons help keep related material grouped. Note that a semicolon is needed after "fruit" and before the coordinating conjunction "and" in the last series.]

- ○ Wrong: *Later, she stopped at a coffee shop to get the following drinks for her friends: a cinnamon latte, with 2 percent milk and no whipped cream, two cherry mochas and a cappuccino, with whole milk and a sprinkling of nutmeg.* [As above, using only commas makes it challenging to keep related items grouped.]

- ○ Right: *Later, she stopped at a coffee shop to get the following drinks for her friends: a cinnamon latte, with 2 percent milk and no whipped cream; two cherry mochas; and a cappuccino, with whole milk and a sprinkling of nutmeg.*

Dashes

Dashes usually serve to separate, often signaling an interruption or an unexpected change in thought in a sentence.

a. Dashes can provide a simple break in an idea. AP style recommends using a space before and a space after a dash:

- ○ *Unlike some other Army recruits, Stella was ready — even eager — to leave for basic military training.*

- ○ *His tenure as president — even if short lived — was noteworthy.*

b. Dashes are also used when phrases that are usually set off by commas contain commas:

- ○ Wrong: *His brother, who is younger, smarter and better looking, was forever getting into trouble.* [The use of commas alone can slow readability and make understanding more difficult.]

- ○ Right: *His brother — who is younger, smarter and better looking — was forever getting into trouble.*

- ○ Wrong: *His latest adventure, if you can call getting drunk, being arrested and spending a night in jail an adventure, happened last week.* [As above, using only commas doesn't offer enough direction for readers to understand related content.]

- ○ Right: *His latest adventure — if you can call getting drunk, being arrested and spending a night in jail an adventure — happened last week.*

Check the AP Stylebook for a couple of other more infrequent uses of dashes.

Colons

These marks introduce material. Typically, what follows the colon further explains, amplifies or specifically names what precedes the colon. Importantly, what precedes the colon should be a complete sentence.

a. Capitalize the first word following the colon if it begins another sentence or is a proper noun. Consider these examples:

- ○ *Forbes magazine named the top-earning musicians of 2017: Sean Combs, Beyonce, Drake and The Weeknd.*

○ *He went to the grocery store to buy several items: soft drinks, eggs, bread, milk and cold cuts.* [However, see the difference in this version, which also is correct: *He went to the grocery to get soft drinks, eggs, bread, milk and cold cuts.*]

○ *She had one principle by which she guided her life: She must be true to herself.* [Note that the material following the colon is a complete sentence, so the first word is capitalized.]

○ *Perry loved one thing in life and one thing only: himself.*

VIEW FROM A PRO
BRIAN CLEVELAND

Courtesy of Brian Cleveland

Brian Cleveland has been a multiplatform editor at The Washington Post since 2012. He shepherds the daytime copy editors and helps run the desk's training, while keeping the local stylebook up to date.

Prior to working at The Post, he was the copy desk chief at The Virginian-Pilot for five of his seven years there, overseeing about a dozen copy editors. He began his career copy editing at the Duluth News Tribune in Minnesota, where he also designed pages and learned numerous other duties.

Cleveland said that his job requires him to look out for all types of errors and that people notice even the smallest of transgressions.

"I think for a time when online journalism was newer, there was a sense that speed was everything and the small things didn't matter," he said. "I don't believe that's true anymore. Now, everyone has an online presence and can get news quickly from a variety of sources. But being first doesn't matter if you're wrong. Credibility is the biggest thing a news organization has to offer its readers, and that credibility is based on getting things both big and small correct. Yes, readers are more understanding about typos and bad grammar when we're quickly updating breaking news stories, but they still notice and they still care."

To meet the needs of his readers, Cleveland said he not only has to focus on keeping things clear, but also using the right platforms and right approaches to reach them.

"I think you have to spend a lot more time thinking about audience than before," he said. "When all you had was a print paper that was delivered regionally, you had a good idea of who was going to be reading a story and when. Now with online, your audience could be much broader and it could be on a variety of platforms."

Although the tone and approach will vary if the story is a longform piece in the print edition of The Post or a quick post to the paper's Snapchat account, the underlying aspects of clean writing and accurate reporting must remain constant, he said.

"Copy editors are reader advocates — we're coming to stories cold like a reader will and it's our responsibility to look at it through their eyes — in terms of clarity, fairness and many other issues," Cleveland said. "We should always be thinking about our audience and how they'll see what we're doing."

In that regard, Cleveland said, editing is both about understanding the rules that govern language and the importance of communicating effectively with the readers.

"As you're learning about editing and language, it's important to get the rules down, because after you've done that, you can start learning when to bend those rules, or maybe even break them," he said. "Language is always evolving and you can't be wedded to how things were done in the past just for the sake of 'that's how it's always been.' Otherwise, we'd still be hyphenating 'teen-ager' and looking ridiculously out of touch. But there's a delicate balance between going along with the latest language fads and respecting tradition and the expectations people have for what words mean and how they're used to seeing them. It's a tough line to walk sometimes."

Although it can be a difficult and seemingly thankless job to some, Cleveland said he finds joy and value in his job.

"Copy editing is more than just spellchecking a story — something I wish more people in the news industry who control budgets understood," Cleveland said. "It's an important step in quality control and, as I said earlier, it's being an advocate for the reader. I really love being a copy editor. It brings together a lot of skills because I work with people from all over the newsroom (diplomacy), I learn about a lot of different subjects (curiosity and critical thinking), and I get to improve the overall quality of the paper (an eye for detail and a bit of perfectionism). Copy editors are the last line of defense in a news organization, and I couldn't be prouder to be among their ranks."

b. Colons also are used with time of day and biblical citations:

   ○ *3:32 p.m.*

   ○ *John 3:16* [Note that the numbers refer to chapter and verse in the Bible.]

c. Colons can be used with dialog or question-and-answer packages. They also may introduce long direct quotations, particularly if they are longer than one paragraph.

SPECIALTY MARKS THAT EXPLAIN

Football fans know that special teams players include gunners, kick returners, long snappers, placekickers, punters and punt returners. Similarly, punctuation has its own special teams players, composed of apostrophes, hyphens, parentheses and quotation marks. Writers don't use these marks all the time, but they would be hard-pressed to get along without them.

Apostrophes

The most common use of the apostrophe is to indicate the possessive, and many rules guide that usage. Until you become familiar with these, you may wish to return to consult this section or the Stylebook to ensure correct use.

a. To show the possessive of singular common and proper nouns not ending in s, add 's:

   ○ *the car's engine*

   ○ *a teacher's classroom*

   ○ *Andrew's job*

   ○ *Louisiana's capital*

b. To show the possessive of singular common nouns ending in s, add 's unless the next word begins with s. Then, just add the apostrophe:

   ○ *the mattress's weight*

   ○ *a fortress's weakness*

   ○ *the mantis's prey*

   ○ *her mistress' sorrows*

   ○ *the boss' seat*

c. To show the possessive of plural common nouns ending in s, add the apostrophe:

   ○ *the shoes' owners*

   ○ *their suitcases' tags*

   ○ *the dogs' food dish*

d. To show the possessive of plural common nouns not ending in s, add 's:

   ○ *her children's teachers*

   ○ *the fungi's growth*

   ○ *the lice's removal*

e. To show the possessive of singular proper nouns ending in s, add the apostrophe:

   ○ *Jesus' name*

- ○ *Arkansas' population*
- ○ *James' menagerie*

f. To show the possessive of common nouns plural in form but singular in meaning, add the apostrophe:

- ○ *his pants' color*
- ○ *the blues' origin*
- ○ *news' legacy*

g. To show the possessive of compound words, add 's or the apostrophe to the word closest to the thing possessed:

- ○ *the passers-by's stares*
- ○ *my attorney general's staff*

h. To show joint possession, use the correct form after the last word of the ownership group:

- ○ *John and Mary's wedding*
- ○ *Huey, Dewey and Louie's uncle*

i. If ownership is individual, however, use the correct form with each member of the group:

- ○ *Stan's and Ollie's talents*
- ○ *Abbott's and Costello's ages*

j. The following special expressions are exceptions to the rules above:

- ○ *for appearance' sake*
- ○ *for goodness' sake*
- ○ *for conscience' sake*

Apostrophes have only three other uses: omitted letters, omitted figures and plurals of a single letter.

k. Use apostrophes to indicate omitted letters, also termed contractions:

- ○ *can't*
- ○ *won't*
- ○ *he's*
- ○ *it's*
- ○ *rock 'n' roll*
- ○ *'tis the season*
- ○ *ne'er-do-well*

l. Use apostrophes to indicate omitted figures:

- ○ *the '90s*
- ○ *the class of '67*

m. Use apostrophes for plural letters:

- ○ *three A's and two B's*
- ○ *p's and q's*

Hyphens

The common use of hyphens is to join words, including these:

- Compound modifiers: These are two or more words that work in tandem to describe, elaborate or change the meaning of a noun.

- Compound proper nouns and adjectives: As proper nouns name specific persons, places or things, so compound proper nouns and adjectives are two more proper nouns or proper adjectives that work together to modify a noun.

- Some prefixes and suffixes: A prefix is a letter or group of letters that attach to the beginning of a word and modify its meaning. Similarly, a suffix is a group of letters attached to the end of a word to modify its meaning.

- Duplicated vowels and tripled consonants: Vowels are a, e, i, o and u. All remaining letters are consonants.

- Numerals: These are words expressing numbers.

- Suspensive hyphenation: This is use of compound modifiers in sets of two or more where some of the repeated words are dropped.

The Stylebook suggests that less punctuation is better and advises using hyphens only when not doing so would cause confusion or misreading. That said, consider these guidelines:

a. Hyphens join compound modifiers, that is, two or more adjectives that offer a single concept and precede the noun they modify:

   - *balance-of-payments argument*

   - *well-known doctor*

   - *first-base umpire*

   - *long-term incentives*

   - *high-growth company*

In addition, when compound modifiers follow a form of the verb "to be," retain the hyphens:

   - *The doctor was well-known.*

   - *The incentives are long-term.*

   - *The company will be high-growth.*

b. Use hyphens to join compound proper nouns and adjectives, particularly when referencing heritage:

   - *Japanese-American*

   - *Anglo-Saxon*

   - *German-American*

However, the Stylebook has two exceptions to this rule:

   - *Latin American*

   - *French Canadian*

c. AP tends to discourage hyphens with most common prefixes and suffixes. The general exceptions are prefixes for words that begin with the same vowel as the prefix ends, for capitalized words and for the rare doubled prefixes. Here are some common prefixes that illustrate the need to regularly check the Stylebook:

- When "ex-" means "former," use the hyphen: *ex-ambassador, ex-mayor.* However, when it means "out of," drop the hyphen: *excommunicate, expatriate.*

- The prefix "anti-" often takes the hyphen, but some common exceptions include *antibody, antiseptic* and *antithesis.*

- Use a hyphen when "pro-" coins a term meaning support for something: *pro-animal rights, pro-business* and *pro-states rights.* When the prefix carries other meaning, drop the hyphen: *proactive* and *prolific.*

- Most uses of the prefix "wide-" require hyphens: *wide-awake* and *wide-open.* One exception is *widespread.*

- When "co-" forms words indicating occupation or status, use the hyphen: *co-founder* and *co-defendant.* Common exceptions include *cooperate* and *coordinate.*

d. Hyphens help avoid confusion with doubled vowels or tripled consonants:

- *pre-election coverage*

- *mall-like atmosphere*

e. Use hyphens with numerals such as betting odds, ratios, scores and votes less than 1,000 on a side:

- *Las Vegas bookies had the Colts as 5-1 favorites in the Super Bowl.* [Betting odds.]

- *Women outnumbered men by a ratio of 3-to-2.* [However, when "ratio" follows the numbers, drop the "to," as in *a 3-2 ratio.*]

- *The Royals beat the Angels 7-2.* [Score.]

- *Elliott won election to the board 315-224.* [Votes with less than 1,000 on a side.]

f. Suspensive hyphenation sounds horribly complicated. Not really. It refers to examples such as those in section (b) above, in which the compound modifiers occur in sets of two or more, and some repeated words are dropped. Consider these examples:

- *He wants to cut the paper into 3-, 5- and 7-inch lengths.* [This is suspensive hyphenation. It allows writers to avoid repeating "inch."]

- *He wants to cut the paper into lengths of 3 inches, 5 inches and 7 inches.* [Not suspensive hyphenation, but correct, because the repeated dimension pairs do not go in front of "lengths."]

- *Their assignment was a 500- to 800-word story.* [This is suspensive hyphenation, which tightens the sentence by dropping "word" in one of the pairs.]

- *The preschool targets gifted 5- and 6-year-olds.* [Also suspensive hyphenation correctly used.]

- *The construction of trans-Atlantic and -Pacific cables was a tremendous boost to worldwide communication.* [This is suspensive hyphenation, but the word dropped in the pairs, "trans," comes first. A side note: AP style calls for hyphens with prefixes, such as "trans," whenever a capitalized word follows.]

HELPFUL HINTS

THE 5-MINUTE AP STYLE GUIDE

The Associated Press Stylebook serves as the "bible" (not Bible, per AP) for media-writing style. The goal in adhering to the stylebook is to create consistency both within a media outlet and among similar media outlets.

Trying to memorize this whole book can feel like catching sand in a pasta strainer: No matter how hard you try, you never catch it all. Even worse, AP tends to change style on some items from year to year, such as its recent decision to allow "they" in some cases as a gender-neutral singular pronoun. For a beginning journalist, the goal of learning AP style shouldn't be to memorize every change or item in the book, but rather to learn the kinds of things that are in the book so you know what to look up.

To help get students used to style, Fred Vultee, an associate professor at Wayne State University who spent more than 25 years as an editor for newspapers, offers his students some quick maxims that account for the majority of the style guide. Here is his "5-minute style guide," reprinted with permission:

THE FIVE-MINUTE STYLEBOOK

10 Percent of the Rules Cover
90 Percent of Style Questions

People

Capitalize formal titles when they appear before names (The message was sent to **President** Vladimir Putin).

Lowercase titles when they follow a name or stand alone (Bashar Assad, the Syrian **president**, fired his **foreign minister**).

Lowercase occupational or descriptive titles before or after a name (The article was written by **columnist** Joe Bob Briggs).

Refer to adults by given name and family name the first time they appear in a news story (**Michelle Obama**) and by family name only on later references (**Obama**).

Children 17 or younger are usually referred to by both names on first reference and *given name only* on later references. Children in "adult situations"—common examples are international sports and serious crimes in which they are charged as adults—are referred to by family name only on later references.

To avoid confusing two people with the same family name, such as husband and wife or mother and son, use both names on later references. A story mentioning Joe Biden and Jill Biden should usually refer to them as **Joe Biden** and **Jill Biden** even after they are introduced if there's any chance of confusion. Sometimes a title can

be repeated to make the distinction (Joe Biden could be "Vice President Biden" or "the vice president" on later references; Jill Biden could be "Dr. Biden"). Only rarely, in some feature stories, will you want to refer to adults by given name on later references.

Do not use courtesy titles (Mr., Mrs., Ms.) in news reports except in direct quotes.

Abbreviate military and police titles before names according to a standard reference list such as the one in the AP Stylebook. Don't abbreviate titles when they stand alone or follow a name (**Gen.** Douglas MacArthur, the **general**). Exceptions are allowed for widely used initialisms (The fugitive CEO was captured at dawn).

Places

Most stylebooks will have a list of cities that are assumed to be understood without having the name of the state (**Boston, New York, Los Angeles**) or country (**New York, London, Cairo**) attached. Follow those guidelines with the usual exceptions for common sense if needed (Books that are popular in **London, Ontario**, might not be popular in **London, England**).

Do not abbreviate the names of U.S. states **except**:

1. In datelines, credit lines, or short forms of party ID: **Debbie Stabenow, D-Mich.**

2. In those cases, abbreviate state names of six or more letters only. (NOTE: the two noncontiguous states, Alaska and Hawaii, are never abbreviated.)

Do not abbreviate such designations as "street" when they stand alone. Only three of these are abbreviated— "street," "avenue" and "boulevard"—and they are only abbreviated when they appear with a numbered address. Do not abbreviate "south" or "north" indicating a part of a road unless it appears with an address (**South Eighth Street; 221 S. Eighth St.; 221 Abbey Road**).

Things

Capitalize proper nouns; lowercase common nouns.

Capitalize trademarks (I drank a **Pepsi**) or use a common noun as a substitute (I drank a **soft drink**).

Use abbreviations on first reference only if they are widely known (**CIA** agents helped overthrow the prime minister of Iran). Otherwise spell out the names of agencies on first reference (The U.S. Agency for International Development; **USAID**). If an abbreviation would be confusing, use a common-noun substitute (the State Law and Order Restoration Council; **the council or the junta**) on later references. When in doubt, err on the side of clarity. Abbreviations are not as familiar as you think they are.

Generally, don't abbreviate units of measure (pounds, miles, hours, etc.).

Capitalize **shortened versions of proper names**: the Michigan Department of Transportation, the Transportation Department, the Department of Transportation.

Time

Use only the day of the week for events within a week of publication (The summit ended **Saturday**. Negotiators will meet **Thursday**). Use "last" or "next" only if needed for clarity (The summit ended Friday, and the negotiators will meet again **next Friday**).

Never abbreviate days of the week. Use "today" to refer to the day of publication only. Do not use "yesterday" or "tomorrow" except in direct quotes.

Use month and day to refer to events happening a week or more before or after publication. Use cardinal numbers, not ordinal numbers, for dates (The summit began **July 11**. The seminar will be held **March 3**).

Don't use the year unless the event is more than a year before or after publication (He died **March 17, 2007**; the tax will take effect **Jan. 1, 2025**).

Do not abbreviate a month unless it's followed by a date (**January; Jan.** 1). Do not abbreviate months of less than six letters (**March; March 12, 1998**).

Use lowercase "a.m." and "p.m." to indicate morning, afternoon and night. Use "noon" and "midnight" rather than the unclear "12 a.m." or the redundant "12 noon." Always use figures for time, in this form: **8 a.m., 10:30 p.m., 1:45 a.m.**

Unless you need to emphasize one element over the others, generally follow time-date-place order: **Trials of collaborators will begin at 2 p.m. April 14 in New York**.

Numbers

The basic rule: Spell out numbers under 10. Use figures for 10 and above.

The main exceptions: Spell out any number, except a year, that begins a sentence (Twelve students attended. 1999 was an important year).

Use figures for **dates, weights, ages, times, addresses** and **percentages**.

For most numbers of a million or more, use this form, rounded off to no more than two decimal places: **1.45 million**, the **$18.1 billion budget**. If the exact number is important, write it out: He received **1,253,667** votes to **988,401** for his opponent.

Spell out numbers used as figures of speech (**Thanks a million**).

Spell out fractions when they stand alone (use **one-half** cup of flour). Otherwise write them as mixed fractions (**1½** cups of flour) or decimals (**1.5** liters of water).

Generally, use a 0 to precede a decimal smaller than zero (**0.75 kilograms**).

Convert metric measurements to English ones.

"5-minute style guide," Fred Vultee. Reprinted with permission.

Parentheses

The Stylebook advises against the use of parentheses because they jar the reader. When you find parentheses in copy, consider replacing them with either paired commas or dashes, as appropriate.

AP also opposes changing any words within direct quotes. However, you may occasionally have a direct quote that needs a clarification inserted using parentheses — never brackets, according to the Stylebook:

- Wrong: *"I blame him [the coach] for our loss," the quarterback said.*

- Right: *"I blame him (the coach) for our loss," the quarterback said.*

- Right: *"I slammed into the pole when it (a dog) came out of nowhere," Andrew Dillon said.*

If possible, though, place the clarification outside the direct quote:

- *"I blame him for our loss," the quarterback said of his coach.*

- *"I slammed into the pole when it came out of nowhere," Andrew Dillon said, referring to the dog.*

Quotation Marks

Journalists use quotation marks frequently, so you must have a clear understanding of the rules involving their use.

a. The most common use of quotation marks is for direct quotations:

   ○ *She said, "Those algebra problems we were assigned for Friday are driving me batty."*

   ○ *"These are the times that try men's souls," Thomas Paine wrote in 1776.*

b. Use quotation marks for compositions, including titles of books, computer games, movies, operas, plays, poems, albums and songs, radio and television programs, lectures, speeches and works of art. Exceptions are the Bible and books that are catalogs of reference material. For additional explanation, see Chapter 6.

c. Less frequently, quotation marks surround nicknames, irony and unfamiliar terms:

   ○ *William F. "Buffalo Bill" Cody, Sen. Christopher S. "Kit" Bond* [Nicknames.]

   ○ *His "mansion" turned out to be a 16-foot Scamp travel trailer.* [Irony.]

   ○ *At this point her Macintosh SE is little more than "chip jewelry."* [Unfamiliar term.]

Three other pointers about quotation marks are worth mentioning.

d. Commas and periods always go inside closing quotation marks.

e. Other punctuation goes inside the closing quotation mark only if the punctuation applies to the quoted material: *She asked, "Will you be late for dinner?"* Otherwise, it goes outside the closing quotation mark: *Are you familiar with the adage "Haste makes waste"?*

f. Use single quotation marks within quotations: *"Let's rent 'Avatar' to watch tonight," she said.*

THE BIG THREE

Here are the three key things you should take away from this chapter:

1. **Punctuation can be split into three categories:** These are end marks that stop, internal marks that pause and specialty marks that explain. As you grasp these characteristics that group punctuation, you can better apply the correct — and most appropriate — mark and rule in your editing.

2. **Punctuation involves knowing and following rules:** Many writers are pretty footloose in their use of punctuation, using marks where they "feel" right or seem to belong. While this smacks of freedom, it actually represents failure to properly use the tools of the writing trade. Ultimately, writers who acquire a strong understanding of punctuation will come to appreciate the control it offers them in their writing.

3. **Editors' primary responsibility is to their readers:** Editors owe it to readers to ensure that punctuation usage conforms to the rules. The less compliance with these guidelines, the greater the difficulty many readers are likely to face in comprehending the written message, and when you make it hard on readers, you may lose them.

KEY TERMS

adverb clause 57

appositive phrase 59

conjunctive adverb 56

coordinate adjectives 59

coordinating conjunction 55

dependent clause 59

gerund phrase 59

independent clause 59

infinitive phrase 57

nonrestrictive clause 57

noun phrase 59

participial phrase 57

prepositional phrase 59

subordinating conjunction 59

DISCUSSION QUESTIONS

1. Of the three main types of punctuation listed in the chapter, which ones do you have the most difficulty using properly? Within that section of punctuation, is there a punctuation mark you find particularly problematic? Which one is it and what makes it hard on you?

2. To what degree do you agree or disagree with the overall importance of punctuation in communication? If the person on the other end of your message understands you, is it a big deal that you have or don't have things perfectly punctuated?

WRITE NOW!

1. Review the following sentences for punctuation errors:

   a. "This is a miscarriage of justice", she said.

   b. The cat put it's ball of string in next to the wall around 9 am.

   c. I never know if I'm doing well or not but I do know I always try hard.

   d. The coach said we never lost a game where we tried hard I believe he is right.

   e. "This [the building floor plan] will help us find our way around the offices," Carl said.

   f. The Cleveland Indians beat the Milwaukee Brewers, 3 to 2.

   g. I met Manny, Moe, and Jack at the store.

   h. The path to the championship game was a long hard road.

   i. Janis lived in a two bedroom house for most of her life.

   j. President, Donald Trump, refused to meet with the diplomat.

   k. I'm a huge fan of 1980's music.

2. Find an example of a poorly punctuated piece of copy that either makes it difficult for you to understand the content or in which the punctuation errors inadvertently change the meaning of the content. Explain what went wrong and then fix the errors.

Visit **edge.sagepub.com/filakediting** to help you accomplish your coursework goals in an easy-to-use learning environment.

IMPROVING SENTENCES AND USING PROPER GRAMMAR

After completing this chapter, you should be able to:

- Understand that choosing the right word is critical to effective media content.

- Rework copy that suffers from wordiness.

- Identify the common usage problems media writers and editors face.

- Decide how best to fix typical usage problems.

- Edit copy to fix common grammar errors in media writing.

Missouri humorist and novelist Mark Twain said it best: "The difference between the almost right word and the right word is really a large matter — 'tis the difference between the lightning bug and the lightning."

Media writers on the hunt for those right words often end up flooding their copy with many poorly chosen, inadequate and unclear words. In this chapter, we will cover techniques you and your writers can use to improve copy. In this regard, each of you assumes the role of wordsmith as you craft and shape the words that constitute the stories in your publication.

The quality of the output, not the quantity of the input, determines value in writing. This must be a guiding force in your editing for a number of reasons:

- It's faster and easier for writers to let their writing be whatever it will be, resulting in what most consider first-draft writing.

- Many digital media writers and some editors don't feel the need to tighten copy, because the web is not bound as much by length limits as print.

- Effective wordsmithing is a sophisticated skill, one that too many writers and some editors haven't acquired.

- Writers learn over time that longer stories tend to get "front-page treatment," whether presented on paper or online. So, adding words may improve chances for better play.

This chapter will focus on a key aspect of microediting: proper word usage. The goal here will be to outline ways to make your writing tighter through stronger sentence structure, good word choices and proper grammar.

HOW TO TIGHTEN WRITING

Tight, well-focused and creatively crafted copy is still a goal, because all readers want to read well-written copy. Although they may be willing to spend time with engaging stories, they won't bother struggling their way through copy that rambles, fails to be concise or is overwritten. A number of culprits get in the way of the right word and clarity and are responsible for wordy copy:

Active Versus Passive Voice

First, know this: **Passive voice** is not wrong. However, like other aspects of media writing, even though passive may be correct, it is not always desirable. For one, things and concepts dominate sentences constructed in passive voice, diminishing the human elements at play.

That said, passive isn't always something to avoid. Sometimes, passive is a better choice for subject presentation and reader understanding. Let's consider its advantages:

- When the doer is unknown. Consider this example: *The book was stolen from the university library [by an unknown thief].* The doer here is unknown, so the bracketed material is correct but often left out.

- When naming the doer is unnecessary, as in this example: *Donald Trump was elected the 45th president of the United States.* Naming the doer of the action here, the voters, seems superfluous.

- When the person or object receiving the action of the verb is more important than the doer of the action. See an example of this: *President John F. Kennedy was shot and killed during his trip to Dallas.* Even though we know the name of the assailant (Lee Harvey Oswald), his name is less important to most readers than the president's.

Now the disadvantages:

- Because it doesn't have to name the doer of an action, passive hides blame and obscures responsibility. Check out this example: *Women have been discriminated against.* This begs the question "By whom?"

- Passive departs from the natural order of "who did what" in favor of "what was done by whom."

- It can sound flat, awkward, convoluted, officious and muddled, as in this example: *Because the car was left unlocked by me, my radio was stolen.*

- Sentences with passive voice tend to be longer, always a drawback in media writing.

The solution to weak use of passive voice is to revise the sentence to use **active voice**:

- Passive: *Because the car was left unlocked by me, my radio was stolen.*

- Active: *Because I left my car unlocked, someone stole my radio.*

- Passive: *The online poll was being conducted by us.*

- Active: *We conducted the online poll.*

- Passive: *My lunch was eaten by my dog.*

- Active: *My dog ate my lunch.*

- Passive: *The green initiative was passed by the Ohio Legislature.*

- Active: *The Ohio Legislature passed the green initiative.*

Form of "to Be" as the Main Verb

Forms of the verb "to be" are common, often appropriate and sometimes even the right word. Notice that the preceding sentence has one as its main verb, "are." No problem here, no need to edit. Likewise with this sentence: *Adrian is the first in his family to graduate from college.*

However, frequent and unnecessary use of forms of "to be" adds words and demands tightening. Look at this example with "was" as the main verb:

- *Sophia was manager of the campus fitness center.*

This is easily fixable:

- *Sophia managed the campus fitness center.*

Fewer words, six versus eight, and a stronger verb to boot. One more example should bring this home to you:

- *Phil will be a runner in next year's Boston Marathon.*

You have to keep the helping verb "will" to indicate future tense, but convert "runner" to a verb to replace "be":

- *Phil will run in next year's Boston Marathon.*

Like the first example, the revision trims two words and strengthens the main verb.

Using the Negative

Writing sentences in the negative is correct but tends to be wordier. Moreover, readers of such sentences understand what is not rather than what is. The what is not tends to blunt meaning in its indirectness. Negative sentences seem hesitating and noncommittal.

- Read this example written in the negative: *Tyrone often was not on time to class.*
- Now read it in the positive: *Tyrone often was late to class.*
- Here's another negatively phrased sentence: *Sandy did not think her writing was strong.*
- And its positively phrased revision: *Sandy thought her writing was weak.*

These revisions trim two words from each sentence. Also, the resulting positive sentences are stronger, more direct and more engaging to readers.

Pronoun Usage

Used well, **pronouns** are wonderful words. They are concise and add coherence. In "The Art of Readable Writing," readability guru Rudolph Flesch argued for a variety of approaches to improve readability.[1] He said we should write like we speak. When we do, our writing is more approachable, more human. To further emphasize the human element, he recommended liberal use of personal pronouns, which he believed enlivened writing and strengthened connections.

Look at these examples, where the first is devoid of pronouns and the second uses a first-person pronoun:

- *The use of computers has enhanced writing.*

- *Our use of computers has enhanced writing.*

No fewer words, but the revision introduces the human element, a plus for readability. Consider this passage. It has no personal pronouns, but it certainly isn't awful:

Antonia Salazar is the top tennis player in the city. The 29-year-old woman, who has played for 22 years, is a 2003 graduate of Rollins College in Winter Park, Fla. Salazar was nationally ranked all four years there and finished fifth in the nation in NCAA Division II. Singles was the game Salazar preferred, though the left-hander had some success with doubles as a college junior.

Now, see how the addition of personal pronouns adds to the revision:

Antonia Salazar is the top tennis player in the city. Having played for 22 years, she is a 2003 graduate of Rollins College in Winter Park, Fla. She was nationally ranked all four years there and finished fifth in the nation in NCAA Division II. Even though she preferred singles, she enjoyed some success with doubles as a college junior.

One of the benefits of personal pronouns is that they tend to fade into the woodwork, so to speak. Although they connect ideas and sentences concisely, they don't draw attention. Also, the revised paragraph above trims six words.

As you edit copy, make sure you and media writers use pronouns freely. Make sure you achieve clarity with appropriate antecedents — the nouns to which they refer — in gender, number and case. Most writers handle gender (female, male and neuter) and case (subjective, objective or possessive) without any hitches. However, number (singular or plural) can be troublesome.

Consider this example: *A student who is seeking financial aid must complete their application in person or online.* The pronoun "their" is plural, but its antecedent, "student," is singular. You have two ways to correct the problem:

- *A student who is seeking financial aid must complete his or her application in person or online.* [This is correct, but some media writers and editors avoid using "his or her," considering it wordy or awkward.]

- *Students who are seeking financial aid must complete their applications in person or online.* [This is the better option, making the noun antecedent "students" a plural noun to match the plural pronoun "their."]

In issues that lack clarity, such as the police seeking a robber whose gender is unknown, and in circumstances that involve gender fluidity, the Associated Press has made exceptions for a singular use of "they." In general, writers should pluralize when possible, but in certain circumstances, to avoid binary gender and English's lack of a gender-neutral singular pronoun, "they" is acceptable. This is not a free ticket to horrible grammar but rather something to consider on a case-by-case basis.

Finally, a word of caution. Pronouns are effective as long as their use is correct. In fact, some editors discourage pronoun use because of potential agreement problems. While you may not wish to ban pronouns from stories, sometimes the easiest fix for problem pronouns is to stick with the nouns involved.

Wordy Modifiers

As you know, **adjectives** describe nouns, and adverbs describe verbs, adjectives and other adverbs. Strings of adjectives or adverbs slow reading and weaken writing. Try these four modifier-cutting tips:

- Replace most adjectives with strong, descriptive nouns.

- Replace most adverbs with strong, descriptive verbs.

- When you find a string of modifiers, keep the best and cut the rest.

- Sometimes, it's best to cut the modifier.

Let's look at examples that illustrate these guidelines:

- Original: *Edgar honed his skills as a funny person in the sixth grade.*

- Revised: *Edgar honed his skills as a comedian in the sixth grade.* [Replaces the adjective-noun package "funny person" with a strong noun, "comedian."]

- Original: *Amy spoke softly to her young child.*

- Revised: *Amy whispered to her toddler.* [Replaces the adverb with a strong verb and opts for a single stronger noun, "toddler," over an adjective-noun package.]

- Original: *The long, dark and deserted hallway led to Bill's tiny, overfilled and crowded office.*

- Revised: *The tunnellike hallway led to Bill's cramped cubicle.* [Replaces strings of adjectives with single, stronger descriptors. Also, replaces "office" with a stronger noun, "cubicle," which carries the idea of tiny without saying so.]

HELPFUL HINTS
WEAK ADJECTIVES AND ADVERBS

The following adjectives and adverbs are example of prime candidates to cut from copy.

- actually
- bad
- basically
- big
- extremely
- good
- hopefully
- interesting
- just
- kind of
- probably
- quite
- really
- short
- usually
- very

- Original: *The new and inexperienced firm successfully obtained its first contract.*

- Revised: *The fledgling firm won its first contract.* [Replaces two adjectives, "new" and "inexperienced," with a single, stronger adjective, "fledgling." Also replaces the adverb-verb package "successfully obtained" with "won," which handles the meaning with a single, short verb.

- Original: *Arturo literally collapsed into his rescuers' arms.*

- Revised: *Arturo collapsed into his rescuers' arms.* [Cuts the weak adverb "literally."]

Here are examples of weak modifiers and how you might correct them.

- Weak: *Chuck was absolutely sure he saw a falling star.*

- Better: *Chuck was sure he saw a falling star.*

- Weak: *The art historian carefully examined the truly special talent of the young painter.*

- Better: *The art historian examined the young painter's special talent.* [Note that the possessive also replaces the prepositional phrase "of the young painter."]

- Weak: *Sara was nice to her parents to successfully obtain their approval of her new boyfriend.*

- Better: *Sara was courteous to her parents to win their approval of her new boyfriend.*

- Weak: *Bob was very nervous when exactly the same dog that bit him last month started chasing him today.*

- Better: *Bob was nervous when the dog that bit him last month started chasing him today.*

Your goal in trimming these is not to sanitize copy but rather to cut the fat and improve readability.

Circumlocutions

These are wordy, roundabout ways of saying something. Some media writers use them because they seem to sound more important. Not so. You should cut **circumlocutions** from copy, replacing each with a tighter choice — the right word — such as those suggested in the list below.

- a large proportion of → many

- concerning the matter of → about

- during the course of → during

- during the time that → when

- in advance of → before

- in the event that → if

- in the vicinity of → near

- made a statement → said

- on two separate occasions → twice

- placed under arrest → arrested

- render assistance to → help

- take into consideration → consider

After you replace circumlocutions, point them out to media writers as an important teaching-learning moment.

Empty Phrases

The name says it all. These phrases don't carry their weight. They're wordy with limited redeeming value. They are never the right word, and they diminish clarity. Consider cutting or replacing with text that is shorter and serves the purpose.

See how you might correct empty phrases in these sentences and their edits:

- Empty: *A combination of drugs and alcohol led to the young mother's death.*

- Better: *Drugs and alcohol led to the young mother's death.*

- Empty: *The students gathered for the purpose of electing a spokesman for their pro-green movement.*

- Better: *The students gathered to elect a spokesman for their pro-green movement.*

- Empty: *Allee is the type of teacher who lives for her third-grade students.*

- Better: *Allee is a teacher who lives for her third-grade students.*

- Better: *Allee lives for her third-grade students.*

HELPFUL HINTS
EMPTY PHRASES

This is a sample list of empty phrases:

- a combination of
- all things considered
- as a matter of fact
- as far as I'm concerned
- at any rate
- currently
- for all intents and purposes
- for the purpose of
- have a tendency to
- I believe/feel/think that
- in a manner of speaking

- in a very real sense
- in my (personal) opinion
- it goes without saying
- it seems that
- needless to say
- one must admit that
- the point I am trying to make
- the reason why
- this is a subject that
- type of
- what I mean to say is that

Redundancies

As heavy as the term sounds, **redundancy** is nothing more than unnecessary repetition using two or more words. The typical redundancy is a product of habit or lack of attention to detail in writing. Many media writers and their editors work under the gun to produce and edit copy quickly; however, that's no excuse to use redundancies.

Consider these examples of redundancies and fixes:

- Redundant: *The tornado completely destroyed three mobile homes at the edge of town.*

- Better: *The tornado destroyed three mobile homes at the edge of town.*

- Redundant: *Recall the old adage, "To err is human, to forgive divine."*

- Better: *Recall the adage, "To err is human, to forgive divine."*

- Redundant: *The consensus of opinion among reporters covering the trial was that the jury ignored the true facts of the case.*

- Better: *The consensus among reporters covering the trial was that the jury ignored the facts of the case.*

Prepositional Phrase Strings

Prepositions are necessary because writers use them to show relationships between a noun or pronoun and other words in a sentence. One-word prepositions number about 70 and include the following examples:

- aboard
- about
- across
- after
- against
- among
- at
- before
- below
- between
- by
- down
- during
- for
- from
- in
- into

- of

- on

- over

- through

- to

- under

- with

Prepositions may be handy, but they also can be pesky when media writers use too many of them. Learn to spot prepositions and the phrases they introduce. Sprinkled around copy, they're fine. Too many strung together, though, slow reading and may invite ambiguity.

See how you might edit these preposition strings:

- Original: *Sidney can deduct the $12,000 for the cost of the hot tub at her new home as a medical expense.* [This sentence has four prepositional phrases.]

- Revised: *Sidney can deduct her new home's $12,000 hot tub as a medical expense.* [This sentence has one.]

- Original: *The professor will take the opportunity for a lecture on improvement of class meeting times for the media students.* [This sentence uses four prepositional phrases.]

- Revised: *The professor will lecture on media class meeting time improvements.* [This version cuts that to one. In addition, the verb "package" is stronger.]

Got the idea? Of course, you don't want to remove so many prepositional phrases that the revision is stilted — perhaps less readable than the original. Let your ear be your guide.

Clichés

Various expressions in English weren't born clichés; they became them. In fact, their early popularity led to their being overused and eventually seeming trite. Sometimes a cliché is a phrase; other times it is a simile (a comparison using "like" or "as"). This is the unwavering rule for clichés: Get rid of every one in copy you edit. You may omit it or replace it with a synonym or another simile. Make sure the replacement is fresh and fits.

Clichés slip into all writing, at least occasionally. See how to fix clichés in these sentences:

- Cliché: *A gunman robbed the liquor store in broad daylight.*

- Better: *A gunman robbed the liquor store at 11 a.m.*

- Cliché: *The Kansas Legislature added insult to injury by passing a bill that taxes unemployment earnings.*

- Better: *The Kansas Legislature worsened the problem by passing a bill that taxes unemployment earnings.*

- Cliché: *A White House spokesman reported that the president was under the weather.*

- Better: *A White House spokesman reported that the president was ill.*

Euphemisms

Media writers can be overly sensitive or squeamish about some terms in English, preferring to substitute an inoffensive replacement for a term or phrase that some may consider blunt, harsh or impolite. It should be no surprise that many **euphemisms** involve sex or bodily functions.

Political correctness has spawned many euphemisms. Others come from government and business, where being less direct about what you mean can be valuable even if it lacks clarity.

Consider the term "ample proportions." Few writers, even good ones, feel comfortable writing "fat." Your first concern as editor should be whether the weight reference is even necessary in the story. If not, cut it. If it's needed, then either you or the writer should use the proper term or an accurate description that shows the condition. See how to edit euphemisms in these examples:

- Euphemism: *Eve's ample proportions were testament to her food addiction.*

- Better: *Eve's 350 pounds were testament to her food addiction.*

- Euphemism: *The former owners of the traveling carnival lived in reduced circumstances.*

- Better: *The former owners of the traveling carnival lived in poverty.*

- Better: *The former owners of the traveling carnival lived on food stamps and unemployment checks.*

- Euphemism: *Wilson didn't realize that the attractive young woman was a lady of the night.*

- Better: *Wilson didn't realize that the attractive young woman was a prostitute.*

- Euphemism: *Gerald Sonderheim passed away* (or *shuffled off this mortal coil*) *following the accident.*

- Better: *Gerald Sonderheim died following the accident.*

Nominalization

This wordy culprit is reminiscent of similar terms discussed above in the section on trimming modifiers. One clue may help you spot **nominalization**: Many nominalized verbs carry "-ion" endings, such as these: "adoration," "application," "conclusion," "destabilization," "education," "expectation," "indication" and "information." Each of these, as is the case of all nominalizations, has a perfectly good verb ready to do a better job.

Consider this example: *Paul's adoration for Evelyn was deep.* The nominalized term is "adoration," a noun form of the verb "to adore." Note, too, that the sentence has another wordy problem: a form of the verb "to be" as its main verb. Fix both problems at once: *Paul adored Evelyn deeply.* Some editors might argue against the need for the adverb "deeply" in the revision, trusting that "adored" is a powerful enough verb to stand alone.

Look at this sentence: *Susan's resistance to the cream puffs was weak.* Revise it like this: *Susan could not resist the cream puffs.*

And one more: *Wilson has no expectation that he will finish his report on time.* Fix it like this: *Wilson expects to miss the deadline for the report.* Note here that besides dumping the nominalization, the revision shifts from negative to positive.

CORRECT USAGE

No one person, organization or institution established our rules of grammar and usage. Instead, they evolved over time. Eventually, standards were codified and written so that we had references to follow.

The rest of this chapter will cover usage, which involves the conventional ways we use words or phrases, and will focus on four aspects: agreement, irregular verbs, problem pronouns and prepositions. It doesn't sound like much, but these four dominate usage issues that can become a minefield for the careless media writer or editor. The best advice is to first become familiar with the usage guidelines here and then be willing to consult the AP Stylebook or a grammar handbook. Coming up with the correct answer typically involves selective fixes that suit the context and follow the rules.

Agreement

Subject-verb agreement and **pronoun agreement** are the focus of this section. Each is a common usage problem that media writers or their editors can correct.

Subject-Verb Agreement

The rule is that singular subjects take singular verbs, and plural subjects take plural verbs. If it were that simple to follow, though, it wouldn't be part of our discussion here. The two things that tend to trip up media writers are identifying the subject and figuring out whether it is singular or plural. This list of trouble spots shows how complex this issue can be:

- collective nouns
- compound subjects
- or, either/or, neither/nor
- not only . . . but also
- linking verb "to be"
- there, here
- words naming mass, quantity or number
- words that may take singular or plural verbs
- nouns plural in form but singular in meaning
- nouns plural in form referring to single things
- intervening prepositional phrases ("as well as," "along with")
- "one of those" constructions

Collective nouns name a group, with the noun taking singular or plural according to whether the group is acting as a unit, as in these examples:

- *The newspaper staff is meeting this morning at 10.* ["Staff" here is a unit and takes a singular verb.]

- *The newspaper staff disagree about how to handle downsizing.* ["Staff" here clearly is not a unit, as suggested by their disagreement. Use a plural verb.]

- *The newspaper staff members disagree about how to handle downsizing.* [Adding the plural noun "members," which becomes the new subject with "newspaper" and "staff" as adjectives, makes the decision about agreement simpler. This always is an option to consider.]

Subjects joined by "and" usually are considered compound and take plural verbs:

- *English and journalism are closely related disciplines.*

- *John and Mary live for rock concerts at the arena.*

- *Mustard and ketchup tend to be standard condiments on most hamburgers.*

However, some frequently paired compound subjects considered single units take singular verbs. Examples of these include "bread and butter," "peanut butter and jelly," and "spaghetti and meatballs."

When a compound subject includes a positive and a negative element, the verb should agree with the positive, as in these examples:

- *The faculty members, but not their department chair, agree to cancel the low-enrolled classes.*

- *The reporter, not his stories, was considered much too conservative.*

- *The ballplayer, but not his coaches, feels the loss most deeply.*

Singular subjects joined by "or" take singular verbs, while plural subjects joined by "or" take plural verbs. When subjects are joined by "either/or" or "neither/nor," they agree with the subject closest to the verb. Consider these examples:

- *Hank or Bill is ready to go over your assignment.*

- *Apples or peaches were the fruit choices on the menu.*

- *Either the players or their coach was responsible for the poor season.*

- *Either the coach or his players were responsible for the poor season.*

- *Neither Maureen nor her brothers enjoy bicycling.*

- *Neither her brothers nor Maureen enjoys bicycling.*

The same rule applies when a "not only. . .but also" construction is used as the subject: The verb agrees with the noun or pronoun closest to the verb, as in these examples:

- *Not only the students but also their teacher was upset over the test results.*

- *Not only the teacher but also her students were upset over the test results.*

Note that "not only" always should be paired with "but also."

As you know, a noun complement is a noun or pronoun that follows a form of the verb "to be" and renames the subject. In those sentences the verb agrees with the subject:

- *Paul's favorite breakfast is pancakes.*

- *Pancakes are Paul's favorite breakfast.*

Sentences beginning with "there" or "here" are simple to handle correctly if you remember that the subject of the sentence follows the verb, as in these examples:

- *There are 50 people applying for the copy editor's job.*

- *Here is the best applicant.*

- *There is no good way to tell the rest they weren't chosen.*

Note that most sentences beginning with "there is" or "there are" will be shorter and stronger if you begin with the true subject, as in *Fifty people are applying for the copy editor's job.*
Words naming mass, sums or number always take singular verbs, as in these examples:

- *Twenty dollars was too much to pay for that meal.*

- *One hundred bushels is all he could harvest from that plot.*

- *Seventy-five years is the average life expectancy for men in the United States.*

"All," "majority," "percent" and "some" take singular or plural verbs according to how they are used in a sentence. The number of the verb matches the number of the noun in the prepositional phrase that typically accompanies them. Used alone, "majority" and "percent" take singular verbs. Consider these examples:

- *All of the pie is gone.*

- *All of the pies are in the refrigerator.*

- *A majority of voters are unhappy with the president's economic program.*

- *A majority is dissatisfied with the food in the union.*

- *Most teachers say that under 60 percent is a failing grade.*

- *Some of the pie is getting old.*

- *Some of the pies were not edible.*

"None" and "number" are special cases. When "none" means "no single one," its verb always is singular. When it means "no two" or "no amount," its verb always is plural. "The number" always takes singular verbs, while "a number" takes plural verbs. Consider these examples:

- *None of the reporters is happy with the new salary proposal.*

- *None of the fees have been collected.*

- *The number of jobs in the media has declined in recent years.*

- *A number of jobs in the media are shifting to online media.*

Some nouns are plural in form but singular in meaning, such as "civics," "economics," "ethics," "gallows," "mathematics," "measles," "mumps," "news," "physics," "shambles," "sports" and "whereabouts." These always take singular verbs.

Other nouns refer to single things but are plural in form and always take plural verbs, such as "glasses," "pants," "pliers," "riches," "scissors," "shears," "tweezers" and "trousers."

Intervening prepositional phrases are those that appear between the subject and verb. Basically, ignore them. Do not let them confuse you as to the actual subject, as in these:

- *The captains on the football team are juniors this year.*
- *The beginning of his many trials and tribulations was losing his younger brother three years ago.*
- *Steve, as well as his brothers, runs a strong 200-meter dash.*
- *College tuition, in addition to numerous other fees, is rising faster than the cost of living.*

"One of those" constructions are common and can be a challenge. Here's an example:

- *Sapphire is one of those young women who love to wear new hairstyles.*

The tricky part is not the main verb, "is"; it's the verb "love" in the relative clause introduced by "who." The temptation is to have that verb agree with the subject, "Sapphire." However, in this construction it must agree with the noun "women," which is the object of the prepositional phrase introduced by "of." A simple check will always help you when editing such constructions. Mentally change the order of the sentence to begin with the prepositional phrase:

- *Of those young women who love to wear new hairstyles, Sapphire is one.*

If you appropriately apply this check, you'll always use the correct verb form.

Pronoun Agreement

Some pronouns always take singular verbs:

- another
- anybody
- anyone
- anything
- each
- each one
- either
- everybody
- everyone
- everything
- neither
- no one
- nobody
- nothing

- one

- other

- somebody

- someone

- something

These pronouns always take plural verbs:

- both

- few

- many

- several

- others

VIEW FROM A PRO
CHRIS DROSNER

Courtesy of Chris Drosner

Chris Drosner spent a lot of his career as a microeditor, serving six years as a copy editor and page designer at the Green Bay Press-Gazette and another six years at the Wisconsin State Journal in a similar role. However, in more recent years, he worked more on the assignment and content side, first as an assistant city editor at the State Journal and now as the executive editor at Milwaukee Magazine.

Throughout his life in media, Drosner said he had a strong sense as to who was in his audience and what those people wanted from him as an editor.

"After 13 years at the State Journal, my news sense was 100 percent in line with what we thought our audience wanted," he said. "I could tell instantly what was a big, drop-everything story and what was inside the Local section."

Drosner said his current job requires him to understand his audience so that he can make the best choices when it comes to everything from story assignments to hands-on editing.

"I get paid for the macro editing. . . . A lot of it is story selection, framing and finding the right writer for it," he said. "After that process, there is a lot of hole-patching, organizational editing and straight-up rewriting. It's much more intensive editing after the writer/reporter files than I did at the State Journal. It's made me appreciate even more my former reporters at the State Journal and what pros they are. All that said, I still do a lot of micro editing, too."

The reason microediting matters is because it shows readers that the publications take their work seriously, Drosner said.

"The audience will believe the publication is as dumb as it looks, and when you misspell something or mess up grammar or are not consistent with punctuation, you look dumb to your smartest, most detail-oriented readers," he said. "Those should be your best readers, your most loyal readers."

Some writing requires flexibility within the rules of style, Drosner said, and he does his best to work with writers who see opportunities to tell better stories if they have some freedom in this regard.

"If a reporter is breaking style or more conventional forms of news writing, and I see what the reporter doing, I might go along with it," he said. "Most of the time, if I'm not getting it, I assume the reader isn't going to get it either. But yeah, for sure, if you've got a reason for writing something in a way that breaks convention, I can go along with it if it works. But we have to agree on this very subjective thing — that it works — and it has to make sense for the story."

Although he knows that content is king, Drosner said he never wants to irritate readers with minor errors that should be caught before publication.

"You might argue that the reporting or the information is what the reader is seeking, and that's probably true," he said. "But when I'm reading a story in a publication and they misspell something or drop a word or use the wrong "their," I *might* keep reading but I'm taking all the information in that story with a grain of salt. It's very hard for me to overcome that . . . I guess it's a breach of trust."

Here are a few examples illustrating their use:

- *His parents are divorced, but both are attending his graduation.*

- *Many are called, but few are chosen.*

These pronouns, though, take singular or plural according to their usage in a sentence:

- all

- most

- any

- some

If a prepositional phrase beginning with "of" follows one of these, check the number of the noun in the phrase. If it's a singular noun, then use a singular verb. If a plural noun, use a plural verb. Consider these examples:

- *All of the pie is gone.*

- *Some of the people are ill.*

- *Most of the stray dogs have been caught.*

IRREGULAR VERBS

Regular verbs have a root form, which is the present tense. They also have a past form, which has "-ed" added to the root, and they have a participle form, which has "-ed" added to the root. Consider the following examples of regular verbs, with the infinitive followed by sentences using the present, the past and the participle:

- **To believe:** He believes in a supreme being. He first believed when he was only a child. In fact, he has believed without question his entire life.

- **To bark:** The dog barks whenever he hears an unusual sound. He barked several times last night. Finally, after he had barked a half dozen times, I got up to investigate.

- **To love:** My daughter loves banana bread. She especially loved the loaf she got for Christmas. To be honest, she has loved the banana bread from her aunt more than the bread I bake.

Media writers have few problems with such regular verbs and the forms they take. However, it's the irregular verbs that can trip up even those well versed in the language. In this section we'll highlight three pairs of irregular verbs that tend to be most problematic:

- "Lay" or "lie"

- "Raise" or "rise"

- "Set" or "sit"

"Lay" or "Lie"

The first step in correct use of these verbs is to decide which fits the context of the copy.

"Lay" means to put something down. It is transitive, which means it takes a direct object, with the action of the verb moving from subject to object in the sentence. Its present form is "lay," its past form is "laid" and its participle form is "laid." These examples illustrate each form in a sentence:

- *When you are finished with the exam, lay it on the professor's desk.*

- *Emily laid hers there before leaving the room.*

- *After all the students had laid their tests on the desk, the professor took the stack back to her office.*

"Lie" means to recline or to be placed. It is intransitive and takes no direct object. Its present form is "lie," its past form is "lay" and its participle form is "lain." These examples illustrate each form in a sentence:

- *Stewart lies in the couch each evening after dinner.*

- *On Monday he lay there until it was time for bed.*

- *He had lain on the couch so long that the cushions have an outline of his body.*

"Raise" or "Rise"

As with "lay" and "lie," you must first decide which verb, "raise" or "rise," is appropriate for the context.

"Raise" means to elevate; to increase in size, value or intensity; or to collect. It is transitive and takes a direct object. It is a regular verb, with its present form as "raise," its past form as "raised" and its participle as "raised." However, it is included here because it often is confused with the irregular verb "rise." The following illustrate each form in a sentence:

- *Few politicians raise more campaign funds than they'd like.*

- *More recently, some raised less money because of the weak economy.*

- *Nevertheless, many politicians have raised more money than they need.*

"Rise" means to get up, to assume a vertical or nearly vertical position or to go to a higher place. It is intransitive and takes no direct object. Its present form is "rise," its past form is "rose" and its participle is "risen." The following illustrate each form in a sentence:

- *Stewart rises each day at the crack of noon.*

- *He actually rose later while he was in college.*

- *He has risen following his own biological clock most of his life.*

A common error some writers make is to add "up" to either of these verbs, as in "raise up" or "rise up." Few contexts need this adverb. It's wordy. Cut it.

"Set" or "Sit"

Again, decide first which verb fits the context of the copy you are editing.

"Set" means to put or to place. It is transitive and takes a direct object. Its present form is "set," its past form is "set," and its participle form is "set." These examples illustrate each form in a sentence:

- *Sandy always sets her drink on the roof of her car while she unlocks the door.*

- *On Monday she set the drink there as usual.*

- *Unfortunately, she forgot she had set the drink there and drove off.*

"Sit" means to take or occupy a seat. It is intransitive and takes no direct object. Its present form is "sit," its past form is "sat" and its participle form is "sat." These illustrate each form in a sentence:

- *George knew that bright students often sit at the front of a classroom.*

- *So, at the beginning of the semester, he sat at the front of his algebra class.*

- *Although he has sat there all semester, he still hasn't done well.*

PROBLEM PRONOUNS

Relative pronouns include "that," "who," "whom," "whose," "which," "where," "when" and "why." They introduce relative clauses, which provide additional information about something in the main clause. You use these regularly in your own writing and will find them in copy you edit. The goal, of course, is to make sure they're used correctly.

We'll review those that are more likely to be troublesome:

- "that" and "which"

- "who" and "whom"

- "who's" and "whose"

- "their," "they're" and "there"

"That" and "Which"

These pronouns introduce relative clauses that refer to things. Use "which" for nonrestrictive clauses, also called nonessential (which we discussed in the commas section in Chapter 5), and set them off with commas. Restrictive, or essential, clauses are introduced by "that" and are not set off by commas. Consider these examples:

- *The afternoon thunderstorm, which hit around 4:10, dumped an inch of rain in 15 minutes.* [Nonrestrictive clause, introduced by "which" and set off by commas. Knowing what time the storm hit, which may be interesting additional information, isn't needed to qualify which storm it was in this context.]

- *The storm that hit today was more severe than yesterday's.* [Restrictive clause introduced by "that" with no commas needed. Here, the information in the relative clause is essential to know because it distinguishes that storm from one that hit yesterday.]

- *The car that his sister drives is a Toyota Highlander.* [Restrictive clause introduced by "that" with no commas needed. The information is required to understand which car the writer is referring to.]

- *The Toyota Highlander, which his sister drives, is not a station wagon or a crossover SUV.* [Nonrestrictive clause introduced by "which" and set off by commas. That the sister drives a Highlander is information not required to understand the rest of the sentence.]

"Who" and "Whom"

These relative pronouns introduce relative clauses about people. Like all relative clauses, they can be restrictive or nonrestrictive, where the former doesn't take commas and the latter does. Importantly, use "who" when referring to the subject of a clause and "whom" when referring to the object of a clause. Subject? Object? Before your eyes glaze over, remember that the subject is who is doing something in the sentence while the object is to whom something is being done. See how this works in these examples:

- *Adrian, who is unlucky at love, has been depressed for months.*

- *Who is the object of his love?*

- *For whom does Adrian pine?*

- *The woman whom he loves is already in a committed relationship.*

A quick trick to help you figure out whether to use "who" or "whom" is to replace "who" with "he/she" or "whom" with "him/her." Let's try this trick with each of the examples above:

- Replace "who" in the first with "he" and "him" to see which fits: *He is unlucky at love. Him is unlucky at love.* Clearly, "he" works here, so "who" is correct.

- Replace "who" in the second with "she" and "her": *She is the object of his love. Her is the object of his love.* "She" fits, so "who" is correct.

- First, change the question in the third example to a statement: *Adrian pines for whom.* Then, replace "whom" with "she" and "her": *Adrian pines for she. Adrian pines for her.* "Her" fits, so "whom" is correct.

- Replace "whom" in the last example with "she" and "her": *He loves she. He loves her.* "Her" fits, so "whom" is correct.

Apply the same trick for "whoever" and "whomever."

"Who's" and "Whose"

Handling these two pronouns correctly can be tricky because they sound the same, but avoiding the errors takes only a bit of clarification.

"Who's" is a contraction for "who is," while "whose" is a possessive pronoun. Whenever you find "who's" or "whose" in copy, do a mental check to see if "who is" fits, as in these:

- *Jared is not sure whose job it is to write the headline.* [Replace "whose" with "who is." It doesn't fit, so "whose" is correct.]

- *The driver who's car spun out of control on I-80 is in critical condition.* [Replace "who's" with "who is." That doesn't sound right, so use "whose" instead.]

- *Whose going to the concert Saturday?* [Replace "whose" with "who is." That works, so you need to replace "whose" with either "who's" or "who is."]

- *The public relations director would not identify whose speaking at the news conference.* [Replace "whose" with "who is." That fits, so replace "whose" with "who's."]

"Their," "They're" and "There"

These three make frequent appearances in copy, and all three sound the same, so knowing how to use each is important.

"Their" is a possessive pronoun indicating ownership by "them." One way to check on its correct use is to mentally replace it in copy with "our," another possessive pronoun, as in these examples:

- *Their luggage was lost between Boise, Idaho, and Louisville, Kentucky.* [Replace "their" with "our." It fits, so "their" is used correctly.]

- *Albert Johnson and his family were waiting their for the bus.* [Replace "their" with "our." It doesn't sound right, so you will need one of the other two. In this case, it's the adverb "there."]

"They're" is a contraction for "they are." As with "who's," you can check on its correct use by mentally replacing "they're" with "they are":

- *The airline passengers spent 45 minutes waiting for they're bags.* [Replace "they're" with "they are." It doesn't work, so "they're" is not correct. The right answer is the possessive pronoun "their."]

- *Many say they're going to complain to the airlines about the delay.* [Replace "they're" with "they are." That sounds good, so either stick with "they're" or use "they are."]

Finally, "there" often is an adverb, though many sentences use it as a noun:

- *There are few Republicans who supported Ted Cruz in his 2016 presidential bid.* ["There" is an adverb used correctly in this sentence. Generally, limit this use of "there," because it is wordy. Revise it to read *Few Republicans supported Ted Cruz in his 2016 presidential bid.*]

- *After the speaker extolled the wonders of Belize, many listeners wanted to go there.* ["There" is a noun and used correctly.]

PREPOSITIONS

It's the rare sentence that doesn't have any prepositions. They're helpful words that link ideas in subtle but vital ways. However, some aren't needed. Others are wordier than need be. Both are our concern in this section.

Unnecessary Prepositions

Many grade-school children still recall being warned not to end a sentence with a preposition, such as in these examples:

- *His approach to punishing his children is one I can't agree with.* [Even though Miss Abernathy would mark this one wrong for ending with "with," most media writers would find it acceptable.

- *His approach to punishing his children is one with which I can't agree.* [That's the one Miss Abernathy would have her students do. And it's grammatically perfect. It also tends to sound too stilted in most contexts.

The better advice is to avoid *unnecessary* prepositions at the end of a sentence — or anywhere else, for that matter, as in these examples:

- *Where did Dad get that car at?* [Both Miss Abernathy and editors would mark that wrong. There's no need for "at." Instead, write *Where did Dad get that car?*]

- *Take that coffee off of the coffee table.* [Here, "of" isn't needed: *Take that coffee off the coffee table.*]

- *Where did the money on the counter go to?* [Wrong again. There's no need for "to": *Where did the money on the counter go?*]

Wordy Prepositions

In addition to unnecessary prepositions, you must be on guard against wordy prepositions that serve only to clutter sentences. Writers use them because they often seem to make content sound more important.

Following is a sampling of these culprits and recommended replacements, which are shorter but not always prepositions:

- as a result of → because

- at that point (in time) → then, now

- by means of → by

- despite the fact that → although, even though

- for the purpose of → for, under

- in close proximity to → near

- in favor of → for

- in the event that → if

- in the immediate vicinity of → near

- in view of the fact that → because

- with the exception of → except

THE BIG THREE

Here are the three key things you should take away from this chapter:

1. **Grammar is nothing new:** The grammar and usage issues discussed here are traditionally taught in elementary and secondary language arts classes. Yet that doesn't make them juvenile or irrelevant. Instead, it heightens the need for you to redouble your efforts to master these basic writing conventions.

2. **Choose the right word:** This demands that you understand which problems with word choices are the ones you'll most likely confront. Flagging problems is the harder part of this battle; once identified, plenty of resources are available to help you fix them.

3. **Of the things that editors must work with media writers to accomplish, trimming wordiness may be the easiest but is certainly among the most important:** Many writers simply ignore the demand for conciseness in their writing. It takes regular reminding, prodding, fixing and coaching from knowledgeable editors to bring their staff members into line with tight writing. And in case you didn't catch it, the title of this item should really drive home this point.

KEY TERMS

active voice 71
adjective 74
circumlocution 75
cliché 78

collective noun 80
euphemism 79
nominalization 79
passive voice 71

pronoun 72
pronoun agreement 80
redundancy 77
subject-verb agreement 80

DISCUSSION QUESTIONS

1. What are the benefits and drawbacks associated with passive voice?

2. Media writing and editing require you to be both grammatically concise and generally clear. If you have to pick between those two elements, which one do you see as most important? Why do you think that way?

3. How important are grammar, structure and style in your daily life? What is it that makes them either important or irrelevant to you?

WRITE NOW!

1. Determine if the following sentences are written in active or passive voice. Rewrite the passive voice sentences in active voice:

   a. James ate most of the cheeseburger.

   b. Chaz was full after dinner.

   c. They were served their food by the waitress.

   d. The concert was sponsored by the university.

   e. The band played several songs from its latest album.

   f. I wasn't served beer because of my age.

   g. Has anyone considered changing the drinking age?

   h. The bartender made a drink for Billy.

   i. Mandy was 17 when she left home.

   j. Leanne gave me a piece of candy.

2. Remove the redundancies from the following sentences:

    a. The Hope Diamond is a unique gem in the history of the world.

    b. Chelsea lived in four different houses before marrying her significant other.

    c. The ATM machine required my PIN number before I could withdraw cash money.

    d. The man's face was red in color after he ran a long marathon.

3. Determine if the following sentences have proper pronoun agreement:

    a. Frank and John went on their vacation.

    b. The group decided they would postpone the amendment.

    c. The cat wouldn't give up her ball of string.

    d. One of the glasses are broken.

    e. All of the pie is eaten.

    f. A member of the Dallas Cowboys refused to sign his contract.

Visit **edge.sagepub.com/filakediting** to help you accomplish your coursework goals in an easy-to-use learning environment.

7 EDITING FOR THE BIGGER PICTURE

The past few chapters outlined how to clean copy on a micro level, picking at punctuation and working through word choices. The need to keep the i's dotted and the t's crossed in copy of all forms matters a great deal, as tiny errors quickly erode your readers' confidence.

However, editing isn't just about knowing when to use "farther" or "further" in a story and when a semicolon should replace a comma or a period. Editing should improve copy on all levels, which means issues of readability, tone, accuracy and more all matter as much as any micro-level errors.

The purpose of this chapter is to help you see the ways in which you will need to edit for the big picture. We will discuss the ways you can find problems at the macro level and help your writers fix them. The goal is to help you see how to work through a piece of copy from that big-picture level and how to work with writers to improve copy as they retain ownership of their work. If you can succeed at these two tasks, you will have a quality staff with improved writers and content that meets the needs of your readers.

LEARNING OBJECTIVES

After completing this chapter, you should be able to:

- Apply the "all A's" approach to reviewing copy and editing a story.

- Engage in a macro-level editing process, including reading a story multiple times, locating bigger-picture problems and reworking copy to better reach your readers.

- Differentiate between the concepts of "editing" and "fixing" when it comes to editorial content.

- Understand the value of constructive criticism and the approach you must take to deliver it to your writers.

EDITING FOR THE BIGGER PICTURE

Throughout the process of editing, you should be looking for all errors, large and small. In addition, you should also spend some time looking at the bigger picture when it comes to the value of the story. Because students like to get all A's, here are a few A's to consider when looking at a story.

Accuracy

You always need to make sure your facts are right, and over your career as an editor, you will develop ways to do this that fit your needs. Some editors read well on a computer screen with an internet browser up on the side, allowing them to check names, numbers and other facts using a search engine. Others love to print the piece and do a "pencil check" in which they cross off each letter of a name and check off each statement of fact during the verification process. Whatever works best for you is the method you should use as you espouse the value of accuracy.

You should not feel bad about asking as many questions of a writer as you need. You also should not feel bad about looking up information and verifying facts. Some writers will become edgy about this, but it is your job to make sure the piece is airtight. If you fail to keep errors out of stories, you aren't much good to your organization, your writers or your audience.

Attention

For years, editors were the gatekeepers of news. They decided what was important and what wasn't. They chose what got the most attention and what got the least. Editors have the right to make something the primary story, the top bit of news or the prominent element on their websites, but they have a lot less influence than they used to.

Journalism purists deride attempts to gain attention for stories as being a cheap marketing ploy that is beneath them, but you need to find ways to attract readers. The best stories in the world will not get read if you can't draw traffic to your publication.

One way to get the attention of readers is through the traditional approach of writing to the interest of the audience, but that's not enough. Many readers rely on search engines to locate stories and websites, so you need to create material that appeals to a search engine. The concept of **search engine optimization** is something you must comprehend and embrace. Failure to do so will lead to your stories, news releases and blog posts being buried under content from other providers who do embrace SEO.

SEO guides how providers of online content construct their headlines, stories, keywords and more with the purpose of making all of it more appealing to search engines. The better you do this, the more easily search engines will find your work and the higher level of prominence it will be afforded in web searches. Most people will not go past the first page of search results a search engine provides to them, so you need to work hard to get your content on that first page. Keep in mind that this is not an exact science, but it is a skill that you can hone through experience and experimentation. We will expand on this later in the book and offer you ways to improve your approach to SEO.

Advantages

Journalists love being first to provide people with information. "The big **scoop**" drives many people in the field to push for big stories. In most cases, those stories don't mean as much as the everyday stories that can affect people's lives. Valuable content can also be lost in stories amid a sea of glib quotes and tortured prose.

When editing a story, look for ways to feature the advantages a story can provide to a reader. Stories about gas prices, tax increases, new businesses and trash collection might seem mundane to writers, but to readers, they can be valuable. When you edit, see if you touch on those key aspects of life that matter to people or if you're downgrading them in your story because they lack sex appeal.

Accessibility

The reason people go to a website, pick up a newspaper, thumb through a magazine or use any other form of media is to be engaged, entertained or educated. The only way any of these things can occur is if the reader can understand the material itself. This is where a good editor can make a huge difference.

Newspapers often target a reading level of between eighth and 10th grade for their copy. Magazines vary widely in their target demographics. Web readers tend to be better read and better educated than consumers of other media. That said, you have to make the material accessible to them. If they can't read it easily, they will go elsewhere for their information. Shape your stories so they reflect the vocabulary, knowledge base and tone you expect your audience to embrace. Make your stories good reads, and people will continue to consume your content.

HELPFUL HINTS
QUESTIONS REGARDING ACCESSIBILITY

At a broad level, you want to make sure the readers have everything they need to fully understand the story. Here are some simple questions you can use to help assess if the bigger issues are dealt with properly:

- Does this piece tell a story?

- Does the lead capture the point of the story?

- Does every paragraph build on the assumptions that come out of the lead, or does the story go on a tangent?

- Is the middle of the story tight, strong and valuable, or is it overwritten and flabby with superfluous detail?

- Do your readers get the background information necessary to understand the story even if they have never read anything on this topic before?

- Does the story answer all the questions it raises?

As with all changes, you want to make sure you do no harm during the edit. If you have a story in which a writer has noted, "Officer Jim Snat said the driver was operating while in a chemically altered state," you can't just say, "Officer Jim Snat said the driver was drunk." These sentences don't mean the same thing. Don't cause an error by carelessly trying to simplify something.

THE EDITING PROCESS

Before you edit a story, you need to understand what the story is trying to do. You should ask the writer to give you a quick review of the piece. The standard "In 25 words or less, tell me what this is about" request is effective in garnering information from a writer. A warning light should start flashing for you if a writer can't give you that synopsis. When writers say, "It's kind of complicated . . ." chances are they don't understand their story. If the writer can capture the story in a strong, simple statement, you can use that information to guide your editing.

Writers often go off on a tangent or do not hammer the point home in the story, because they intuitively know what they think the story should be. Sometimes, what they want to say can get lost between their brains and the computer screen. If you know what the story is supposed to be about, given what the writer has told you, you can help keep the story on track.

Once you have a sense of what you will read, you need to read the entire story thoroughly before you edit. You need to read the story the way you think a reader would, for several good reasons.

First, you want to see the whole piece before tearing into it. If you start tweaking grammar and rewriting sentences before you get a feel for the story, you're not doing anyone any favors. The goal of an edit is to improve the copy, but you need to assess the state of the copy before you can improve it. Changing things before you see the big picture is a bad idea.

Second, you might be able to bring more out of the story than the writer initially thought existed. A small nugget in the fourth paragraph might make for a much better lead. A tack-on item at the end might make a good sidebar. A giant hole might emerge that will require the writer to go back and make some more calls. The writer needs to fix all of these things before you waste time picking at grammar and style.

Finally, you will feel more comfortable with the piece if you read it and digest it before you edit it. In approaching the piece the way a reader would, you will make better decisions as to what to change and what to leave alone. In addition, you will get a better sense of how much editing you will need to do or if the reporter needs to do more work before you start editing. Will this be a story that needs a little polishing, or are you going to have to bulldoze the whole thing and send it back to the reporter? The first read gives you a feel for that.

EDITING VERSUS FIXING

In the classic newsroom movie "The Paper," a reporter keeps asking if someone has another word for some word he's already used twice. Finally, in a moment of frustration, his editor says, "I've got another word for all of them." The editor then proceeds to rewrite the whole story. This serves as a nice bit of movie magic, but it isn't what you should do as an editor.

Editors often find themselves pressured to fix information on the fly. The lack of time, space or patience drives editors to do a lot of quick cuts and short fixes without involving the writers. This is not an ideal situation for any editor.

Editing and fixing are different things. Editing involves discussing the positives and negatives with the writer and going through what makes something good and what parts of the story need improvement. This can be done face to face, if the reporter is around, or via digital technology, if geography makes this prohibitive. In either case, the writer and the editor come to a sort of agreement on what works and what needs to be repaired. Then, the writer goes back and works on the story on the basis of that discussion. When the writer is finished, she will come back to the editor with the improved story, and the process continues until both parties are satisfied with the outcome.

Fixing is when the editor takes over, changes things and sends the story along without input from the writer. Fixing can also be when an editor demands that the writer change things to fit the editor's whims.

This process of changing things yourself or forcing your writers to perform rote actions without any input will teach them nothing. By fixing the story, you prevent your writers from learning anything, and in most cases, your staff will resent you.

If you do more editing than fixing, you will find that your staff members will continue to improve their copy before you see it. A good editing session allows them to see why you think things need to be changed and how best to change them. In addition, you will find that you won't have to fix the same problems each time you get a story.

Think about it this way: When you were 4 or 5 years old, you were probably learning to tie your shoes. Your mom or dad could do it a lot faster and a lot better, but they wanted you to do it yourself. You probably tried and failed a lot, but in the end you figured it out. Had they not forced you to do the work yourself, you never would have learned this skill, and you'd only able to wear flip-flops.

People who do the activity will learn the skill much better than people who have the activity done for them. Keep that in mind when you work with your writers.

THE FIRST PASS

When you start your first edit of a story, it is a good idea to have the writer nearby, if possible. Talk through the story with the reporter as you are reading it. This will allow you to see what the reporter was thinking during the writing process. It will also allow you to ask the reporter specific questions as you encounter them.

For example, you could ask, "Wait a minute, you said in the third paragraph that the bill was approved, and now it seems that you're saying the opposite. How does that work?" The writer could either see how the two paragraphs were incongruent and allow you to fix the problem or show you how you misinterpreted these ideas. Either way, it helps you figure out if you are reading things properly or if the reporter lost something during the writing process.

Also, you should use this process to ask the reporter for help on parts of the story that need rewriting. If you don't understand what a paragraph is trying to say or if you find a sentence that is too long, you can ask the writer for help. When the writer tells you the underlying meaning of the paragraph, you can work together to find a clearer way of expressing that thought. This allows you to fix the problem, but it also allows you to keep the piece in the writer's voice.

Finally, you can use this opportunity to make some last-minute checks on key facts in the story. You can ask simple questions like, "Are you sure 'Donowski' is spelled right?" or "Are you sure Carlton is a Republican and not an Independent?" You can also poke at some more complicated statements: "Are you sure that this type of land-use policy has never been used in the state before?" or "How did you figure out that the state will need six years to repay this bond debt?" In challenging these things, you can make sure that the writer is confident in the facts. Verify everything before publishing the story.

THE DEEPER EDIT

Once you pick through the basic levels of editing associated with that first cut, you will need to look for other aspects of the writing that will determine how well this piece will meet the needs of the audience. As much as spelling, grammar and style can trip up a piece, the larger issues listed below also matter a great deal in the overall value of a story:

Edit for Value

Media organizations essentially enter into a contract with readers each time they produce content. The organization promises to provide something of worth to the readers in each piece of copy. The readers, for their part, promise to consume the content and return to that organization in the future for additional pieces of important information. To keep this loop operating efficiently, editors must work through copy in such a way as to find the sweet spot between copy that has holes in it and copy that is flabby and overwritten. Consider these questions in determining value:

What Is the Most Important Thing Here?

The answer to this question should help you structure the piece (which we'll get to later), but it should also help you determine the overall value of a story. If you can locate the primary focus or the main assertion within a story, you can then ascertain how valuable this will be to the readers. A story that has a wide-reaching impact of both a quantitative and qualitative nature will require more sources, a higher word count and better overall play in your publication. A story that might matter to a few people, but not in any meaningful way, should receive reductions in all of these areas. If you don't know what is most important, you can't figure out how much value it will have to your readers.

How Does Each Piece of the Story Matter?

When you work in an inverted-pyramid format, the goal is to move from the most important piece of information to the least important piece of information. What this means is that you are asked to weigh the overall value of facts, sources and quotes to determine the degree to which it should be in a story and where it should be. For each paragraph, source and quote, you should be able to explain exactly why this element has merit and how it helps the readers understand the story. If you can't, you should check with the writer to see if you are missing something. If the writer can't explain the value behind that part of the story, you should cut it. If the writer explains it well enough to retain the piece, make sure the writer's explanation matches the story itself. If you "get it" on the basis of the explanation but not the writing itself, have the writer rework that part of the story to clarify its value to the readers.

Are There Parts of the Story That Don't Matter?

Writers occasionally will do something called "notebook emptying," in which they toss in an extra source, a superfluous fact or a random quote. The idea behind this is that the writers feel that because they got the facts, they deserve to be in the piece. Your job as an editor isn't to preserve the efforts of your writers, but rather to refine copy so it best serves your readers. To that end, you should look at each piece of the story through the eyes of a reader and determine if it needs to be there. If the piece has value, keep it. If it doesn't, remove it.

Edit for Tone

Music, movies, novels and other forms of art have varying levels of "feel" to them that will provide the audience members with a sense of how they should emotionally engage them. Sharp, shrill string instruments paired with films can provide viewers with a sense of foreboding in horror movies, while bright colors and soft lines can give a painting a generally pleasant feeling. The same thing is true of media-based writing, in which the overall tone of the piece will make the difference in how the readers perceive it.

The type of story your writer has assembled will determine the tone the piece should have. A city council story or a speech on pork belly futures can come through with a straight-forward, fact-based tone that conveys information in a perfunctory manner. A long-form narrative or personality profile will rely more heavily on description and emotion to create a sense of connection between the story's subjects and the readers. The goal of the editor is to accentuate these tonal areas as needed to improve readability and connectivity.

The editor should also look for poor taste or incongruity between the subject matter and the tone. A story about someone dying in an explosion is no place for a "He went out with a bang" joke. Similarly, not every profile story should lapse so deeply into angst and melodrama as to annoy readers. The goal of an editor is to find the right vibe for the story.

Edit for Pace and Flow

A well-constructed story is like a tree, in that the branches sprout seamlessly from larger limbs, and everything connects back to the trunk of the structure. A poorly constructed story is like a bundle of twigs: The branches all exist in the same space, but they lack connectivity and they fail to create a larger whole. They stick out in every direction and they fail to exist in a cohesive unit, and the parts can fall out of the bundle easily, creating a disjointed mess.

The two areas that help create a well-constructed story out of a collection of sentences and sources are pace and flow. Pace refers to the speed at which a reader can move through each sentence and subsequently through the entire story. Flow refers to the way in which the audience can smoothly move from point to point while reading the story without confusion or interruption.

The use of sentences that range from 17 to 23 words in most traditional inverted-pyramid pieces will create natural pace for the piece, regardless of platform. This does not mean you should never use longer or shorter sentences, but it does mean that you should use shorter or longer sentences for a purpose and that you should understand what they do to the pace and flow of the piece.

Short sentences of about 8 to 12 words lead to sharp breaks in the overall movement of the piece. These sentences can be used to force readers to "slam on the brakes" at a specific point of interest in story.

Example

Ted Alport picked up his mail after work, the same way he had each day of the 11 years he lived at 1127 E. Smith St.

Amid the bills and charity solicitations, he found a thick, padded envelope that came without a return address sticker.

Alport was splitting his attention between a ringing phone and his barking dog as he poured the envelope's contents onto his kitchen counter.

After he calmed the dog and answered his phone, he glanced back to see what he received, only to stop and scream.

It was a severed hand.

The buildup in this piece is done mainly with medium-length sentences; the quick "punch" is done with a short sentence at the end. This approach stops the readers at a crucial point in the story and forces them to pause upon reaching it.

Longer sentences that go beyond 25 words will create a sense of longer, rolling scenes or rambling and careening text. This can lead to improved movement in a piece and a quickened pace that creates a sense of excitement or danger.

Example

Cliff Jenkins stood on the rickety porch, picking at a small piece of paint on its railing as he watched the sun go down on his 120-acre farm, when he noticed the yellowish clouds and blue sky converge into a foreboding green.

Suddenly, the green mixture began pouring toward the earth, spinning in a counterclockwise direction and creating a coolish, damp mixture of air that rushed at him in a rough, fast and violent manner.

Before Jenkins could call inside the house for his wife, Erma, to lend a second opinion on what was happening, the twister had descended to the ground and begun to tear through every speck of corn he had planted earlier in the day, tossing aside fence posts, farming equipment and livestock like a raging toddler having a fit.

The construction of these longer sentences can give the readers a feeling of speed in moving through the piece. Depending on the topic and the verbiage, this approach can make a story feel fast and precise or rapid and chaotic.

Although pace can lead to flow, it doesn't necessarily always create it. Flow requires the seamless moving from point to point in a story on the basis of the content itself. The implementation of transitions will assist you as you work from topic to topic and point to point.

The type of story can determine the best way to create flow. For example, in a standard news story, a paraphrase-quote pairing can create flow nicely between paragraphs when the paraphrase sets up the quote. The quote can then elaborate on topic and add value to the paraphrase.

Example

Valedictorian Miguel Sanchez said this year's graduating class brought its own sense of style and value to the school.

"We were smooth and polished half the time and ragged and worn the other half," he said. "But we made sure that Henshaw High was a better and stronger learning environment for future classes."

If you are working on smoothing transitions between paragraphs, you can look for ways to touch on similar or oppositional topics that will allow you to demonstrate cohesion of ideas.

Example of Similar Ideas

City councilmember Jesse Witford said the decision to remove residential restrictions from the Oak Lakes area would lead to overcrowding and pollution.

"The whole point of passing these restrictions in the 1970s was to prevent corporations from dumping toxins into the lake," he said. "Without these restrictions, it will be the wild west out here in terms of environmental destruction."

The city's environmental director, Cassey Vilt, also said any hazardous materials that entered the lake would create an irreversible and negative impact.

"You can't unring a bell," she said. "If you let a business treat the lake like a toilet, you will be stuck with whatever ends up in there forever. You can't flush a lake and start over."

Example of Opposing Ideas

City councilmember Jesse Witford said the decision to remove residential restrictions from the Oak Lakes area would lead to overcrowding and pollution.

"The whole point of passing these restrictions in the 1970s was to prevent corporations from dumping toxins into the lake," he said. "Without these restrictions, it will be the wild west out here in terms of environmental destruction."

Developer Mitch Malone said fears of destruction were overblown and that businesses aren't always "the bad guys."

"We're an easy target, because we like money," Malone said. "That said, business interests and environmental interests are not incompatible and we want to show that responsible regulations and responsible corporations can lead to beneficial outcomes for this city."

To best edit for overall flow, look for those simple links between paragraphs in which one supports the other. Then, seek ways to show similarities or differences between those chunks of information. This can be the repetition of a word or phrase or it can be just based on a similar topic that reflects a cohesive understanding of the information. As you continue to piece your ideas together, you can create a whole picture, much like one that emerges from a completed puzzle.

Edit for Balance

When it comes to news pieces, editors often worry about getting "side A" and "side B" into a story to create a sense of balance between opposite factions within a story. This means that if a plan to build a school is going to require a referendum, the editor would want people who favor the referendum and those who oppose it. If a city is picking between two candidates for its new police chief, the editor normally wants someone who favors candidate A and someone who favors candidate B. This is a form of balance that you should consider when you work on a story, but you shouldn't stop there.

Balance is about looking to see that all important angles of a story are present and properly represented, so when a reporter simply grabs what appears to be sources that are on side A and side B of the issue, you should push that person to look for other potential sources. Simply saying, "Well, we got the Republican! Let's go grab a Democrat" is reductive and pointless. That doesn't mean you shouldn't have either of those two people, but it means you should push the writers to think more deeply about the ideologies, experiences and values each source brings to the story. This will also help you determine if any of those items are unrepresented in the story.

All editors should seek balance in other ways as well. Consider how much one source dominates a piece of copy and what that says about a topic. If you are editing a press statement

VIEW FROM A PRO
REED FISCHER

Courtesy of Reed Fischer

Although he said he spent almost 100 percent of his career in news organizations, Reed Fischer has worn a wide array of hats over time and for a good reason.

"I'm a 38-year-old writer, reporter, blogger, editor, project manager, and strategist," he said. "I've also dipped into social media marketing, app development, and website redesign. . . I include all of these descriptors because I quickly learned that the people who said 'I don't know how to do that' or 'I won't do that' were more likely to get laid off, or get passed over for promotions."

This "jack-of-all-trades" approach has allowed Fischer, who is currently the senior editor at Minnesota Monthly magazine in Minneapolis, to thrive in a field that has evolved greatly since he graduated from college.

"The ground underneath us is moving, and it will continue to move," he said. "Keep learning new skills."

Fischer said that on top of learning new skills, editors have to keep abreast of the needs of their readers. He has freelanced for a variety of publications, including Rolling Stone and the Village Voice, while also working for altweeklies and consumer magazines, each of which has a niche that his work sought to fill.

"If you're writing to a highly informed audience, then you don't have to spell so much out for them," Fischer said. "If you're doing hard and serious topics, best not to muddy your prose with lots of clever asides. If you're doing a personality profile, best not to write it like an instruction manual. Be intentional with your choices throughout to serve the audience."

Good managers and good editors rely on data to help make decisions, he said, but Fischer doesn't believe in being "a slave to Google Analytics."

"Now that we can know so much more about demographics (and even sub-demos when you compare the audience reading you online vs the one reading you in print), it's essential to make use of it. . ." he said. "Ideally audience numbers provide a chance to help you eliminate stuff from what you produce that already seems to have less value and fulfillment associated with it."

The editing process "will bleed into every aspect of your life eventually if you do it long enough," Fischer said, noting that good editors will consistently take a logical approach to improving copy on both the micro and macro levels.

"Ideally a good editor reaches a point where they just look at any block of text and start to run through a mental checklist in their minds," he said. "They see the extra spaces at the same time they're thinking, 'This quote is pointless.' I have to do a lot of both micro and macro at Minnesota Monthly. I'm helping writers at the beginning of the process avoid bad choices (unclear angle, lack of quality sources) that will make it hard for them to complete their assignments, and then when they sometimes do still make bad choices (confusing organization, incorrect hyphen use), I clean it up on the sentence level. It's a small enough organization that I still am doing editing every day."

In the end, although he has moved from a writer to an editor to a top-level manager, Fischer said the love of editing still gives him joy.

"I always liked a thing that an editor of mine once said: 'Amuse thyself,'" he said. "If that's not part of your job in journalism, you're doing it wrong."

about the merging of two companies, do both of these organizations get an equal amount of space and say within the piece? Does one group's representative provide the majority of the content, with the other group's representative serving only as someone who "agrees" with every element?

Also, look at who gets prominence in terms of placement within the story. The higher up within a piece someone is presented, the more valuable that person appears to be to the readers. It can seem easier to stick with one source through a series of paraphrases and quotes before hopping over to the second source, but editors need to look for a way to balance information within the piece to keep things fair. Thus, an editor may need to restructure a story to weave comments from a second source into the first few paragraphs of a story to keep things equal in terms of value on the basis of placement.

CUTTING COPY

The benefit of writing for digital media is that time restrictions and space limits no longer dictate how much story you can tell. However, just because you can write forever, it doesn't mean your audience will read forever, which is where editors come in as arbiters of story length.

Cutting copy requires editors to understand a story completely and then make decisions on how best to remove problematic elements, eliminate redundancies and shrink a story's size. The quality of the editor will determine if the cuts mimic those of a skilled surgeon or a third-rate butcher.

Traditional editors who believe in the purity of the **inverted pyramid** will espouse a "cut from the bottom" approach, arguing that the less valuable information will be lower in a story, if that story is written properly. This format of writing, standard for most forms of straightforward media writing, dictates that content should be written in single-sentence paragraphs in descending order of importance.

While this may be the simplest path to reducing the size of a story, it clearly isn't the best. This presupposes that the writer built the story in an inverted-pyramid form and that the writer did so perfectly. In addition, a few more insightful edits elsewhere in the piece might tighten the piece enough to prevent a need for that kind of chopping.

A good rule of thumb is to let the lead be your guide for whether each paragraph you read is adding to the sum of human knowledge. If you're reading a feature, use the nut graph or the general sense from the first few paragraphs to guide you. Each paragraph has to support or augment the lead in a meaningful way.

Newer editors often won't cut from the bottom, but will instead eliminate many of the quotes in the story, arguing that the paraphrase leading into them tells the story well enough. Again, some quotes can be superfluous or repetitive, but it doesn't mean you should play a game of seek and destroy with every quote in a piece. If you do this, you could reduce an engaging piece of copy to a flat and dull recounting of fact.

The best thing to do is look at each pairing of paraphrase and quote to determine if it has value. If the pairing conceptually fails to add value, eliminate the whole thing and then move on. If the paraphrase repeats the quote, ask the writer to rework the paraphrase to improve its value. If the quote is bland, remove it and have the writer seek a better quote to pair with the paraphrase. The goal is to have quotes that add spice and feeling to the story, so eliminating them as a matter of course makes as little sense as retaining boring quotes simply to make sure you have quotes in a story. Editing is about finding the sweet spot between too much and not enough, and this applies to cutting or adding quotes as well.

FILLING HOLES

A **hole** in copy is created when a writer raises an issue that interests a reader but doesn't provide enough information to satisfy that interest. Editors develop an intuitive sense over time as to where holes exist and what is required to fill them. Here are some simple examples of holes and how to fill them:

A Question With No Answer

Writers often spend enough time working in a specific area of interest that they start to understand things that go beyond what readers will intuitively know. It can be jargon, historical references or "inside baseball" issues, and in most cases, the writer will assume that others know these items as well. A hole can develop in a story when a gap emerges between what the writer knows and what the readers do. Here's an example:

Francisco Smart took over as San Antonio's mayor six months ago, completing the end of his predecessor's term.

This situation raises at least two questions:

- Who was the predecessor?

- Why was he or she unable to complete the term?

You can easily fill in the hole with a simple edit:

Francisco Smart, who is completing Carol Jafkey's term as San Antonio's mayor, took on his current role six months ago when Jafkey moved to Arizona.

This might raise additional questions, such as "Why did Jafkey move to Arizona?" That said, you have plugged the bigger holes, and you can address the additional questions later.

Any time you see a statement that has you asking a question the writer hasn't answered later in the story, you need to acknowledge the presence of a hole and find a way to fill it.

An Accusation With No Response

News traditionally requires balance, but that's not just an ideal associated with newspapers. Unless you want people to see you as a slanted source of information, you need to look for fairness when you are editing. In some cases, a source will fire a shot across the bow and accuse someone else of something nefarious. The first question you should ask is whether that accusation needs to be in your piece in the first place or if it's just a cheap shot that lacks value. If it merits inclusion, see what truth there is to the accusation or afford the accused an opportunity to respond so you don't end up with a hole like this:

Paul Lazlo has filed suit six times against Rich Wood, accusing his neighbor of running an illegal gambling ring in his basement.

The accusation is pretty serious, so make sure you don't just let it linger:

Paul Lazlo has filed suit six times against Rich Wood, accusing his neighbor of running an illegal gambling ring in his basement. In each of those cases, the court has dismissed the case as being without merit.

Here's another approach:

Paul Lazlo has filed suit six times against Rich Wood, accusing his neighbor of running an illegal gambling ring in his basement. Wood testified in court each time that this was nothing more than a friendly poker game that Lazlo detested because he was not invited to participate.

The goal is to make sure that you don't leave the door open on an accusation when you can easily close it and give your readers a more complete version of the truth.

An "Oddity" With No Context

Oddity is an interest element writers often emphasize in their work to give readers a sense of how special an outcome or issue is. However, when a writer fails to provide context for that information, the readers often feel lost or don't have a full appreciation of this rarity. Here's an example:

Mel Purvis of the Cincinnati Reds pitched an opening day no-hitter, marking only the second time in major league history that a pitcher accomplished this feat.

A couple questions are left unanswered here:

- Who did it first?

- When did he do it?

Mel Purvis of the Cincinnati Reds threw an opening day no-hitter, marking only the second time since 1940 that a pitcher accomplished that feat.

Or this:

Cincinnati's Mel Purvis joined Bob Feller of the Cleveland Indians as the only pitchers to throw opening-day no-hitters in major league history.

However, to plug both holes, you need to reconsider your approach a bit:

Cincinnati's Mel Purvis became the second player in the past 78 years to throw an opening-day no-hitter, joining Cleveland's Bob Feller who first accomplished the feat in 1940.

That plugs both holes and helps the readers understand the rarity of the feat.

Any time you have an oddity, you run the risk of having a hole in the story. Make sure you edit to provide context and meaning to help your readers more fully understand the magnitude of what you want them to know.

HOW TO CRITICIZE EFFECTIVELY

Constructive criticism is a useful tool in the editing process. Most editors think they are offering constructive criticism, but people who have to deal with them think the editors are just being critical. Criticism can cause harm for the editor-writer relationship when editors don't do it well, but it can help writers improve their skills when editors take the time to criticize effectively.

When you edit a piece, you need to point out the good as well as the bad. You can reinforce growth when you point out specific good things the writer did in the story. You can then offer suggestions of how the writer can improve the copy now and in the future. This approach will show your writers that you appreciate the work they do while explaining what doesn't work and why it doesn't work.

If the material needs more than a few minor corrections, send it back to the writer for revision. When you let your writers do the revisions themselves, you will find that they not only keep the work in their voice, but they also might improve it better than you could. The editing process might take one rewrite or several, but as you review drafts, you will see improvement.

Finally, you should take time to do a postmortem with your writer. Once deadline is gone and the piece has gone to bed, give each other some breathing room, but make sure you come back to the piece and spend some time with it. Talk about what went right and what went wrong. Explain what you liked and what you didn't like, and ask the writer for feedback. Once you're through with it, you both should have learned something.

THE BIG THREE

Here are the three key things you should take away from this chapter:

1. **Look at more than the small stuff:** Editing requires you to pick at the spelling, grammar and structure errors of copy, but it also requires you to make sure a story reaches your readers in a clear and effective way. This is where the "all A's" approach comes into play. Make sure your copy is accurate, draws a reader's attention, is accessible and emphasizes key advantages. If you do this, you will serve your readers well in showing them the bigger picture.

2. **Editing takes longer than fixing, but it's worth it:** The goal of an editor is to make a writer better, thus

limiting the amount of editing that will occur in future drafts and future assignments. If all you do is fix the stories and don't help the writers improve, you will continue to fix the same mistakes over and over again. If you work with your writers and give them a sense of what works and why as well as what doesn't work and why, you will have a much stronger writer at the end of the process.

3. **Find ways to improve tone, balance and flow within stories:** The goal of good editing is to

smooth out the rough spots you find in stories so that the readers get the best possible version of the piece. This is something you can do by making sure the tone of the piece is appropriate, the story maintains a sense of balance and it flows well from the top to the bottom. When you are able to do this, you help the writers refine their craft and also give your audience a complete, clear and valuable piece of copy.

KEY TERMS

flow 98
hole 102
inverted pyramid 102

notebook emptying 98
pace 98
scoop 94

search engine optimization 94

DISCUSSION QUESTIONS

1. How well do you take criticism of your writing? What helps you grow, and what do you feel leads you to react negatively? How have your experiences with criticism shaped your approach to criticizing the work of others?

2. Of the A's listed in the chapter, which one is easiest for you to accomplish in writing and editing? Which one

is most difficult for you? Why do you think this is the case?

3. How important is tone in the writing that you enjoy? What is it about the tone of those pieces you like that makes them effective for you? What kind of tone do you dislike when you read content? What could make it better?

WRITE NOW!

1. Find a story in a local media outlet and review it for pace and flow. Does the piece move well between points, or is the writing stilted and rough? Does the piece move quickly from point to point, or does it slowly meander in its storytelling approach? How do the pace and flow of the piece affect your overall enjoyment in and engagement with the story? Write a short essay on your thoughts.

2. Fill in the holes associated with these statements:

   a. In the 2017 season, the Cleveland Browns became only the second NFL team in history to post an 0-16 record.

b. Hurricane Nate was the fourth hurricane to make landfall in the United States in 2017.

c. Nabi Tajima was the world's oldest person when he died at age 117 in 2017.

d. The White House worker who said senators should ignore Sen. John McCain's opinion on the president's CIA director because "He's dying any-way" no longer works for the administration.

3. Compare and contrast the concepts of editing and fixing, outlining the pros and cons of each approach to improving copy. Outline your thoughts in a short essay.

$SAGE edge™

Visit **edge.sagepub.com/filakediting** to help you accomplish your coursework goals in an easy-to-use learning environment.

8 HEADLINES

The headline has changed over time, on the basis of the needs of the medium for which it was written. Newspapers place multiple stories on a single page, necessitating headlines of varying lengths and font sizes. Newsletters and other specialty publications rely heavily on strong service-oriented headlines, which tell readers how to solve problems. Corporate websites and public relations campaign blogs use persuasive messages to draw readers to content that will benefit the group and the audience.

With the web, headline writers must contend with medium-based needs as well. While a newspaper hoping to get attention can simply make the headline bigger, web headlines don't work that way. A mysterious headline on a company's blog post could entice readers already on the site, but might not make the first page of results from an internet search. A strong "how to" headline that might be honest and truthful in print could draw suspicion from online readers who are inundated with hoaxes and schemes as they surf the web.

The purpose of this chapter is to help you understand what makes headlines work and what limits their effectiveness. We will examine issues pertaining to grabbing the attention of readers as well as capturing the interest of search engines. We will also discuss the best ways to write effective headlines while avoiding making the mistakes that can make you look foolish.

HOW HEADLINES WORK

Headlines let readers know what a piece of copy will contain. The goal of a good headline is to engage, entertain and interest a reader enough to invest time in the remainder of the piece. Here are some of the key things a headline can do if you write it well:

Draw People to Stories They Want to Read

Readers often scan headlines for topics of interest. A good headline on a website or in a set of search engine results can help you grab the readers and let them know the piece is worth reading.

HELPFUL HINTS

HOW TO WRITE AN AUDIENCE-CENTRIC HEADLINE

People read stories to satisfy specific needs, and your headline should tell them how the story will meet those needs. To make your headlines more audience-centric, consider drawing on the following items as you write for your readers:

- *Self-interest:* Readers want to know "What's in it for me?" If you can show your readers a personal benefit through a strong headline, they will likely stop and give the story a second look. Find an aspect of the story that tells the readers what's in it for them and make that a dominant element of your headline.

Example: If you get a story on a city council's decision to add money to the park department's budget to improve and add playground equipment throughout the city, a simple, noun-verb-object style headline can get the job done:

City council gives park department financial boost

However, there's a clear benefit here that goes underreported in that headline: The city has just added more fun things for kids at its parks. Parents of young children will likely want to know this information, and they will consider it useful. Rework the headline to emphasize that element of self-interest:

More playground equipment slated for city parks

- *Curiosity:* People want to know how things work. If you can write a headline that makes people ask, "How did that happen?" you've got a chance to pique their curiosity and make them read on.

Example: A story involving two local sports teams can always have a simple and straightforward headline that tells the story clearly and directly:

Knights defeat Pirates, 3-2

The headline tells the story, but it does little to make the audience want to read on. Nothing in that headline makes your readers ask, "How did that happen?" Instead, focus on things that might make your readers want to know more:

Hobbs hits game-winning homer, sends Knights to World Series

This headline puts emphasis on two points: It was a comeback win, and the Knights are going to the World Series. Both of these items can arouse interest in your readers and encourage them to read the story.

- *Problem-solving opportunities:* Media outlets that practice service journalism rely on stories that help readers fix things. Men's and women's magazines provide articles on how to repair a damaged relationship or how to talk to a child about an unpleasant topic. Trade and hobby magazines teach people how to fix a leaky pipe or refinish a piece of furniture. Niche organizations offer advice on how to lose weight or avoid credit card debt.

A headline that tells people how to do something can provide knowledge and help solve problems. Too many headlines of this nature rely on hyperbole ("How to get the best, cheapest, most sensational makeover ever!") or have been heard hundreds of times before ("How to lose weight without dieting!"). To craft an effective headline of this nature, you need to focus on what distinguishes this article from the dozens others just like it.

Example: A headline on repairing a broken garbage disposal can be boring but necessary, especially if your sink is full of food scraps and your disposal doesn't work. A simple headline is easy enough:

How to remove, replace or repair your garbage disposal

However, if you want people to pay attention to your article, you'll want the headline to focus on something that makes the article appealing to a reader who is not mechanically inclined:

Five "no-tool" fixes to try on your broken garbage disposal

This headline is clear and concise, but it also emphasizes something different about the article (fixing something without tools). It also has keywords likely to show up on a search of the web (broken, fix, garbage disposal).

Let People Know Which Stories They Don't Want to Read

Readers, especially in the internet age, have niche-based interests when it comes to what they read. While readers might receive dozens of emails, tweets and "push" alerts each day, most people won't read even 20 percent of the full pieces behind the headlines. If you write a clear and concise headline, your readers will be grateful that you helped them find things they want and avoid things they don't.

Show Readers Things They Didn't Know That Are Important

Doing what's good for you isn't always your first choice. Parents force children to eat their vegetables, doctors tell patients they need to exercise more and professors extol the virtues of studying harder for tests. We might not want to do these things, but we know they are important. Headlines can influence readers in the same ways that parents, doctors and professors influence those people under their watchful eyes. A good headline gives people a reason to look at stories they might otherwise avoid.

Example: A story regarding massive changes to the country's tax code will not draw many readers if the headline is written in a simple and straightforward way:

House, Senate vote to change federal tax code

However, the changes can have a significant impact on readers. A good headline will put that impact front and center:

Tax changes to double penalties on late filers

Give Readers a Sense of the Relative Importance of the Story

In traditional media, editors run headlines higher on a page and in larger type to indicate the importance of a story. A headline that stretches across the entire front page of a newspaper in 60-point type will tell a reader that the story is more important than one that runs in 30-point type across two columns of text.

On your site, you can rely on font size to some degree to impress upon your readers the importance of the topic. You can also attempt to determine which headlines get additional attention through prominent placement on the site. However, when it comes to impressing search engines, these things matter significantly less. Later in the chapter, we will discuss how you can use other techniques to find your way to the top of internet searches.

HELPFUL HINTS
BASIC TERMS OF HEADLINES

To better understand some of the terms associated with headlines, here is a cheat sheet you can use. Some of the terms cross over from traditional to digital media, while others do not. Even so, you should understand the language of all platforms.

Point: An old printer's measure that equals 1/72 of an inch. **Point** size measures the font's height. A headline that uses a 36-point font would be approximately half an inch tall. A 12-point body copy font would be approximately 1/6 of an inch tall. In both digital and traditional media, a headline needs to be larger than the

subsequent body copy. However, the size of the headline is less of a concern in digital media than it is in traditional media.

Deck or *deck head*: A secondary headline element that goes below the main headline and elaborates on the information in it. A **deck** is often useful as a secondary step for readers who might be enticed by the headline but are unsure if they want to read the whole story.

Hammer: A headline treatment reserved for large stories in traditional media. These have three or fewer words and are displayed in large, bold type. **Hammer** headlines will always need to be rewritten for the web, as they lack the elements to attract both readers and search engines.

Kicker: A small headline that runs above the headline and uses a word or a few words to indicate what the story's main topic is. In other cases, a **kicker** is a short phrase that leads into the main headline.

Title tags: A web coding process that determines what information will appear at the top of the browser window's bar. Search engines like Google will display the first 50 to 60 characters of a title tag in their results lists, but that's a rough estimate, so shorter is often better. The information in the **title tag** lets visitors know what site they are on as well as what the content for that page should be. Each page should have a unique tag and should include the keywords you want the search engine to find.

Header tags (or *H tags*): Used as headlines, decks and subheadings for webpages. These tags run from H1, which is a primary headline, to H6. Traditionally, **headers** like H1 and H2 are used the way a headline and deck head would be used in print media. Subsequent heads can be used to break up text. Search engines pay attention to these headers, so it is important to put keywords into them. However, you should not sacrifice readability in an attempt to appease the search engines.

Font: Also known as a typeface, a **font** refers to the style in which the letters and numbers appear in a headline or text.

Serif: A small stroke found at the end of each edge on a letter or number. **Serif** also applies to a font family that makes use of these strokes. Fonts of this nature are said to be easier to read in small print, which is why they are often used for body copy in traditional media.

Sans serif: Meaning "without serifs," this refers to a font family that does not use the small strokes at the ends of the letters and numbers. **Sans serif** fonts are used in traditional media as headline fonts because they are easier to read at large sizes. On the web, both serif and sans serif fonts are used for headline and body copy.

Leading: Pronounced "ledding," the space between lines of type. Tight **leading** means that there is very little space between the lines, while loose leading means that there is additional space between the lines. Improper leading can harm the readability of your text.

Kerning and *tracking*: Often used interchangeably, although they have slight differences. Generically speaking, these terms refer to the addition or reduction of horizontal space between letters to improve readability or fit. **Kerning** is selectively adjusting the spacing of specific letters, while **tracking** applies this principle to an entire block of text.

THE CORE OF A GOOD HEADLINE

A good headline has a mix of structural and grammatical components that accomplishes the tasks noted above. A headline should have a strong noun-verb-object structure, which contains concrete nouns, vigorous verbs and obvious objects. Headlines with this structure are clear and easy to understand:

Man bites dog

Firefighters extinguish blaze

Johnson Corp. wins construction bid

When composing a headline like the simple ones above, you will notice two things that are standard for good headlines:

Good headlines are written in present tense. The action associated with the story has already occurred, but most headlines get present-tense treatment because it conveys a sense of immediacy and timeliness. Some variations on this theme include the following:

Infinitive form: *Trump to run for second term*

Present participle: *Trump running out of time to pass bill*

Even when you have a story that relies on a past action or a headline with a past tense verb, you can provide a present tense tie to it:

Washington never chopped down cherry tree, historians say

Johnson murdered wife, jury decides

One thing you will want to avoid is the use of modal verbs. These are helping and "condition-based" words that don't tell your readers something concrete. For example:

Zika virus may be linked to three area deaths

Johnson might be running for senate

When you write a headline this way, you aren't giving your readers any real information. You could just as easily have written the headline "Zika may not be linked to three area deaths" or "Johnson might not be running for senate." Instead, tell your readers what you know:

Heath department studies link between Zika virus, area deaths

Johnson explores senate run

Good headlines are written in active voice. The use of noun-verb-object structure leads to strong active-voice sentences. In some instances, you will want to flip the headline components to emphasize news value, as in this headline regarding the assassination of President John F. Kennedy:

President slain in Dallas

The most important thing was the death of the president, and therefore, the passive-voice construction was acceptable. Early editions wouldn't have had the name of the shooter, Lee Harvey Oswald. Even if they did, editors would have been unlikely to make him the focus of the headline.

Good Headlines Then Get More Specific

Once you have those main components, here are some key additions you can make to increase the value of your headline:

Adjectives and adverbs: The use of key descriptors can improve the clarity of your headline and give your readers additional context as they decide whether to read on. However, use them sparingly.

Time and place elements: Timeliness is an element of news value, which means newer information is better than older information. When you add a clear time element to your headline, you can give your readers a sense that the news is fresh:

Five great grilling ideas for Labor Day barbecue

You can also use the time referent to provide a time peg for history-based headlines:

50 years after epic homer, Mazeroski still a hero in Pittsburgh

Place elements are crucial because proximity is also an element of news value. People pay more attention to events that happen closer to them. These locations can be a state (*Trump visits Wisconsin*), a city (*Milwaukee gets new stadium*), a roadway (*Crash on Interstate 3 kills Wautoma plumber*) or any other geographic referent that you think will get your readers to pay attention.

Explanatory elements: These elements clarify why a person should care about the article below. These clauses provide the reader with context regarding the subject of the article. Obituaries use them to remind readers why the person who died was important. Here are a few examples:

Michael Jones, Smithville's first mayor, dies at 92

Carlton Kasmerski, founder of Pizza Acropolis restaurants, dies at 75

HELPFUL HINTS
HEADLINES AND STYLE

Headlines follow basic rules of grammar and style. They require noun-verb-object construction. They must be clear, concise and correct. They must be grammatically sound. However, headlines allow for some variations when it comes to grammar and style. Here is a list of the main ways headlines differ from other forms of journalistic writing. Keep in mind that these are guidelines more than rules.

- *Articles:* Omit articles when you write your headlines. "A," "an" and "the" are usually unnecessary in a headline:

  Mayor blasts city council over convention center contract

  Habitat for Humanity builds home for area woman

  However, you can still use an article when you need to emphasize a point or as an important descriptor:

  Kanye says he remains "the best of the best"

  I'm a star among stars, Hayes declares

- *Verbs:* Eliminate "to be" verbs and other helpers that can be implied:

  Muncie man arrested in hotel robbery

  Lillibrook named pageant winner after statewide search

- *Punctuation:* Commas are used as substitutions for conjunctions, while semicolons are used to indicate separate thoughts. Quote marks are still used for movie, book and other composition titles, but use single rather than double quotes:

  'Moonlight,' 'La Land' take home top Emmy Awards

  Garner, Affleck file for divorce

  City Council voids building contract; mayor calls decision 'offensive'

  Simpson injured in car crash; police suspect foul play

  Also, other characters that are usually spelled out can be used in headlines:

  Smith earns council win with 56% of vote

  ABC Manufacturing earns #1 ranking for customer service

- *Numbers:* You don't have to spell out numbers under 10. You can also start a headline with a numeral:

  55 people promoted at Smith Corp.

  2 dead, 9 injured in bus wreck

- *Abbreviations:* The rules on abbreviations vary from place to place. On the web, abbreviating doesn't make much sense, as your abbreviations might not match the search terms of your readers. However, you can use abbreviations if they are likely to be things your readers would know:

  WWE plans 'Wrestling Apocalypse 2020' for NYC

THINGS TO DO BEFORE WRITING A HEADLINE

Read the Full Piece

A piece of writing that uses the inverted pyramid will present the most important information in the first two paragraphs. However, some writers bury the lead deep in the story, either through the use of a narrative introduction or because they wrote poorly. To ensure that you've fully understood the point of the piece, read every word of it at least once. If you can't figure out why the piece matters, have the writer explain it to you. It could be the writer's fault for not making things clear, or the point might be there and you just missed it. Either way, a writer likely knows the story better than you do, so asking for clarification once you've read through the piece makes sense.

VIEW FROM A PRO
LINDSAY POWERS

Courtesy of Lindsay Powers

Lindsay Powers has spent much of her professional life trying to get your attention, and being quite successful in doing so. She has spent the past 13 years as a writer and an editor, with 10 of them being in digital media. She is currently the vice president of lifestyle and entertainment for SiriusXM, and she previously served as the editorial director of lifestyle at Yahoo and the editor in chief of Yahoo Parenting. During her time at Yahoo, she literally wrote the headlines that appeared on Yahoo.com, a site that reaches more than 600 million people a month, making it one of the most read websites in America.

"My goal is to keep headlines succinct so they're not cut off on mobile and social (platforms), to insert an emotional tag and give a little while holding back," she said. "For example, 'Mom's Brave Move Saves Daughter's Life.' I like this because 'mom' is a word that connects people, you get a bit of a taste of the story but you want to know more and it's a nice adjective."

Powers said that throughout her career, digital media needs have altered how people write headlines.

"Ten years ago, headlines were similar to print — i.e. not as specific and more along the lines of 'mayor embezzles funds,'" she said. "Then (search engine optimization) grew in popularity, and headlines became very formulaic, like: Oscars 2017: Photos of Best Actress Winners' Dresses. . . .Then after many websites got their SEO in order, you saw more emotional headlines with the growth of social media over search engines. For example:

'You'll Never Believe What Charlize Theron Wore to the Oscars.' But after social media began deprioritizing click-bait headlines, you're now seeing voice-ier headlines to increase engagement, i.e.: 'Charlize Theron's Daring Oscars Dress.'"

In terms of digital considerations, Powers said she keeps various aspects of tagging and SEO in mind, but still relies on quality writing when crafting her headlines.

"I think SEO is important, but writing a good headline is only going to take you so far if your product loads slowly or your Google sitemap is poorly set up," she said. "It's not sexy, but optimizing your product to play nicely with search engines and social media is so important, as is making sure your meta tags and H1 tags are properly set up in your CMS. I think this probably sounds like a different language for most print editors, but digital editors know success relies on a good relationship with product and engineering."

When it comes to her approach to headlines, Powers said she applies the core values of journalism to her work while still tempting readers to further engage the content.

"My personal favorite headline is something that gives some of the story away but holds a little back," she said. "You want to give people a reason to click on your story, but not tease them too much, which is just annoying. But if you give the whole story away in the headline, why would people read?"

As much as algorithms, tags and SEO determine what headlines land where in a reader's search, Powers said the key to good headlines will always be the degree to which they connect with the human readers.

"Tug at the heart strings, use odd numbers, don't use the word 'this,' keep your voice active, avoid gerunds, use connecting words — mom, dad, teen, grandma, cop — instead of names unless the person is super famous, keep nationwide stories from reading too local and minor, don't just write boring SEO headlines," she said.

Think About Why the Story Is Important

Take a moment to digest the story once you've read through it. Ask yourself what the story is trying to tell you as a reader. If it helps, try completing the sentence "This story matters because . . . ." Whatever you come up with should be reflected in your headline.

Select Several Words That Capture Key Elements of the Story

After reading through the story, go back through it and pick out key words that capture the story's essence. Look for the "who did what to whom" aspects of the piece. Then build the core of the headline from those elements. From there, you should add words that will attract readers as well as search terms that will attract bots. You should also use words that reflect the tone of the story. This is particularly important with regard to verbs. For example, a person can address an issue, refute a claim or attack an allegation. Each has a specific tone to it, so make sure the words you choose fit that tone.

Try Several Words Before Settling on One

Consider all the word choices available when you're writing a headline. Try a few nouns to see which one makes the most succinct subject. Test several verbs to figure out which one creates the proper sense of action. Examine the direct object in the headline and see if it is receiving the action of the verb or if it's just filling space. Some editors can nail a headline on the first try, but those editors are rare. Don't be afraid to take a second pass at a headline — or a third — even if you think the first was good.

If There's Any Chance You Might Get Into Trouble for Writing It, Don't Write It

Journalists have long been known for an eclectic sense of humor. The late hours and pressure-filled deadlines can lead to a terse or even vulgar response to an uncooperative headline. In other cases, a general lack of maturity can create a giggle-worthy headline inside the newsroom and a major headache outside it. If you find yourself about ready to write something glib, insulting or obscene, move away from the computer until the urge passes. Even typing a headline with the intention of deleting it later can get you into trouble if it somehow manages to get published. "I didn't mean for people to see that" does not make the subject of your sarcasm feel any better nor does it serve as a defense in a libel suit.

KEY ELEMENTS OF WRITING A HEADLINE

Emphasize What Is New and Distinct

Readers receive a constant stream of information from a variety of sources and platforms. To help grab their attention, you should tell them something they didn't know already, which is usually the newest aspect of a developing story. As you write headlines, look for ways to infuse new and distinguishing information into your work.

Let's say you are running a public relations campaign for a local fraternity that is fundraising for a scholarship to commemorate a member who died of cancer. The group hopes to raise $30,000 in a month and wants your help to inform the press about its efforts. Your first news release might have a headline like this:

Zeta Beta Tau seeks to raise $30,000 for Buckston Memorial Scholarship

As the fundraising drive gets going, you want to put out additional releases, but you wouldn't want to focus on the same information in the headline. You would want to focus on what's happened since the last release:

Zeta Beta Tau halfway to $30,000 fundraising goal for memorial scholarship

At the end of the month, people would probably want to know one thing: Did the fraternity succeed? Your last headline for the final release of the campaign should answer that question:

Zeta Beta Tau more than doubles $30,000 fundraising goal for Buckston Memorial Scholarship

Explain What Has Happened, Not What Hasn't Happened

Imagine a newscast that began with the anchor intoning, "Top story: The president was not shot tonight. He remains unharmed and in good health. In other news, the United States did not declare war on the sovereign nation of China . . . ." Sounds ridiculous, doesn't it? However, editors often write headlines that explain what didn't happen:

Gulf Coast unable to avoid Hurricane Irma's wrath

(Did we think the coast was going to move?)

HELPFUL HINTS

MISTAKES THAT CAN LEAD TO BAD HEADLINES

- *Bad trades:* In an effort to not repeat a word or to make a headline fit in a smaller or larger space, editors can swap words that have similar meanings but fit the editors' needs a bit better. "Caught" can become "captured" or "arrested." A "victory" can become a "win." However, not all words are created equal. "Robbery" isn't the same thing as "burglary."

  In an infamous snafu, the Crystal Lake, Illinois, Northwest Herald, ran a story about a protest by World War II veterans regarding the bombing of Japan, and the headline called it "Enola homosexual" exhibit.

  They meant the Enola Gay, the name of the plane used to drop the first atomic bomb on Japan during World War II. They made a bad trade, swapping "gay" for "homosexual," and it led to a horrible headline.

- *Too many adjectives and adverbs:* The better you are at picking good nouns, the less you will have to rely on adjectives. The same idea applies to verbs and adverbs. If you are writing a headline with multiple adjectives and adverbs, take a second look at your noun and verb to see if you might improve them.

- *"Ing" heads:* As noted in earlier chapters, gerunds are words that sound like verbs but act as nouns and end in "-ing," such as "swimming is good exercise." Headlines like this can create problems for your readers. For example:

  Running can be dangerous

  Needing more nurses

  The first example is a gerund; the second is not. However, they have several problems in common. The headlines don't inform you as to who thinks running is dangerous or who needs nurses. The verb is weak in both headlines as well. An "-ing" word seems like it does a good job of using a strong verb and helping clarify the sentence, but the opposite is true. Focus on using a good noun-verb-object structure:

  Doctors say running destroys knee ligaments

  Hospitals need more nurses, administrators say

- *Vague or uninteresting head:* For a story to have value, something interesting must have happened. You need to extract that interesting element from the story and place it in the headline. When you don't, you produce headlines like this:

  Speaker arrives in Madison, gives talk at convention center

  Board of trustees holds meeting

  Instead, look for things that matter to your readers and highlight them. Seek specific actions and outcomes:

  Ex-NRA official calls for gun ban during Madison speech

  Trustees back 15 percent tuition increase

- *Too complicated:* Headlines are supposed to be informative and easy to understand. When editors rely on abbreviations and acronyms, they run the risk of turning a good headline into a pot of alphabet soup:

  SGA, OSA vow to kill CCC bill

  GOP OKs DACA restrictions

  These heads are bad for print and even worse for the web because OSA, SGA (student government association acronyms) and GOP (shorthand for the Republican party) aren't common search terms for the underlying concepts.

  Other headlines become too complicated because the editors try to cover every angle of the story in a few words. The key to a good headline is to have a primary focus that captures the theme of the story. The more elements you put into the headline, the more problematic it will become.

President can't get health care repeal past Senate
(Did he try tiptoeing?)

Journalistic writing requires action, so use your headline to announce that action. It will lead to stronger headlines, better construction and improved readability:

Hurricane Irma pounds Gulf Coast
Senate rejects president's health care repeal

Stick to the Facts

Headlines should add nothing to the story beyond what the text itself provides. If a blog post you wrote says your company is likely to earn a government contract, the headline should reflect that. You should not write the headline as if the money's in the bank. If a person is arrested on suspicion of killing someone, the headline should not state the person has been arrested "for murder."

Nuance is integral to storytelling, and it needs to be reflected in the headlines. In a web setting, it's easier to do this, as you have fewer problems with space limits. However, the underlying principle remains valuable here: A headline should say only what the rest of the piece says. No more, no less.

Reflect the Tone of Your Piece and Your Publication

When you go to a job interview, you dress a certain way to make a specific impression. When you go out with your friends to a concert, you probably dress much differently, something suitable for the occasion. The situation you find yourself in will largely dictate how you dress because it will determine how you want people to perceive you. Headlines act in a similar fashion, providing readers with an important first impression. They give your readers cues as to what they should expect from a story. Bad headlines don't convey that tone:

First-graders work on art skills

Will this piece be a cute profile on first-grade students making handprint turkeys, or is it about the ways education fails young students? Will it talk about how art is becoming more integral to education or how art is being cut to help cure budget shortfalls? Is it a story about kids who have fun and get special art classes or a story about how educators are finding it more difficult to teach art to young children because of diminishing skills? It could be anything.

Give your readers a chance to see what the story is about by glancing at the headline:

Middleton-area first-graders use Thanksgiving art to brighten local retirement home

THINGS TO DO AFTER WRITING A HEADLINE

Once you finish the headline, you need to make sure you haven't made any mistakes or created any problems for your readers. In many cases, a headline goes through several revisions, thus allowing the introduction of errors or the omission of words you swear you put in there. Consider these tips for checking up on the headline you just wrote:

Make Sure the Headline Is Accurate

A headline that incorporates important search terms, that has a good noun-verb-object construction and that appeals to your human readers isn't worth anything if it is inaccurate.

When print journalists put headlines together, they often struggle to make words fit into specific spaces. To make things fit better, they use shorter words in the place of longer ones. They also sometimes use vague terms in the place of more concrete ones. This can lead to an inaccurate headline. A web headline doesn't have the kinds of space constraints of print layouts, but it can have similar problems. Once you've written the headline and you are satisfied with it, go back through and question every word and every implication. Make sure you are right.

Make Sure You Deliver on Promises

If you write a headline that promises your readers "Five ways to lose weight," the subsequent piece must include five ways to lose weight, and you'd be wise to count them. If the headline states that the Senate has passed a bill to revamp the tax code, the story needs to include content regarding the Senate, the bill and a tax-code bill that has passed. Failure to do so leads to confusion and resentment among your readers. Once the headline is ready for publication, give it another look and be certain the headline doesn't make a promise that the story can't keep.

Read It Aloud and Emphasize Various Words

Certain words sound different depending on how you read them or how others might have read them. Notice that the first part of this paragraph provides you with a perfect example of why this is important. The first use of the word "read" is pronounced like "reed," while the second one is pronounced "red." However, as the words sit silently on the screen, they look identical. When you are done writing your headline, go back and read it aloud. Place emphasis on different words and look for words that can trick or confuse your readers.

Examine the Headline for Jargon

Some folks call this headlinese or editor-speak, but journalists of all kinds use words that aren't part of the vernacular. Editors use some of these words because they sound interesting or they fit well in small spaces.

For print journalists, these words can be somewhat helpful. A punchy headline can entice readers who are glancing at a newspaper box on the way down the street. The use of "nab" or "hike" can be great for a one-column headline, but you don't have these problems on the web. The problem you do have is trying to help both the reader and the search engine find your story. So, while you could say a company executive was "canned," chances are your readers wouldn't. Therefore, they're not going to type that word into a search engine, and your story won't show up in the search results. "Fired," while common and less jazzy, is probably a better choice.

Read From the Perspective of a 12-Year-Old Boy

Headlines can lead to huge headaches when you inadvertently write something that is a double entendre. If you can imagine how a 12-year-old boy with a crude sense of humor could twist the words into something rude, you can avoid serious problems. Some headlines, like this one that ran in a Missouri newspaper, seem fine at first glance:

Lamb remembered for big heart, caring personality

It would have been a touching headline had the woman in the obituary not died of an irregular heartbeat caused by an enlarged heart.

Whenever you write a headline involving sex, make sure you're saying what you think you are saying:

Church looks into sexual abuse

Sex education delayed; teachers demand training

Sexual slang can lead to problems as well. In 2011, the city of Fort Wayne, Indiana, wanted to honor a former mayor who died in office during the 1950s and decided to name the city's new government center after him. This would rarely make news outside of Indiana, but the man had an unfortunate name: Harry Baals.

The former mayor pronounced it "balls," while his descendants changed it to sound like "bales." On the printed page or computer screen, however, it looks like a bad joke. It's not the fault of the headline writer that this man was unfortunately named or that he was famous, but the writer still has to deal with it in a decent and dignified way. In the end, the city declined to name the center after the former mayor, but the web remains full of "Harry Baals" headlines.

If a 12-year-old boy can snicker at it, it's bad. Change it.

Check for Minor Errors

Some computer programs don't do well to alert you to spelling errors. Others will bring up every name and abbreviation, which leads some editors to hit the "skip" key repeatedly without paying attention. That approach isn't smart and can create a problem if you accidentally skip the wrong thing, such as a name that you spelled one way in a headline and a different way in the deck head.

Also, something can be spelled right but not be the right word. Every so often, a headline will trumpet the opening of a pubic library, alert readers to the time of a pubic meeting or issue a notice to the general pubic. In each case, the word is spelled correctly. In each case, that's not what the writer meant. When you think you are done with the headline, give it one more look for minor errors.

Have Someone Else Read It

Before you publish your work, ask someone else to read the headline. The extra set of eyes will tell you if the headline works or not. This fresh read can help you see the headline as your readers

---

HELPFUL HINTS
HEADLINE CHECKLIST

The best way to determine what makes for a good headline is to read as many headlines as possible. If you scan a general interest website for headlines, you should keep track of the things that you clicked on. Once you have a fair sample of headlines that engaged you, ask a few of these questions:

● What drew me to this headline? What is interesting about it?

● Did content match well with the headline?

● Would I click on similar headlines in the future? Why or why not?

● What kinds of keywords are present in this headline?

● Was there anything I learned from the story that should have been in the headline?

Also try looking at headlines you didn't click on right away. Follow the same logic:

● What made me avoid this headline?

● If a headline on this topic were better in some way, would I click on that headline?

● Are there errors, vagueness or other problems with this headline that turned me off to it?

● If I ended up clicking through, is there anything in this story that might improve the headline?

will. Editors often read and reread a story to the point where they know so much about it that they assume the reader has the same background. A new person might ask, "Who is Jones?" or "What's FISA?" Readers will likely ask similar questions if the headline isn't clear.

SEO AND HEADLINES

As we noted earlier, you aren't just trying to impress people with your work. You need to get the search engines and their "bots" or "spiders" to pay attention as well. According to recent statistics, about 80 percent of web surfers won't go past the first page of search engine results. You can't rely on luck to land in the 10 spots on that page. You have to work at improving your headlines with an eye toward what the search engine likes and doesn't like. This is called search engine optimization.

The website Copyblogger espouses an 80/20 rule: 80 percent of the people will read your headline, but only 20 percent will read your story. Recent research supports that idea, noting that users decide to stay or leave your site in eight seconds or less, and headlines are the one piece of copy that users will read.

With those facts in mind, your headlines and your approach to SEO take on added importance.

How Is SEO Comparable to What I'm Already Doing?

Bots attempt to find information that is relevant to readers by matching search terms with headlines and keywords. In that way, they are similar to your readers in that they want important information and they will take the easiest path to get it.

When a bot scans the net, it wants headline and search terms that:

- *Are clear:* The inverted-pyramid or noun-verb-object structure helps the search engine understand the story as much as it helps the human reader. A "Clown kills governor" headline will draw the human eye and the search engine's interest.

- *Are concise:* Size matters in print, where only a certain number of characters can be crammed into a headline hole. The same adage applies in web heads to some degree. The search engine reads about 65 characters worth of a headline before it moves on. This means keywords and keyword density are vital.

Both readers and search engines like to know what the story is about right away. So, the closer to the front you can put your keywords, the better off you'll be.

A keyword tells a bot to pay attention to your article when that word is used as a search term. However, given the 65-character limit of a bot and the short attention span of an average reader, you want to avoid cramming too many keywords into your headline.

- *Use "main idea" words:* As a journalist, you should work to know what your readers specifically look for when they read your work, and you should write accordingly. If you are aware of how your audience will seek information online, you can use the same terms they will and thus improve their chances of finding your work. For example, when readers want to find a review for a specific movie, they will likely type in the keywords from that movie's name and the word "review." When they want a recipe for chicken Kiev or directions on how to fix a car's alternator, they will pick several key words specific to their needs. Focus on the "main idea" of the search when you build your headlines, and you will be in good shape.

How Is SEO Different From What I'm Doing?

Even though it has been called "mass media," journalistic output always had a specific and defined audience in mind. Newspapers tend to cover specific geographic areas. Magazines have audiences that seek specific types of niche information. Corporate websites target people who share common interests in charities, companies or organizations. PR firms try to entice the media and other sectors of the public to take an interest in an event or a cause.

A web search casts a net across all of these things. A reader who types a few words into a search engine might receive information from newspapers, magazines, TV stations, blogs, corporate webpages and more. The web crawler that retrieves the information for that individual does not ponder if it should or shouldn't do something. It simply finds information and brings it back.

To help the search find your work, here are some things you need to do:

- *Get more specific:* If you are from a small town or a large city, a headline in the local newspaper trumpeting "Mayor robs convenience store" is likely to get a lot of attention. If you're writing a headline for that local paper that announces the return of an injured high school athlete, a headline of "Smith to play at state tourney" might garner similar attention.

However, a worldwide audience doesn't know which mayor is involved in the robbery or who Smith is. A search will only locate content if it relates to the terms the reader entered. By including more specific information, you will improve your chances of being found:

Use first and last names as well as titles and context clues:

Lackbow Mayor Rob Wax accused of robbing Quick Mart
Sheboygan North's Jim Smith to play in Wisconsin basketball finals

In both instances, you've given your search engines a lot more to work with, and you've still kept to that 65-character limit.

- *Write multiple headlines:* Deck heads and subheads often support and augment the information contained in a traditional print headline. On the web, you have similar options as you write your headline. The web head that is most akin to a traditional print headline is the H1 headline. However, you have several headline options below that headline (H2 through H6) as well as the title tag, which places the words in the bar at the top of the browser window. You should make use of several of these items as you attempt to entice the bots.

The Dark Side of SEO Headlines

In the early days of print media, publishers relied on sensational stories, giant headlines and gossip-driven content. The logic was simple: The bigger the headline and the more salacious the innuendo, the more likely people would buy the magazine or newspaper.

In the case of the internet, the more key terms you include in your headlines and the more you rely on terms that are trending well, the more often a search engine will find your work.

In both cases, it's about popularity and money, but those tactics can backfire.

When readers find out your story isn't what you say it is in the headline, they will abandon your piece and consider your future work with suspicion. In terms of SEO, search engines have become more sophisticated in their approach to keywords and search terms. Some content sites use "keyword stuffing," in which someone attempts to use specific keywords repeatedly to make a story more prominent in a search. Search engines are now aware of this practice and will penalize sites that use this technique by pushing the site lower in search results.

Journalists can't be like snake-oil salesmen of the 1800s, who put their wares into a covered wagon and sold magic elixir out of the back as they moved from town to town. By the time the townsfolk realized the magic serum was worthless, the salesman had their money and had moved on to the next town. As a journalist, you won't survive this way, especially on the internet, where information about deceptive practices can spread like wildfire. If your organization develops a reputation as one that offers nothing of value or tries to entice search engines with false promises, your readership will desert you.

One thing worth remembering about headlines is this: They are only the beginning. While a sharp headline with good keyword usage can attract both a bot and a person, if the story itself falls flat, you have still failed as an editor.

Headline writing, while important, is only one part of the job.

THE BIG THREE

Here are the three key things you should take away from this chapter:

1. **Nail down the basics, then add more:** Good headlines start with a solid noun-verb-object structure that focuses on the key elements of the story. Begin your headline with a concrete noun and a vigorous verb before you worry about what else you want to say. After you feel confident in your headline's main idea, augment it with adjectives and adverbs that will entice readers and capture the attention of search engines.

2. **Take time to write, edit and review:** A headline is the most prominent and important part of your work with a story. It is a small piece of copy, which can lead you to blow it off or give it little attention. Don't skimp on time and effort when it comes to the headline. Write it as clearly as possible, analyze what you have written and then review it multiple times to improve its effectiveness.

3. **Honesty and accuracy count:** The web has given rise to hyperbolic headlines and false promises. As much as it seems like a good idea to use wild claims and keyword stuffing to drive traffic to your piece, remember that you are a journalist and that means something. Don't sacrifice your ethical principles, your professionalism and your commitment to the truth for the sake of short-term gains. Keep your headlines accurate and honest above all else.

KEY TERMS

deck 108
font 109
hammer 108
headers 109

kerning 109
kicker 109
leading 109
point 108

sans serif 109
serif 109
title tag 109
tracking 109

DISCUSSION QUESTIONS

1. Of all of the elements listed in the chapter, which ones do you think lead to the best headlines? Which elements are the ones at which most writers fail? Why do you think this is the case?

2. The importance of headlines has shifted from the overall size of the type of the headline to the ability to entice readers with specific verbiage. Given your experiences with print and digital media, what draws

you to headlines the most? Is it the booming size of printed headlines or is it the clickbait-style pieces that try to grab your attention? Is it something else entirely?

3. In looking at digital headlines on sites that promote themselves via social media, how often do you click on them, and how often do they provide what they have promised? Do you feel satisfied or cheated more often? How has this changed your approach to consuming content online?

WRITE NOW!

1. Use the first half of the headline checklist provided in the chapter to review content that you have recently consumed. Look at the various elements in the checklist that drew you to the content and explain how they worked well for this. Also, consider headlines that you didn't click on any website you frequently visit and apply the second half of the checklist to those pieces. Write a short essay that explains your findings.

2. Select three stories from a local publication that you think fail to meet the standards outlined in the chapter above, such as the use of active voice and the use of present tense. Also review the headline for things such as accuracy, clarity and engagement issues. Rewrite the headlines in a stronger format, fixing these shortcomings, and then write a short paragraph after each headline to explain what was wrong with the previous headline and what makes your version better.

3. Select three stories from a print publication, such as a newspaper or news magazine, and rewrite the headlines for the web, emphasizing clarity for nonlocal readers as well as SEO potential. For each one, explain in a short paragraph what was lacking in the original version and how you improved it with your rewrite.

Visit **edge.sagepub.com/filakediting** to help you accomplish your coursework goals in an easy-to-use learning environment.

9 PHOTOGRAPHY

The cliché "A picture is worth a thousand words" serves as a reminder of the value of visuals when presenting content to your readers. Visuals attract the attention of readers, capture slivers of time in a single frame and help readers best understand specific actions or outcomes. Some people learn more from visuals than they do from text-based information, so images also have the benefit of reaching audiences that would otherwise be left in the dark.

Photography has benefited all forms of media over the past two centuries, with photojournalists nabbing iconic visual representations of joy and heartbreak as well as war and peace. Photographs also augment common stories and showcase interesting moments within a community. The power behind the visuals they collect can shift opinions, engage readers and trigger emotions like no other form of media can.

As an editor, you play a vital role in the value these visuals create for your readers. You need to coach your photographers before, during and after a photo shoot so they put themselves in the best possible position to get quality images. In addition, you help select the best possible frames from the many your photojournalists shoot and then edit them to accentuate their best storytelling attributes. Your efforts can improve or destroy a photographer's work.

This chapter will examine the essential elements of photography from an editor's standpoint. We will discuss what makes for compelling images and how to improve them ethically and legally. In addition, we will discuss issues of image selection and ordering, on the basis of the shoot and the way you plan to use the content. We will also look into the coaching aspects associated with the editor-photographer relationship and how it can benefit everyone concerned.

ELEMENTS OF A QUALITY IMAGE

The goal of a photographer is to tell a story with visual elements in much the same way a writer tells a story with words. Whether those elements come in a single frame or multiple shots, the photographer needs to stimulate viewers and make them want to take a second look at the content. As a good editor, you want to help your photographers select the best possible images and then shape them appropriately to accentuate their best attributes. To do this, consider these four concepts when you examine photographs:

Interest

A photo has to engage your viewers, because not only is it there to tell a story, but it should help draw readers into any connected content as well, such as other images or a text-based story. As an editor, you should understand what the point of the photo is at first glance.

For example, a photo of a top-tier tennis coach might depict her standing in her office among the dozens of trophies and plaques her teams won over the years. This image integrates both the subject of the photo and the background to explain that this person has been extremely successful. In other cases, a wide-shot photo of a farmer standing on unplanted crop land can use the background to provide a sense of isolation. Even more, a strong close up on the expressive face of a circus clown can give readers a sense of amusement or joy. Regardless of the shot, the composition of the image needs to tell a story.

Aesthetics

Certain basic rules apply to standard photographs. The rule of thirds helps you organize the content within the frame so that the most important elements receive the highest level of attention. The quality of the lighting, the crispness of the subjects in the frame and the presence of action and reaction all lend something specific to the aesthetics of the shot. Understanding these basic rules as an editor will help you cull the frames that don't meet these basic standards and thus avoid images that will create problematic visuals for your audience.

It is worth noting that just as in writing, some rules can be broken for specific reasons. A horizon can be tilted if the photographer needs to convey some lack of balance. A shot can be blurry if the photographer wants to communicate confusion. You should consider the rationale of the photographer when you pick through the images. This is why a quality coaching relationship between shooters and editors matters.

Significance

In cases of breaking news, the significance of the moment presents itself clearly. If you run a photograph of a fire or a car crash, you don't have to worry too much about nuance or context when it comes to explaining the importance of the shot. Beyond those instances, the ability to dig deeper into the context to help your readers see why this moment matters will take work.

If you can connect the writer and the photographer before they begin their work, you can help them get on the same page for how the photos and text should complement each other. If the writer has already completed the reporting work, see if you can get the photographer a rough draft of the story, so the shooter can get a sense of who is important in the story and what is the tone of the story. This will create a better opportunity for the photographer to succeed in gathering significant images for the package.

Emotion

Photographs convey emotion in a way that text cannot, as they capture a sliver of time and allow readers to view it for as long as they care to. The use of standard images or stock art, like photos of ambulances or buildings, don't convey that emotion, so you need to select images that will evoke a sense of feeling from your readers. Instead of using a team photo with a story of a championship game, you should look for celebration or defeat images taken at that game. You can also look for images of gleeful children at county fairs or angry citizens protesting at a city council meeting. These shots give people a sense of tone and feeling that words alone cannot.

Emotion can also be a concern if you work with breaking news images. If a family is grieving at the sight of a car crash, where a loved one just died, running a photo of people sobbing might be in poor taste. Even more, a photo of emergency workers prying a bloody body out of the wreckage could really upset your readers. Some papers use what they call the "breakfast test," which is to say that they wouldn't run images that might make people who read the paper during breakfast nauseated. The question of what to run or not to run in this situation often comes down to the ethical standards of the publication itself. That said, emotion remains a key element of visual communication.

HELPFUL HINTS
SHOTS AND VALUES

Photographers have three primary types of photographic shots they can use when they want to tell a story. Here is a breakdown of those shots, what they are good for and when to avoid using them:

Long Shot

This shot, also called a wide shot, is used to show a lot of action within the frame to provide the viewer with a sense of "the big picture." The long shot is often used to establish a scene. Photographers can take a shot of a crowd of high school students who are cheering for their football team. They also can take a wide shot of a crowded street or an empty church. This shot is almost always at the front of a photo story to place the viewer at the scene of the story.

Use it when you want to:

- Establish the scene.
- Show the massive size of something (crowds, desolation, devastation).

Avoid it when:

- Details are important.
- It leaves too much wasted space within the frame.
- You have a primary speaker within a frame.

Medium Shot

This shot frames the action of one or more individuals or provides a small slice of a larger event. When we talk to another person, we are almost always viewing them the way we would see a medium shot. A small family dinner, a person typing in a computer lab, a mechanic working on an engine and hundreds of other real-life situations are best viewed as medium shots.

Use it when you want to:

- Focus on an action-reaction sequence between people or within a small group of people.
- Provide the viewers with a small piece of action within an event.
- Provide a more intimate shot than a wide shot.

Avoid it when:

- The participants can't be adequately framed in this fashion.
- It fails to provide the impact that a different shot would provide.

Close-Up Shot

This is also known as a detail shot. It is meant to provide your viewers with a tight shot of a small piece of action. The key to a close-up shot is that it must be easily identified and provide value within a photo package.

Use it when you want to:

- Focus on a detail that would otherwise be overlooked.
- Provide the viewers with an intimate look at something.
- Capture a small action.

Avoid it when:

- You can't tell what is happening in the frame.
- It jars the viewer because the action doesn't translate at that level.

WORKING WITH PHOTOGRAPHERS

As mentioned in Chapter 2, editors often serve as coaches, in that they want to put their team members into the best possible position to succeed. In terms of working with photographers, the goals of editors remain exactly the same as working with any other individual on staff: Help them figure out what they need to do, help them if they have trouble accomplishing their tasks and help them see what worked well and what didn't once they are done. With this in mind, consider this solid walkthrough of how to work with photographers throughout the process of an assignment:

Before the Assignment

In the best circumstances, you should work with both the writer and the photographer together. In some organizations, photography staffs have their own editors, so getting this person in on the conversation also would be a good idea. In any case, you want to have some sort of conversation among the journalists who will work on this assignment at any level. The more time you can spend preparing the journalists on the front end of the assignment, the better chance they will have to succeed during the assignment.

Part of the coaching you do here should include explanations as to what the photographer could encounter on the assignment. For example, you might know that the gym where the big basketball game takes place has really bad lighting. Passing this on to the photographer and suggesting some lighting or equipment options can help the photographer plan the shoot. In other cases, you could know that a profile subject is more engaging at home instead of at work, thus allowing the photographer to suggest holding the shoot at the subject's home.

It also doesn't hurt to discuss the idea of angles, taking a 360-degree walk around the scene and other basic concepts with the photographers to see how they plan to shoot the assignment. Even if you aren't an expert on lenses or lighting, you should share as much information as possible prior to the shoot.

You should also discuss how the images the photographer will take will be used. If you need one photo to serve as the primary image on a promotional poster, the photographer has to look for that one great shot that tells the story. However, if you need a series of 30 photos for a slideshow on a website, the photographer will need to look for multiple moments from a variety of perspectives and use a range of shot types. It also helps to let the shooter know how much time the subject has available or when you expect the photos to be ready for publication. This can help the photographer better apportion the time spent on the shoot.

During the Assignment

Much of what will happen on assignments will force your photographers to rely on their instincts and experience, so unless they need to reach you, you can pretty much leave them alone. However, much like a coach during a game, if you notice something problematic has emerged, you can call a "time out" and talk to the photographer about the situation. You might have a shooter out at a July 4 celebration, taking pictures of families and parades, when a jumbo jet explodes while landing at a nearby airport. This would be the right time to pull that photographer from the celebration and get that person over to the crash.

It could be something less catastrophic than that, on the basis of a last-minute change from the subject or your organization. A planned shoot at a golf outing might need to move to a nearby country club if rain hits while the photographer is in transit. A client might change its design approach, thus making it crucial to shoot more horizontal images than verticals. If you need the shooters or the shooters need you, make sure you are available to each other. If not, you should let your shooters handle their business as they see fit.

After the Assignment

The conclusion of the shoot provides you with two opportunities as an editor: the chance to select images for publication and the chance to coach the photographer. Depending on how tight the deadline is, you might need to push the latter back a bit, but don't forget to return to that coaching opportunity before all is said and done.

In selecting the images, you need to work with the photographer (and photo editor if one is on staff) to determine which photos will do the best job of storytelling, on the basis of the written piece and the packaging of the content. It's not always about the best individual frame, but in many cases, it's about the right shot or combination of shots. As you make these selections for various platforms, such as a single shot for a printed product and 20-some shots for a slideshow, be sure to solicit input from the visual journalists. This will help you make better choices and give your staff members a sense that you care about their perspectives.

In terms of coaching, you need to review the images that made the cut and those that didn't to explain not only what didn't work, but also why it didn't work and how the shooter could improve for the next time. If you notice that the photographer has developed habits that aren't conducive to storytelling, such as relying heavily on horizontals instead of mixing in verticals or using a specific type of lens, you can mention that as part of your coaching. Simply saying "This is bad" won't help your photographers in the long run, and continued improvement should be a goal for you and your staff. In the same manner, make sure you explain why something is good. This will help your photographers repeat their successful actions and build on them as well.

VIEW FROM A PRO
WILL VRAGOVIC

Courtesy of Will Vragovic

The importance of visual communication has always mattered in the field of sports journalism, and photojournalist Will Vragovic has spent much of his adult life making sure his readers get the best he has to offer.

Vragovic now serves as the team photographer for the Tampa Bay Rays, covering every aspect of life associated with a major-league baseball team. Prior to transitioning to his current job, Vragovic worked as a photojournalist and photo editor at the Tampa Bay Times, where he covered the Rays as well as the football teams for the University of Florida and Florida State University. He also helped out with the paper's coverage of the NHL's Tampa Bay Lightning.

Even with this sports-heavy portfolio, Vragovic said he always considered himself "a general assignment kind of guy."

"That's why I got into newspapers in the first place," he said. "Everything from features to spot news and lit portraits, I've always prided myself in being someone that my bosses could look to no matter what the needs of the day are."

Vragovic said photographs can evoke emotions in a way that other forms of storytelling cannot, making them a valuable element in any form of media.

"What I think is so powerful about photography is that it knows no language barriers," he said. "You don't have to speak English to understand what is happening in my photographs. I didn't have to understand Arabic to feel the emotions of Syrian refugees landing in rubber boats in Lobos. Great photographs make you understand concepts subliminally before your eyes even seek out a caption for more detail."

Over the course of his career, photography and its place in media evolved considerably, transitioning from print needs to digital requirements, including the heavier use of color and the need for additional publishable images. Vragovic said the biggest changes, however, came in terms of photography editing.

"Early on, what went into the paper went online, as the web was essentially a digital copy of what you'd find in print," he said. "After a while, big click-through galleries became a thing. The web almost became a dumping ground for piles of content. There were a couple of different ways that looked over the years, but fast forward to today where everyone is a little more 'digital first' and I think what we are seeing now is well curated, tightly edited, and beautifully presented storytelling in photos. Which is what you used to see in print."

To help avoid dumping piles of content in that way, Vragovic said he works with his photographers to isolate images that communicate the key aspects of the story they are trying to tell.

"Every editing session with a photographer begins with me asking them to tell me the story as we quickly run through their take," he said. "I want to get a feel for what they're trying to say and what are the most important pieces of that story, as well as just get a sense of what they were seeing. And I really do mean quickly run. I might look at 500 photos in the two or three minutes that they're talking. Then we'll go back again from the beginning, and start tagging photos that hit those key pieces, people, and moments of the story."

As they work together to piece together a simple print package or a complex story with dozens of images, they look for specific visual and narrative elements, he added.

"We're looking for the holy trinity, Moment, Light, and Composition," he said. "You can have a successful photo with any of them, you can have a really successful one with any two, and if you have all three. . .well, you certainly don't need any advice from me. Beyond the strength of photos as individuals, I'm looking for how photos work together to tell a story. Sometimes, one photo is all you need. Other times, a sequence tells the story."

Vragovic said his photography and photo editing rules are fairly simple: Don't add, delete or deceive. He did say that moving from news to promotional photography has allowed him to approach his craft in different ways.

"In a news gathering role, there is a lot of restraint in how you handle photos after they've been taken," Vragovic said. "For the most part, crop, contrast, color adjustment. . .you're basically trying to make sure things look as you saw them. . . .The rules are different away from journalism. Image manipulation is probably closer to the rule than the exception. That said, I don't feel any pressure to change how I approach my work. If an image is going to be manipulated, I feel that it should be in such a way that's clearly been done so for an artistic/creative purpose. This job will allow me the freedom to do a fair amount of freelancing, so it's important to me that editors can trust me to uphold the standards of authenticity in news gathering situations."

Of all the things he has learned over the years, Vragovic said one constant exists among all the roles he's seen in the field of media.

"The most successful people I know in this business are those that people *want* to work with, not just because of crazy talent levels, but because they can collaborate and communicate and make the whole process fun and rewarding," he said. "It's a small community, there are rarely more than two and a half degrees of separation between most photographers. Your reputation will always precede you."

IMPROVING IMAGES AS AN EDITOR

Depending on the field you enter, the ability to alter images will be limited or expansive. Advertising images are almost always retouched to remove blemishes or to accentuate specific aspects of a product. News images are supposed to be as close to reality as possible, with limited manipulation or alterations. The ethical codes of the various disciplines will outline what is and is not acceptable.

Below is a list of ways in which editors in all media fields can improve images, along with some suggestions for how best to use these methods:

Sizing

An image's size will vary on the basis of a number of aspects of the publication, including the overall value of the image in telling the story and the relative importance of the image to other elements around it. The goal of an editor in terms of this aspect of photography is to weigh the size of the image against its overall value and then run it accordingly. For example, if you profile a new school superintendent, people will want to see what this person looks like. A simple mug shot will suffice, and that shot can run fairly small on a printed page or computer monitor. No matter how large you make that shot, it won't improve the value of it. It is just as valuable if the head of the person is about the size of a quarter or if you run it over the entire front page of a newspaper. Thus, you should run it at that quarter size, because the value of the image is best reflected at that size.

Conversely, if you have a shot of the winning goal celebration from the state finals of a soccer match, you have to run it larger to get any kind of value out of it. A thumbnail-sized image won't allow your readers to see the joy on the faces of the players or the excitement of the moment. This could run large enough to cover the entire width of a magazine spread or as a splash page on a website. Sizing isn't about trying to cram as much as possible into a tiny space or about blowing up images so they cover everything. Instead, it's about balancing the size of the photo with how well it tells a story at that size.

Cropping

The idea of framing a photo is to take the raw image and select the most valuable portion of it for publication. To do this, you will engage in cropping, something editors and photographers have done with everything from razorblades and printed images to digital technology. **Cropping** selects the people or things that need to be in the image and eliminates the elements of the photo that shouldn't be in there. The best way to make this assessment is to determine what pieces add value to the storytelling you want the photo to do.

Some things are a distraction and should be eliminated for that reason. A photo of a group of veterans honoring fallen comrades during a Memorial Day ceremony might have a blimp in the sky above them or a kid picking his nose in the crowd behind them. A tighter crop will remove those pieces that draw attention away from the subject of the shot. This is also true for everyday items that don't add to the story, such as a glowing exit sign in a photo of a theater owner posing in front of his biggest screen or overhead lights in a photo of office workers. Don't be afraid to tighten the crop, but do so for a valid reason. In other words, don't trim off the top of someone's head or exaggerate a crop just because you can. Whatever you do, do it for a purpose.

Toning and Contrast

These terms are often used interchangeably, but they touch on two specific things. **Contrast** is about the spectrum of white to black and how the image shades in perspective to the other elements of the frame. One way of thinking about this is to consider converting a color image to black and white. If you photographed a football player in a red jersey with white numbers on it, the contrast between the bright white numerals and the dark red jersey might be quite striking in color. However, in converting it to black and white, you might notice that the white doesn't stand out as well. You would want to improve the contrast of that frame to make the white stand out more.

Toning is about the brightness or darkness of an image. In that same example, the red on the jersey in color might look too pink or too burgundy to accurately represent the color of the shirt. To improve this, you would work with the toning to make the pink darker or the burgundy lighter to get the shirt's color closer to reality. Many textbooks on photography go into this in much more detail.

HELPFUL HINTS
TYPES OF PHOTOS

The type of photo you use will depend greatly on what you hope to accomplish with the image and what options are available to you in terms of image types. Here are a few types of images and when you will likely use them:

Mug Shots

This simple head shot of a person within the story is used to put a face to a name. Most run at about a thumbnail size, and the head of the person needs to be at least as big as a dime. **Mug shots** can be cut from larger images or created as posed photos. The image is usually cropped between the neck and the chest and just outside of the shoulders.

Environmental Portraits

These photographs intend to pose a person in a way or in a situation that accentuates the purpose of the story. Consider a story of a mother who lost her daughter during a combat mission overseas: The image might be a photo of the woman posed in her home while holding a framed photo of her daughter. Another story that would benefit from an environmental portrait would be a story of someone who owns the largest bobble head collection in the state. A picture of this person standing in front of his entire collection while holding a bobble head of himself would provide a sense of size and personality. **Environmental portraits** work well when you want to attach not only a name to a face, but also a concept to the story.

Action Shots

Most photographers take action shots when they cover sports or news, capturing a sliver of time and preserving it for the readers and viewers of the media outlet. The goal with these shots is to capture a real moment, without intrusion by the shooter.

Editorial Illustrations

As the name implies, **editorial illustrations** use raw images and content manipulation to tell a story in a complex way. Editorial illustrations should be labeled as such, so people don't erroneously believe the event or object depicted exists in real life. However, good editorial illustrations should be so obvious as to not deceive readers into thinking something could be real. A good example of this approach would be pairing a story about the housing market crash with an illustration where photos of houses are being sucked down the drain of a sink. The idea is valid and explanatory (the housing market is going down the drain), but no one is likely to think, "Gosh, I wonder where they found that giant house-eating sink!"

Stock Art

This form of photography relies on images that are related to the content but not directly attached to the story itself. A **stock art** approach would have you running a generic photo of an ambulance with a story about hospitals. Your staff didn't take the ambulance shot, it isn't paired with anything specific in the story and it doesn't add a lot of value. However, the image provides a visual cue for readers that the story is about medicine, hospitals or health care, so it can draw readers to the text itself. When possible, it's best to avoid this kind of photography and rely more on staff-produced images that are directly germane to the written content.

Sharpening

The purpose of **sharpening** a photo is to pull out details within the frame in a process of fine tuning the image. People often misinterpret sharpening as finding a way to make an image less blurry, which is actually impossible. When you sharpen an image, you increase the contrast between the pixels in the image, thus creating the illusion of a less blurry photo. However, this is merely the human eye interpreting the contrast as being sharper. If you keep this in mind, it will save you a lot of time trying to salvage blurry images through heavy sharpening in digital-editing programs.

However, the process of sharpening does have benefits for good images that just need a tweak or two. If you photograph an automobile mechanic, you can sharpen the image so that the name embroidered on his shirt is legible. Pulling out a detail like this might augment the story you want to tell, so sharpening does make sense in this case. However, like every other tool in your toolbox, make sure you use it for the right job.

CAPTION WRITING

Images can tell stories, but they often need some text to help readers more completely understand them. To do this, you need to write quality photo captions that accompany the images. Here are three types of **captions**, or "cutlines," that you can write and how to write them well:

Standard Captions

With most standard action photos, you want to write two-sentence captions. The first sentence tells your readers what is going on in present tense without being patently obvious. It captures most of the 5W's and 1H and gives the readers a sense of what they are seeing.

Bad Example

Jim Ertz does a presentation Tuesday morning while members of Otto Corp. look on.

The "no duh" element of this caption makes it pointless for your readers. The only things they learn are the time element and the name of the person at the center of the shot. This isn't enough value, so you would need to provide more context for the action in the shot.

Better Example

Financial consultant Jim Ertz outlines his "Get Lean and Mean" strategy Tuesday morning for members of Otto Corp., a business on the verge of bankruptcy.

Pixabay/robinsonk26

This gives you more of a sense of who the main person in the photo is, why he's there and what value he provides.

The second sentence should provide the readers with depth and context as to why this image and the subjects within it have value. Using the better example from above, consider this second sentence as one that provides context for a story on the strategy.

Example

Financial consultant Jim Ertz outlines his "Get Lean and Mean" strategy Tuesday morning for members of Otto Corp., a business on the verge of bankruptcy. Since 2012, Ertz has used this strategy to save 98 percent of the 240 businesses that hired him after they experienced a severe financial downturn.

Here's another example of a second sentence for a profile on Ertz:

Financial consultant Jim Ertz outlines his "Get Lean and Mean" strategy Tuesday morning for members of Otto Corp., a business on the verge of bankruptcy. Ertz helped bail out his first business when he was in college and has since become the most experienced financial salvation expert in the United States.

Here's one for a piece on the company:

Financial consultant Jim Ertz outlines his "Get Lean and Mean" strategy Tuesday morning for members of Otto Corp., a business on the verge of bankruptcy. Otto Corp. lost more than 80 percent of its value in six months and has until the end of the year to pay off its $45 million debt or it must close for good.

The point is to focus that second sentence on the "why" elements of the frame, which means you need to fully understand the point of the story before you write the caption.

Extended Captions

When a photo must stand alone, editors often want a few more lines of text to provide depth and meaning to the image that would traditionally come from a written story that accompanied the image. This use of an extended caption essentially combines the first two lines of a standard photo image with additional information that helps enrich the readers' sense of value. Start with this simple caption:

Mishawaka resident Will Makker explains his opposition to the Hartwell Industries project to the city council during its Monday meeting. Makker was one of 23 people to argue against the plan to build a factory for the international toy maker on the shore of the Milton River, arguing it would pollute the area.

This works as a standard two-sentence caption, so it's a solid starting point for the readers. What likely matters now is some additional information on what happened at the meeting and what will happen next. This is where additional lines of text can help:

Mishawaka resident Will Makker explains his opposition to the Hartwell Industries project to the city council during its Monday meeting. Makker was one of 23 people to argue against the plan to build a factory for the international toy maker on the shore of the Milton River, arguing it would pollute the area. The project has been one of controversy for Mishawaka over the past six months, with some citizens arguing the jobs would be welcome and others fearing potential environmental damage. The meeting was the city's fourth open forum on the topic, and the council expects to vote on the issue at its May 8 meeting.

This gives your readers both a look back and a look ahead. It also helps provide a balanced look at the issue itself.

Historical Lines

You may not always have a current photo of a person you wish to feature with a story, so it might be necessary to run an archival photo. You also might want to run an older image as part of an obituary on someone famous or an anniversary of a landmark. To make the captions effective, you need to approach the content in a slightly different way:

Bill Robbins and his wife, Gayle, cut the ribbon at his first "Eat 'Em Up" restaurant in Belleville on Aug. 14, 1967. Robbins, who successfully franchised his self-serve restaurant idea into a global food empire, died Wednesday at age 83.

In this case you can see the time element in the first sentence provides a sense of when the event occurred, and the second sentence still explains why people are seeing this image now, even though the event happened decades ago.

THE BIG THREE

Here are the three key things you should take away from this chapter:

1. **Photographs should tell a story:** The purpose of including a visual element with a text story has to be more than just to break up the grayness of the text block. Photographs need to stimulate and engage readers as they provide information to them and evoke emotion within them. If the photos don't tell a story, they lack value to the readers and you should avoid them.

2. **Coaching is crucial:** Photographers are skilled craftspeople who understand a great deal about their job, but even the greatest skill players need a coach some times. Work with your photographers before, during and after the shoot to help them make the most of each assignment. The goal of coaching should be long-term improvement, so find the positives to reinforce and explain reasons why certain things didn't work out as well as they could have.

3. **Captions count:** A lousy caption can destroy the best image in the world. Make sure the captions provide context and relevance for the images. Not only should the "who did what to whom" elements outline the importance of the frame, but the caption should also explain the "how" and "why" elements of the shot as well. A well-written caption and a perfectly captured image can tell your readers a great story.

KEY TERMS

caption 130	editorial illustrations 129	mug shot 129
close-up shot 124	environmental portrait 129	sharpening 129
contrast 128	long shot 124	stock art 129
cropping 128	medium shot 124	toning 128

DISCUSSION QUESTIONS

1. How important is photography to you as a reader in terms of getting you to engage with the material? Do photos draw you in, or are you more attracted to other elements of a media package when choosing what you want to consume?

2. How often do you read captions with photos? To what degree do you agree or disagree with the chapter's assessment that captions matter a great deal in telling a story with an image?

3. Have you ever been fooled by an editorial illustration or thought a photo was too good to be real? How do you view photos overall after those experiences, and to what degree do you think this makes it more difficult for media editors to effectively use truly great images in communicating with readers?

WRITE NOW!

1. Review a local publication's use of photography and identify as many of the types of photographs outlined in the chapter as you can find, including mug shots, environmental portraits, action shots, editorial illustrations and stock art. Which of the photos are used most often within your publication? Which ones are used the least or not at all? How effective do you find this use of photography and why do you think this way? Use examples as you write a short essay on your findings.

2. Select several photos you have taken recently and write a standard caption for each of them. Remember that action shots work best for this kind of work, so try to avoid posed photos. Use the first sentence to explain what is going on in the photo and then the second sentence to add value and context to it.

3. Select two photo slideshows from any media outlet you like and evaluate them for their mix of shot types and their overall image selections. How many photos are long shots, medium shots or close-ups? Does the approach the photographer selected to each shot work well for the image and its ability to tell a story? Also, do you think there are too many, too few or just the right number of images to tell the story effectively? If you think the slideshow has too many images, which ones would you cut and why? If you think it has too few, what would you like to add? Explain your thoughts in a short essay.

Visit **edge.sagepub.com/filakediting** to help you accomplish your coursework goals in an easy-to-use learning environment.

10 INFORMATION GRAPHICS

LEARNING OBJECTIVES

After completing this chapter, you should be able to:

- Understand the purpose of information graphics as storytelling tools.

- Understand the key aspects of a graphic, including a headline, chatter, information layering and information density.

- Define and differentiate among types of charts, lists and boxes.

- Determine which types of graphics will best help you inform your audience in which types of storytelling situations.

- Construct a simple graphic to augment a content package you plan to publish.

- Define and differentiate among the types of web-based, interactive graphics available to you as an editor.

In the early 1980s, USA Today began nationwide news dissemination. The paper used splashy color, truncated stories and large images to draw the attention of readers. In addition, the paper's pages were heavily laden with charts, maps, boxes and other graphics.

Critics derided the paper as "McNews," arguing it was a fast food version of more substantial reporting and writing. However, in the 30-some years since it was first published, USA Today has not only become the No. 1 paper in terms of print circulation, but also a leader in the use of graphics. The staff members at USA Today realized that graphics could help readers understand certain things better than text-based stories would. They also realized that people had less time to consume the news, so using color, breakouts and other visual cues to draw their attention to things that mattered was a smart idea.

Information graphics describe things that can't be captured well in a photo and can't be explained easily in text. They combine an artist's touch and a reporter's insight to give people what they need to know in a visual and textual fashion. The web has provided news organizations with even more opportunities to use information graphics and other visual appeals to draw readers. As an editor of any publication in any field of media, you will need to understand the full range of graphic options available to you and how to best use them.

In this chapter, we will explore the types of graphics that you can use, when you should use them and how you can integrate them into your work. Although high-end graphics require additional training that goes beyond the scope of this book, we will show you some examples of well-done interactive graphics. However, don't worry if you aren't an artistic person. Simple graphics require almost no artistic skill and can be quite effective.

BASIC THINGS A GRAPHIC SHOULD DO

The term "graphic" tends to conjure images of art-driven, multifaceted, multicolor explosions of information. Graphics can be large, intricate and filled with information, but they can also be simple visual elements in your publication. In many cases, simple graphics can be among the most useful parts of your coverage. A good graphic of any size or type should do the following things:

Add Value

The purpose of a graphic is to give the audience members a broader, deeper, clearer or better look at information than they could get without the graphic. If a story discusses how a bridge fell apart because of years of neglect, a graphic can illustrate the step-by-step process of the decay and collapse. Although a story can explain what happened, a graphic can do much more to show people how it happened. This adds value to the story and helps the audience members better understand the situation.

Many graphics become "dead art" because they serve no purpose in furthering the story. If the aforementioned story came with a drawing of what the bridge looked like when it was first built 50 years earlier, you have added nothing to the story. Photographers also run into this problem when they take "building shots," which can include things such as a photo of a bank taken two days after the bank was robbed. In both cases, this art doesn't do anything for the audience members. If you include a graphic with a story or as a primary storytelling element, make sure it adds value. Don't have art for art's sake.

Be Accurate

Many organizations have transitioned the job title for graphics personnel from "graphic artists" to "graphics reporters." The shift in the vernacular is small, but it reveals something important in how these organizations view graphics. Although artists might only need to make something look good, reporters need to make sure the piece is factually correct.

Accuracy remains the primary goal of all good journalism. If you work with a graphic, you must make sure that it is correct in every way. The colors must be right. The elements must be drawn to scale. The text that describes the image must be free from errors. A beautiful graphic that can dazzle the eye and excite the mind is worth nothing if it is factually flawed.

Tell a Story

A graphic doesn't have to be large, colorful or interactive to have value, but it must tell a story. The story can be simple, such as "here is how you get to the Fourth of July parade," or complex, such as "here is the way in which an ultrasonic particle generator converts liquid into fine particles." Graphics reporters and graphic artists must use visuals and text to tell a story the same way their writing colleagues would.

Good stories have a beginning, a middle and an end. The beginning is engaging, the end provides closure and the middle matters. They also help people learn something and give them a sense that the story was worthwhile and satisfying. Incomplete stories leave the readers feeling frustrated and lost.

A graphic should follow that same approach and include all of the elements a reader would need to make sense of the content. Don't rely on artistic ability alone to "wow" your audience members.

Clarify Information

A good graphic will help people understand what something is, how something works, what something looks like or why something exists. It can also clarify information for people so they can place the graphic into their own frame of reference.

When basketball star Shaquille O'Neal made his first trip to Milwaukee as a rookie, a city newspaper ran a story about him to explain how large a 7-foot-1-inch, 330-pound man is. To help convey that message, the paper used a graphic representation of one of his shoe prints. The visual allowed people to get a clear sense of how big he was by comparing their feet to O'Neal's size 23 shoe.

Look at your graphics and decide whether they add clarity to your readers' experience. Make sure the graphics show the readers something important in a clear and concise fashion.

Embrace Simplicity

Technology has made it easier to build graphics, apply effects and use interactive elements. Web graphics can blink, beep, zoom and fly. Video and audio can mix with text and illustrations to create massive visual experiences that rival those in the movies. However, just because something can be done doesn't mean it should be done.

HELPFUL HINTS
THE ANATOMY OF A GOOD GRAPHIC

James Abundis/*The Boston Globe*

Let's take a look at what makes for an effective graphic:

1. *Headline:* Notice that the graphic has an engaging headline that is large enough to draw your attention to the rest of the visual. The headline is at the top of the image and provides a simple and yet interesting statement to let you know what this graphic will tell you: how self-driving cars work.

2. *Elements:* Each time the artist chose an element, he did so for the right reason. For example, to show the various places the technology will be installed on the vehicle, the artist built a car element to showcase the sensors and cameras. However, he also used a second car graphic to show how current driver-assisted systems work to protect drivers in specific ways.

3. *Chatter:* Under the headline, the artist uses some text to inform the readers about the purpose of this graphic. The sentence here, which is similar to the lead of a story, is called **chatter** and serves to set the stage for the rest of the graphic. At a minimum, the chatter should explain what the graphic will be about and why the audience members should care.

4. *Information layering:* The artist uses multiple elements here to tell particular stories. For example, the main car contains information about where the self-driving elements are installed on the car as well as what each element does in helping the car drive itself. The second car shows how radar and ultrasonic technology provide the car with information on when to brake, turn, accelerate and more. This use of information layering provides the reader with a lot of crucial information through several layers of information.

5. *Information density:* If a graphic has too much information, readers feel overwhelmed and have difficulty making sense of the piece. If it has too little information, the piece will have large blank spaces that will distract your readers. In this graphic, the artist makes good use of space.

Some of the best graphics are the simplest because they convey information effectively. Although multimedia graphics can have value, they aren't always necessary, and in some cases the interactive elements are distracting.

When in doubt, use simpler tools to do the job well. Before you add a rollover, a blinking feature, sound effects or other gadget-style elements to a graphic, ask yourself why you are doing so. If it's because it provides your audience members with a better overall experience, that's fine. If you are adding elements just to show off, figure out another way to placate your ego instead.

THE SPECTRUM OF GRAPHICS

Graphics range from simple visuals through detailed and interactive experiences. Editors and artists can build graphics in various stages of complexity, depending on the approach they take to the material. The important thing to remember is that the content is king when it comes to graphics. As we noted above in the "Embrace Simplicity" section, layering a graphic with unnecessary bells and whistles because you can doesn't make sense.

This section of the chapter will provide you with several types of graphics and will touch on specific reasons to use these graphics. We will discuss these graphics as being simple or complex, but keep in mind that you can always augment simple graphics in a variety of ways to give your audience members a deeper and richer experience. As with everything else in journalism, you should have a reason behind why you are using a graphic and why you are applying specific types of elements to it.

Boxes

The breakout box is among the simplest things you can do for your readers to give them something of value in a way they are less likely to miss. Let's take a look at some of the more common versions of the breakout box.

Take Action

This box provides people with key information that allows them to do something on the basis of the material contained in the story.

An **action box** can include time, date, and place information for an event. It can also provide additional travel information, such as driving directions and parking information. Other information, such as whether the event requires tickets, what the tickets cost and whether food or drink will be available, can be helpful.

This box meets all of the needs mentioned above. It's short and to the point, and it gives the people what they need to know if they want to attend the event. Instead of forcing your readers to wander through a whole story to figure out where they need to go, you can do it simply with this breakout.

Another example of when to use a box like this is when a charity or an organization is seeking help. Instructions on how to volunteer for a local soup kitchen or an address where people can send money for a memorial fund are great bits of information for a take-action box. Whenever you have something in

Example of an action box.

"Into the Woods" brings fairy tales to life

by Emily Miels

mielse64@uwosh.edu

The Oshkosh Community Players theater group, which includes a number of UW Oshkosh students, is redefining "happily ever after" in its production of "Into the Woods."

"It's kind of a twisted fairy tale," director Joe Ferlo said. "It takes four Grimm brothers fairy tales and puts them together into one by adding a fifth tale."

According to Ferlo, the four tales used throughout the play are "Cinderella," "Little Red Riding Hood," "Rapunzel" and "Jack and the Beanstalk."

Ferlo said audiences should expect an upbeat, energetic show. He compared the first part of the production to the movie "Princess Bride."

"By the end of the first act, everyone's wishes come true," Ferlo said. "The second act is what happens after 'happily ever after.'"

Sarah Gorski, an Oshkosh student playing Cinderella's stepsister, Florinda in the show, said "Into the Woods" is a musical people of all ages can relate to and enjoy.

"Every girl wants to be a princess and every boy wants to be Prince Charming when they're young," she said. "It's fun to see them twist it in this way."

According to the Grand Opera House website, "Into the Woods" has a cast of 21 people, plus the crew and "will arguably be the most elaborate community-based production on The Grand's stage in the last 10 years."

"It's a massive undertaking with people with varying amounts of experience," Justin Spanbauer, a UW Oshkosh sophomore playing Rapunzel's prince in the show, said.

According to Spanbauer, cast members' acting experience ranged from very little to several years.

The music for "Into the Woods" was written by Steven Sondheim, who is well known for productions such as "West Side Story" and "Sweeny Todd: The Demon

Barber of Fleet Street."

Because the Grand Opera House was recently renovated, Ferlo and the theater group wanted to showcase what the theater could offer, including new audio technology.

"The orchestra is generated digitally," Ferlo said. "Even though there's only a couple of people in the orchestra pit, it sounds like a full orchestra."

Spanbauer said the music was one of his favorite parts of the production.

"It's a really challenging score," Spanbauer said. "It's so catchy and there's some really brilliant lyrics."

Gorski said she particularly enjoys a song that Little Red Riding Hood sings called "I Know Things Now."

"It's a song about life lessons learned," Gorski said.

Ferlo said they chose the play partially to help generate interest in the Oshkosh Community Players group.

"The Oshkosh Community Players really wanted to do a show that would kind of

reboot the organization," Ferlo said.

Spanbauer heard about the production through the Theater Arts Board and decided to look into it.

"There's not a lot of theater presence in Oshkosh, especially at a community level," Spanbauer said.

He encouraged anyone interested in acting or theater in general to check out the show and get involved in the community theater.

If you go...

WHEN:
• April 15-17

WHERE:
• Grand Opera House

TICKETS AND INFO:
• www.grandoperahouse.org

Advance-Titan, University of Wisconsin Oshkosh, "'Into the Woods' brings fairy tales to life" by Emily Miels.

Example of a mug and chatter box.

Word has it:

"What do you think about people who choose a vegetarian lifestyle?"

"I think it's a personal decision, and I have a lot of respect for those who chose that lifestyle because it takes a lot of discipline."

-Brooke Wetor
Journalism major,
sophomore

"I don't really have a position on if someone is a vegetarian. I personally would not do it, but if they have the will power to cut something like that out of their life, then good for them."

-Tony Grandprey
History major,
sophomore

"I don't understand how they can live without meat. There are a lot of nutrients you get from meat."

-Janna Johnson
Criminal Justice major,
sophomore

"I would not prefer to live that lifestyle, but for some people it makes them feel better about themselves, which is always good. It's not a diet; it's a lifestyle change and shouldn't be treated as a fad."

-A.J. Daczyk
Business major,
junior

Advance-Titan, University of Wisconsin Oshkosh

a story that could compel people to do something after they read it, pull that information out of your story and place it in a box so it is easier to find.

The use of a small image and a quote can provide both a good visual and an opportunity to highlight a particularly meaningful piece of dialogue. By using a small photo of a person's face and a quote, you can turn a few words into a valuable graphic.

You can use this approach effectively with multiple quotes and photos. If an issue brings about some discussion or provides readers with a sense of outrage, you can give your readers an opportunity to be heard.

You can use this type of graphic as part of any section, ranging from news and opinion to sports and entertainment. You can provide this in a slideshow format or as a static set of images. You can augment this with audio or let it sit flat. You have many options with this kind of box, and it can be as simple or as complex as you want it to be.

Biography

This is a way to advance the **mug and chatter box**, especially when you're working on a profile of some kind. **Biography boxes** can help stories that relate to a hiring or firing, a promotion or demotion or even a death. The story will likely go into a great deal of depth, but to get the simplest set of facts regarding the person, you can use a small breakout box.

This biography box works well for a number of reasons. It gives your readers the name, age and other demographic information they will want to know, such as the person's education and previous places of employment.

Fast Facts

This is a common box that allows you to highlight several key items for a reader. You can use a box like this to summarize the most important points of an article. In many cases, a **fast-facts box** answers the "What?" "So what?" and "Now what?" questions. The box provides the essential information for people who glance at the story and are uncertain if they want to read the whole thing. If the information in the box appeals to them, they might read the full story. If the box doesn't pique their interest, they can take the small bit of knowledge they gained and move on to the next story.

Other boxes like this include a "by the numbers" perspective, such as this budget box:

Example of a biography box.

Joseph A. LeMire

LeMire

- Took interim police chief position after former police chief Michael Melland reitred in July 2010.
- Served as lieutentant at UWO for two years prior to taking position as interim chief.
- Previously served as part of the Escanaba Safety Department.

Advance-Titan, University of Wisconsin Oshkosh

Example of a "by the numbers" box.

Finding Funds in a Recession

Chancellor Richard Wells used strategic planning to reduce the impact of the slumping economy. Here's how UW-O found enough money to pay for this initiative:

Rescinded 2% pay increase	$2.2 million
Rainy day fund	$2.5 million
Mandatory furlough days	$3.3 million
5.5% tuition increase	$3.3 million
2.5% unit-wide budget cuts	$3.7 million
TOTAL SAVED	**$15 million**
TOTAL NEEDED	**$13.6 million**
REMAINDER	**$1.4 million**

Advance-Titan, University of Wisconsin Oshkosh

Courtesy of Kori Rumore

As a graphics producer at the Chicago Tribune, Kori Rumore's job involves both the artistic and the journalistic elements of storytelling. She researches and reports on topics of interest, doing so through data visualizations, explanatory graphics and more for the digital and print publications.

"Though I'm a suburban Chicago native, I never imagined I'd have the opportunity to work at either of the city's major newspapers, the Sun-Times or the Tribune," she said. "My previous experience was working in graphics at small newspapers in two of the finest retirement communities in the U.S. — Naples, Florida and Tucson, Arizona. But, those experiences really prepared me to take on breaking news topics, flesh out project ideas and teach myself how to use new technologies."

Rumore said good graphics must communicate important information effectively.

"An effective graphic, in my opinion, tells a story in and of itself," she said. "Sure, graphics are usually partnered with stories — but they're much more than window dressing. A simple chart showing the number of homicides or carjackings in Chicago by year can show a trend that might otherwise take several paragraphs of a story to explain, for example."

The expansion of technology and the heavy reliance on digital content have changed the way Rumore says she does her job now as opposed to back when she started in journalism. Even when she started at the Tribune in 2013, she said her team built graphics for print only, but gradually moved to more digital projects.

"Though the technology will continue to change, I think it's important to remain flexible and open to these changes," Rumore said. "Really, there's no better way to learn a new program or system than to just stay positive and open-minded, dive in and see how it works. It's challenging, but fun!"

Even with the switch to a digital-first paradigm, the way her team approaches graphic reporting remains based on the importance of the content, the value to the audience and the time available to build the piece, she said.

"The types of graphics that my team pursues all must include information that is: local, timely and involves at least some data," Rumore said. "If a project meets those standards, then we can determine the format. Format might be determined by the amount of time we have to pull a project together. If something needs to be turned quickly, then maybe it's a chart or a map embedded into a Chicago Tribune webpage. If we have more time to complete the project, then maybe we create a story page for it and a video. All of our projects must work on phone (iPhone and Android), tablet, laptop and desktop breakpoints. Plus, we're mindful that we want to build an audience who, hopefully, sees our work and wants to subscribe to continue seeing our work."

The graphics must also be representative of reality and contain accurate information, she said. Although some people use graphics to distort the truth or push an agenda, media professionals can't warp the truth with visual content.

"Any graphic — map, chart, diagram, whatever — requires some skepticism on the part of its viewer," Rumore said. "Yes, there are groups who use statistics to deceive — yes, they create fake news! Be aware of that. Also, consider the source of the information that's presented. Is it reputable? Or, is it from a politically biased organization? We have to trust our sources and the information we use from them. My team only uses statistics from reputable sources."

Regardless of the changes to the field or technology, Rumore said the underlying aspects of journalism will never change in regard to how graphics should work.

"Here's what I think will always remain important: great reporting skills, solid writing backed up by a thorough copy editor and mastering of the tools required to build a digital or print graphic quickly," she said.

The story mentions a $1.4 million surplus within a budget. This is interesting, but many readers will wonder how the university achieved this surplus. The box does the math for them, and it shows specific financial areas that contributed to the surplus. Additionally, pulling the numbers out of the story not only highlights them but also prevents them from bogging down the text of the story.

Graphics Beyond the Box

The box can be an effective tool, but other visual representations of events, data and processes can tell good stories for your readers. Below is a list of items that serve as more complex graphics, but are still within the ability of most computer-savvy online editors.

You are here

Pixabay/nix1111

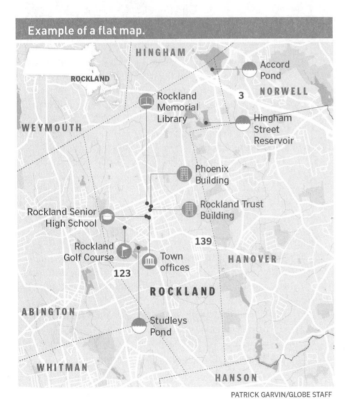

Example of a flat map.

PATRICK GARVIN/GLOBE STAFF

Patrick Garvin/*The Boston Globe*

Maps

These visual representations of space are meant to provide readers with a sense of placement. Maps can be a small section of a neighborhood or a detailed examination of the universe. They can include a few minor points of interest or they can be laden with information, like the USA Today weather map.

The best maps balance detail against space. Those maps that don't will lack focus and be as useless as the one on the left that shows our place in the universe.

Although clearly a joke, this exaggeration brings up an important point on maps: they must give your readers a sense of value. A giant map of Texas with three bits of information on it isn't much help. However, a 4-inch map crammed with dozens of lines and hundreds of words isn't much good either.

Look to the left for an example of a solid map.

When you use a map on a website, you should strive to go beyond a simple flat map. Sites such as MapQuest, The Weather Channel and Google Maps have provided the underlying technology that allows you to provide your readers with digital, interactive maps with little effort. You can link to the site for the map if you choose, or some sites will allow you to embed their content into your pages.

By embedding maps into your site, you can provide readers with opportunities to see weather updates, get directions to an event or see where traffic is bogging down because of an accident. You should look for opportunities to take advantage of these maps and provide your readers with access to interactive and valuable content.

Tables

A table is used to break information out of a story and show a side-by-side comparison. If you wanted to show how enrollment at your school has increased from last year to this year, a table would allow you to input numbers and demonstrate those changes. You can augment the table to include things like the change from last year to this year in actual students or on the basis of percentages.

Charts

These graphics provide you with another good way to make figures clearer. Many computer programs offer you the ability to translate numbers into various types of charts, on the basis of the type of data involved. People often have difficulty with numbers, but they tend to understand them better in a visual form.

Bar charts represent numbers with vertical or horizontal columns of color, and they are helpful for your readers when they are looking at a static set of numbers or trying to visualize quantities.

In this example, you can see multiple comparisons here. One shade of a bar represents 1980, and the second represents 2015. Each column represents a particular university, and each row represents the race of the students that attend each of the institutions. The bars allow you to compare which races make up the highest percentage of students in each case, and you can see comparative growth, or lack thereof, in each case.

Fever charts, or line charts, use a line to show quantity change over time. You can build these charts so that each point of change along the x-axis represents anything from seconds to centuries.

This example displays a common use of a fever chart: a look at financial changes over time. The journalist who created this piece included specific points of interest to highlight where those changes occurred and the specific numbers the Dow Jones Industrial Average hit at those points in time.

The **pie chart** is a circle that shows what part of a larger whole is represented by each division. These charts can provide people with information about election results, the components that make up their soil or the quantities of jelly beans that are produced in each color in a jelly bean factory.

Bubble charts allow you to compare quantities in a simple fashion, akin to the way a bar chart would, or they can be used in a much more complex fashion. In the case of the bubble chart used here, the sizes of the bubbles indicate the magnitude of the topic at hand, namely, the numbers of lawsuits filed against each of the presidents listed.

That said, you can also use the bubbles in other ways, such as placing them on a map to show which states have the largest number of incarcerated citizens. You can also use them as plotted points on a graph to create an additional data dimension for your readers. The goal

Example of a bar chart.

Diversity in the Boston area's largest universities

Even as international student enrollment in the Boston area has skyrocketed, the percentage of black students has remained low. Here is a look at diversity at the region's three largest universities:

	Boston University	Harvard University	Northeastern University
White	1980 84% / 2015 48%	79% / 45%	91% / 46%
Black	4% / 4%	5% / 5%	4% / 3%
Hispanic	2% / 9%	3% / 8%	1% / 6%
Asian	2% / 12%	3% / 14%	2% / 10%
International	9% / 24%	10% / 23%	3% / 32%
Multiracial	* / 3%	* / 4%	* / 3%

Numbers may not add up to 100 percent because of rounding.
The data include students on all levels at universities that offer at least a bachelor's degree or above, and exclude students who did not report ethnicity. Racial groups that made up less than 1 percent are not shown.
* 2015 numbers include multiracial, a category introduced in 2008. In 2015, students who are Hispanic and at least one other race are counted as Hispanic.

SOURCE: Department of Education, Integrated Postsecondary Education Data System   GLOBE STAFF
Staff/*The Boston Globe*

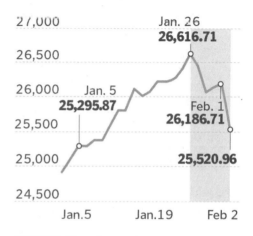

Example of fever chart.

Dow downer

Stocks had their worst week of the Trump presidency.

SOURCE: Dow Jones   YANWU/GLOBE STAFF
Yan Wu/*The Boston Globe*

Example of a bubble chart.

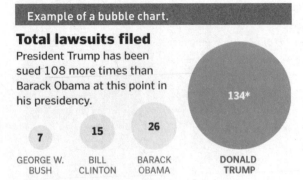

Total lawsuits filed

President Trump has been sued 108 more times than Barack Obama at this point in his presidency.

7	**15**	**26**	**134***
GEORGE W. BUSH	BILL CLINTON	BARACK OBAMA	DONALD TRUMP

When the president is named as a defendant or respondent, through May 5 of the first term.

JAMES ABUNDIS/GLOBE STAFF

James Abundis/*The Boston Globe*

Example of a list.

Which Cambridge restaurants paid for liquor licenses and which got free ones?

In this stretch of Central Square, roughly half the restaurants bought liquor licenses and the other half received free ones in recent years, with records showing prices ranging from $35,000 to $250,000.

● PURCHASED LICENSE   ● FREE LICENSE

	Name	Address	Alcohol	Purchase
1	Shanghai Fresh	735 Massachusetts Ave.	Beer/wine	Paid
2	730 Tavern Kitchen & Patio	730 Massachusetts Ave.	All alcohol	Paid
3	Mainely Burgers	704 Massachusetts Ave.	Beer/wine	Free
4	Dosa Factory	571 Massachusetts Ave.	Beer/wine	Paid
5	Pepper Sky's	20 Pearl St.	Beer/wine	Free
6	Viale	502 Massachusetts Ave.	All alcohol	Free
7	Little Donkey	505 Massachusetts Ave.	All alcohol	Paid
8	Happy Lamb Hot Pot	485 Massachusetts Ave.	Beer/wine	Paid
9	La Fabrica	450 Massachusetts Ave.	All alcohol	Paid
10	Patty Chen's Dumpling Room*	907 Main St.	All alcohol	Paid
11	Pagu	310 Massachusetts Ave.	All alcohol	Paid
12	Darwin's Ltd.	313 Massachusetts Ave.	Beer/wine**	Free
13	Naco Taco	297 Massachusetts Ave.	All alcohol	Free
14	Roxy's	292 Massachusetts Ave.	All alcohol	Free
15	Oath Pizza	181 Massachusetts Ave.	Beer/wine	Free
16	Saloniki	181 Massachusetts Ave.	All alcohol	Free

*Closed Oct. 28

**Also serves cordials/liqueurs

Map shows restaurants with liquor licenses issued in 2015-2017.

SOURCES: City and state records; Mapbox; OpenStreetMap   SACHA PFEIFFER, PATRICK GARVIN/GLOBE STAFF

Sacha Pfeiffer, Patrick Garvin/*The Boston Globe*

with this graphic, as is the case with every graphic, is to tell the story effectively and clearly. If you involve too many data dimensions in your bubble chart, you can create more confusion than clarity.

Lists

When material is too cumbersome for a story but not visually appealing enough for a graphic, a list is often a good option to try. Here is a good example of when a list can be handy:

In this case, the journalist combined the value of a map with the simplicity of a list to create an informative visual element. In the list portion, the journalist provided the name and address of each business, as well as what types of alcohol it served and whether it paid for its liquor license. All of this information could not be crammed onto a map without creating a mess, so this paired approach makes the most sense.

Process Diagrams

These visual representations are occasionally referred to as "use case diagrams" or just "diagrams." The purpose of a **process diagram** is to explain how something works in a step-by-step fashion. Icons or images represent participants and elements while lines demonstrate motion or sequence.

This piece breaks down the physics and artistry associated with the "bottle toss" trend. The step-by-step explanation shows how to set up the bottle to create the greatest likelihood of a successful outcome. It then breaks down how to toss it, what happens inside the bottle and why it lands on its bottom if it is tossed properly.

Example of a bar chart.

Future of online grocery shopping

Online food and beverage purchases in the United States could reach $100 billion by 2025.

	Online sales	Percent of total retail*	Grocery store equivalent**
■ Current ■ Estimate			
2016	$20.5b	4.29%	764
2025 Conservative	$44.6b	8.51%	1659
2025 Moderate	$72.6b	13.86%	2702
2025 Aggressive	$103.3b	19.72%	3844

*Total food and beverage retail sales (excluding nonconsumer) are estimated to reach $523.8b by 2025.

**Number of grocery-store-equivalent digital retail models.

SOURCE: Food Marketing Institute, Nielsen   YAN WU/GLOBE STAFF

Yan Wu/*The Boston Globe*

These diagrams can show people how a new type of engine will work, what process is used to turn a bill into a law or how to write a sappy romance novel. When you have a procedure that can be outlined in a chronological fashion, consider using a process diagram to show your readers how that procedure works.

Timelines

Anytime there is a story developing over time, you should consider using a graphic. Chronology can bog down a story and kill readability, so you want to make sure you look for ways to pull that content out of your story.

If you have the opportunity to do more interactive pieces, you should consider doing so. The web is an active medium, so look for ways to take advantage of that. By having several sections of a **timeline** with pieces you can click on, you will provide your readers with an opportunity to scan the chronology of a piece or to skip past parts of the timeline that are of little interest to them.

Interactive Graphics

The web has always provided editors with more chances to engage the readers via visuals. The wider array of colors, the limitless space and the opportunity to empower readers are at the heart of the medium. Graphics built specifically for the web allow the editor to emphasize several pieces of information via multiple forms of storytelling. In many cases, these graphics contain the traditional elements of stories, photos and print graphics. However, the elements are used in a different fashion to enhance the viewers' experiences.

Online graphics have become more advanced over the past decade, because of the multitude of options available to website editors and graphic designers. Graphics can be animated, allowing the reader to see how something should move or how a process can develop. Graphics can be interactive, as they allow readers to touch, move or react to things that they might otherwise never experience.

In her book on multimedia journalism, Jennifer George-Palilonis[1] placed interactive graphics into several succinct categories:

Narratives. The purpose of this kind of graphic is to provide readers with a simple review of a story, engaging them from a visual perspective. The stories told in these formats often have a distinct point of view and provide the audience with information about an event, an idea or a topic. **Narrative graphics** often incorporate video, still images, music and other elements.

This graphic on the evolution of same-sex marriage throughout the United States links directly to the text-based content within the story. As the reader scrolls down through the history of this issue, the graphics change to reflect which states performed same-sex marriages, which ones had legalized civil unions and which ones had banned any form of same-sex marriage. This allows the reader to see where this issue first took hold within the country and then how each state came into play on the topic.

Example of a process diagram.

Breaking down the bottle toss

The act of flipping a water bottle through the air to achieve a perfect, upright landing on the table in front of you is part art form, part science.

ARTISTRY IN THE DELIVERY

SCIENCE IN THE TOSS

1. Begin by holding a plastic bottle, filled a third of the way up, from the top. At this point, the center of mass lies with the water at the bottom of the bottle.

2. Toss the bottle in a forward and upward motion. The bottle rotates, but most of the water doesn't because it is free to move around within the bottle instead.

1/3 full

Center of mass

Spin slows

Angular momentum

3. As the bottle continues on its downward path, the spin of it is reduced and transferred to the heavier, contained water. The "spin" refers to a concept known as "angular momentum."

Gravity

4. The bottle soon reaches a point at which it is barely spinning at all, and it falls straight to the surface because of gravity. The weight of the water, as well as the flat bottom of the bottle, contribute to the bottle landing upright.

SOURCES: James Bird, assistant professor fluid dynamics, Boston University; Iain Stewart, physics professor, MIT

SONIA RAO, JAMES ABUNDIS/GLOBE STAFF

Sonia Rao, James Abundis/*The Boston Globe*

Example of a narrative graphic.

The Boston Globe, 09 January 2016. Screenshot retrieved from http://www.bostonglobe.com/2016/01/09/same-sex-marriage-over-time/mbVFMQPyxZCpM2eSQMUsZK/story.html.

Example of an instructive graphic.

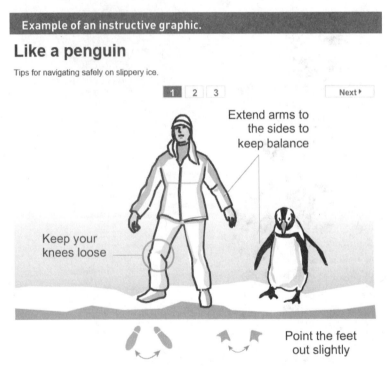

"Like a penguin" from Boston.com. Screenshot retrieved from http://archive.boston.com/interactive/graphics/2008/20090107_ice/.

Instructives. These graphics are similar to diagrams, as they use step-by-step instructions to show people how something works or how to accomplish a task. The value in a graphic like this is that it provides movement and interactivity to give readers a sequential understanding of an event. Although a diagram can provide sequencing and information, **instructive graphics** use motion to help readers more fully comprehend action. Below is an instructive that is simple and yet effective:

In three steps, the artist explains how to walk safely on icy sidewalks with a step-by-step examination of how best to avoid falling and what to do if you do fall.

Other instructive graphics can be used to show people how to do something. In most cases, these are not steps that can be accomplished at the computer. Instead, instructives provide users with an example and a visual description of how to do something so that they may learn how something works and then apply this knowledge elsewhere.

How to fix a leaky toilet would make for a good instructive. The graphic artist can demonstrate the specific steps a person should take while seeking out the leak and the steps she should take to repair it. A book with written instructions might convey the same approach, but the visuals will allow the user to better assess if she is in the right area, touching the right thing and adjusting items properly. It can also show her how to do things that might not make sense if she saw a text-based description.

Simulations. These graphics allow users to experience something in a hands-on fashion. This is one of the more interactive forms of graphics, as it puts the control of the situation in the hands of the audience members. Web quizzes, video games and other similar projects are simulative graphics. They allow the participants to test their knowledge, dunk a basketball or engage in a spy mission. However, news organizations can use these types of graphics for their work as well.

This **simulative graphic** uses 1980s "Nintendo-style" elements to allow the user to play a game. In this case, the simulation is how to find a parking place after a snowfall in Boston. As the user quickly realizes, this is not an easy task.

When considering if you should use a simulative graphic, remember that the topic will dictate the approach. If the topic lends itself toward simulation, such as "how to play a guitar," use a simulative graphic. However, if it involves things that don't make for a good simulation, such as how to plant a garden, consider using an instructive approach.

Data Visualizations

One of the more recent trends in online graphics is the use of complex data visualizations. The concept is not a new one, as newspapers and magazines have been using pie charts and bar charts for years to show people data in a more visual fashion. However, with the advent of more complicated data programs and innovations in graphic design, **data visualizations** have exploded in terms of use and variations.

These visualizations combine rich data with graphic arts to make difficult content easier to understand. Although they are based on numbers, these visualizations can be creative and interactive. Here's an example of a visualization that would have good value to readers of a news site:

In this representation, the artist uses color and shading to provide the readers with the opportunities to see where most of the wealth and poverty resides throughout the state over the past 45 years. The users can watch as certain areas become more or less affluent over time by clicking each decade.

Data visualizations allow you to show the readers data in ways in which it makes sense to them. Many good online tools exist for you to help push the boundaries of how you want people to view data.

Example of a simulative graphic.

PATRICK GARVIN/GLOBE STAFF

The Boston Globe, "Do you have what it takes to park in Boston after a snowstorm?" 14 March 2017. Screenshot retrieved from https://www.bostonglobe.com/metro/2017/03/14/you-have-what-takes-park-boston-after-snowstorm/F4mRCqQmXhUG3IUD0QRrCN/story.html.

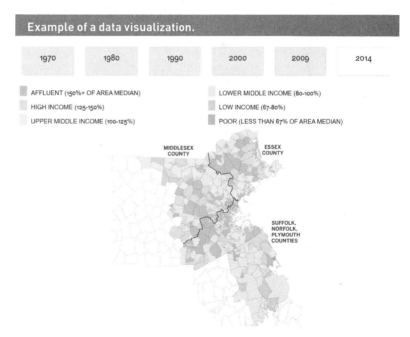

Example of a data visualization.

The Boston Globe, "Boston's struggle with income segregation" 06 March 2016. Screenshot retrieved from https://www.bostonglobe.com/metro/2016/03/05/segregation/NiQBy000TZsGgLnAT0tHsL/story.html.

THE BIG THREE

Here are the three key things you should take away from this chapter:

1. **Graphics are an important element in storytelling:** People often learn more from a coherent graphic than they will learn from an extended story. Good editors can see potential in graphics and apply them as a primary

or secondary storytelling element in their publications. Whether it is a simple chart or a complex interactive graphic, these journalistic elements can make a big difference in reaching your audience effectively.

2. **You don't have to be an artist:** You might not be an artist or a gifted user of high-end graphics programs, but you can use simple graphics to help your readers better understand key pieces of information. Boxes, charts, diagrams and more can be easy to produce and helpful to your readers.

3. **Have a reason for doing what you're doing:** A core premise of this book is to use the right tool for the right job. This is particularly true in the case of graphics, where you can find yourself developing graphics for almost everything you do. Before you use a graphic, make sure the story you want to tell would benefit from the graphic. If all it will do is add a striking visual element, eliminate it and stick to the tool that does the job best.

KEY TERMS

action box 137
bar chart 141
biography box 138
bubble chart 141
chatter 136

data visualization 145
fast-facts box 138
fever chart 141
instructive graphic 144
mug and chatter box 138

narrative graphic 143
pie chart 141
process diagram 142
simulative graphic 144
timeline 143

DISCUSSION QUESTIONS

1. What experiences have you had with interactive graphics? Which of the types of graphics listed in the chapter have you encountered? How valuable were these graphics to your overall understanding of the material?

2. What do you see as the benefits and drawbacks of graphics-heavy publications?

3. Graphics expert Kori Rumore notes in the chapter that graphics can be misleading, stating, "Any

graphic — map, chart, diagram, whatever — requires some skepticism on the part of its viewer. Yes, there are groups who use statistics to deceive — yes, they create fake news!" How much effort do you put into analyzing graphics you encounter in media outlets? Have you ever been deceived by a graphic or felt a graphic didn't tell you the whole story?

WRITE NOW!

1. Select a graphic from a local media outlet and examine it for the key elements of a graphic on the basis of the Helpful Hints box in this chapter: headline, elements, chatter, information layer and information density. How well does this piece do in meeting those standards? Also, analyze the graphic on the basis of what the chapter considers to be the basic things any graphic should do. Does it meet those standards? Write a short essay on your findings.

2. Locate a news story, press release or piece of marketing material that you think would benefit from the inclusion

of a chart. Use a simple chart generator, like those included in Microsoft Word or a free online service, to create a pie, bar or fever chart that would augment this coverage. Then write a short analysis of why you think this adds value to the piece of copy you selected.

3. Review a local publication for instances of graphics and note which ones are most used and which ones are least used or not used at all. How graphics-heavy is this publication? Could it benefit from more or less graphic elements? Explain your thoughts in a short essay.

$SAGE edge™

Visit **edge.sagepub.com/filakediting** to help you accomplish your coursework goals in an easy-to-use learning environment.

11 PUBLICATION DESIGN

The ability to create a visually appealing package of content can make the difference between having an engaged and interested audience and having readers bypass your publication without thinking twice. A quality design requires an editor to use various elements to create a complete story: Photos, graphics and text must work in concert as they provide the readers with information. Beyond those issues, editors must choose appropriate fonts, colors and page structure as to accentuate key aspects of the story they wish to tell.

Design is often viewed as different from the rest of your journalistic efforts. In truth, the ability to design is about the ability to communicate. Just like writing, you need structure, coherency and clarity. Just like photography, you need visually appealing aesthetics and some eye-grabbing material. In short, the same approach you take toward quality writing or photography should apply to your design.

In this chapter, we will outline the basics of design as they will pertain to your job as an editor. Our purpose here will be to introduce you to the primary elements of what makes for good design, what elements of design to avoid and how to let form and function mesh to improve your readers' experiences with your publication.

BASIC PRINCIPLES ASSOCIATED WITH DESIGN

As with all other forms of journalism, design requires the editor to research the purpose of the publication, analyze the ways in which he or she can best reach the publication's readers and provide quality material in a valuable way. The difference between design and other forms of media communication comes from the array of tools at the editor's disposal. Taken another way, you can think of this like you would an orchestra: Text, graphics, photos and other elements are like sections of the orchestra, with each one doing its part to create something. Design is where the editor becomes the conductor, accentuating specific orchestral sections or instruments to create a complete experience for the audience.

Below are a few basic things you should consider as an editor when you determine how to approach design for your publication:

Assess Your Audience

If you were to write a story on a new dental procedure for a newspaper, you would include information about the benefits of the procedure, the process people undergo and what experts and participants think about it. If you were to write that same story for a dental professionals' magazine, you would include more technical details, a broader explanation of how the procedure works and ways in which it can be sold to patients. If you were to write about the procedure for a parenting website, you might focus on things that matter to moms and dads, explain the benefits for children and show parents how to help their children deal with the procedure and the aftercare. The underlying audience determines your approach to the topic.

Design is no different. If you design for a site that sells princess costumes and children's toys, you will likely use script fonts, include bright soft colors and focus on elaborate visuals. If you are designing a standard news publication, you will have a more muted color palette, a more conservative text font and standard photography.

Publications geared toward preschool children need to have more visuals and fewer words, because children can be easily distracted and often lack strong literacy skills. Publications geared toward scholarly readers, such as doctors and researchers, need text to be a dominant element, because the users have longer attention spans and a thirst for knowledge. Keep the audience in mind when you are putting together the elements of your site.

Capture and Retain the Readers' Attention

People today have more choices than ever for their reading and viewing pleasure. When they come across your publication in print or on the web, you want to grab their attention and hang on to it. If you want to get your readers' attention, you need to do more than use giant visuals and screaming headlines. You need to have balance among your elements on the page. You need to show the readers a dominant visual, a solid headline and additional layers of information.

Be Consistent

Consistency allows readers to feel grounded as they consume your content. The use of specific visual elements in a consistent fashion within a publication and between editions of that publication will provide the reader with a sense of comfort and stability.

Newspapers use common markers to identify separate sections, while some magazines use a consistent font for headlines and text. Websites use the presence of common elements, such as the banner at the top of each page, a standard set of navigational elements and a standard color palette, to help establish consistency across the site.

You should also consider using a common set of fonts, backgrounds and headlines. The more you use those elements in the same manner, the less attention you will draw to them, leaving your readers better able to focus on your content. In addition, you will help your readers sense the cohesion of the publication.

DESIGN CONSIDERATIONS FOR COLOR AND BACKGROUND

Your audience should determine which colors you use for your site. Jennifer Kyrnin, a web design expert, notes that several factors are important when considering color choices[1]:

Culture: Kyrnin says colors contain cultural meanings. In some parts of the world, white is the color worn for funerals, while in other places, it is the color of weddings. Red can be seen as lucky or triumphant or as dangerous and angry. As you put your publication together, you need to be aware of these differences and even more subtle ones as well. For example, if you were building promotional material for the U.S. Olympic team, the use of red and blue, two of the colors on the country's flag, would be a logical choice. However, if you were building a website for fans of the University of Missouri, red and blue would be horrible choices, because they are the colors of the University of Kansas, a bitter rival.

Age: Brilliant and splashy colors often appeal to children, but adults prefer calmer colors and tones. If you want to appeal to kids, bright reds and neon blues make sense. If you want to appeal to their parents, you need to take a more muted approach.

Class: Publications designed for people of a working-class background should contain common colors, Kyrnin says. Although upper-class people enjoy obscure hues, those in the middle class prefer colors they can identify easily. If you are working on a website for unionized factory workers, you should keep this principle in mind and rely on standard tones. If you want to entice doctors and scholars with your publication, you will want to look for a more intricate color palette.

Gender: Despite efforts to create gender-neutral patterns, some stereotypes die hard. Boys are blue, girls are pink. Kyrnin also explains that men tend to prefer cooler colors, such as blue or green, while women like warmer shades of pink and orange. In pitching football garb to women, NFL marketers latched on to this idea and produced player jerseys in pink. They became an instant hit.

If you are trying to sell an extreme wilderness vacation to Harley-riding male bikers, pink might not be your best choice. Conversely, using funeral colors to sell parents on a daycare program will likely cause problems as well. Although too much gender association with color can become a detriment or be seen as pandering to a stereotype, you should consider this issue when you develop your design approach and your color palette.

Trends: As fashion goes through trends, so do designs. If you flip through a bound volume of old newspapers, you will notice the stylistic changes in the photos and fonts over time. Although you shouldn't redesign your publication every week to match trends in colors, you should keep an eye on those trends. You don't want to look dated or stale.

Beyond those concerns, you will also want to ask these questions:

Is the background distracting? A burn, in which a photo, a color or some other visual element is faded into the background, has long been a tradition in print media. When done well, it can be helpful in conveying meaning and improving the readers' overall experience. When done poorly, it can make for a difficult reading experience. For example, your team's mascot or a school logo can be a valuable element, but dropping several hundred of them underneath your text as a background can give your readers fits.

Does it make sense? Color choices and image choices can lead to what we call "shiny object syndrome." Just as bright lures can attract fish, something that "looks cool" can draw the attention of a reader. Before you let a giant photo of a muscle car or the image of an oil painting serve as the background for your website, consider whether it makes sense to do so. The same thing needs to apply with colors. A metallic purple with a high-gloss finish might look incredible on a fully restored 1969 Ford Mustang, but it might look horrible in a magazine or on your website.

HELPFUL HINTS
COLOR THEORY

Color theory involves the ways in which certain hues and shades work well together while others tend to clash. The theory is more than 500 years old, but is often traced to Isaac Newton in the 17th century, when he presented his thoughts regarding color usage and presence.

The discussions on this theory revolved around the concept of three primary colors (red, blue and yellow) and the variations that could be derived from mixing them. Although it is interesting, much of what the founding fathers of color theory discovered goes beyond the scope of this book. However, some aspects of color theory can be enlightening and helpful to you in selecting colors.

The theory uses a color wheel that shows the primary, secondary and tertiary colors. If you wish to select colors that work well together, you want to pick colors that are in harmony. Visually speaking, harmony is something that creates order, balance and pleasure for the eye. You can pick harmonious pairings in a few easy ways:

- *Analogous colors:* Any three colors that are side by side on a 12-part color wheel exist in harmony. In this approach, the colors are similar enough to work together but different enough to show contrast. The use of analogous color is simple and effective in creating a color scheme for your site.

- *Complementary colors:* Any two colors that are opposite each other on the color wheel work in a complementary fashion. These colors can create contrast and stability within your color scheme. Complementary colors provide your readers with a palette that is easy on the eyes and that works well to help convey meaning and value.

- *Natural colors:* Nature has a way of creating things of beauty. Flowers, trees, rocks and other natural formations provide aesthetic value and pleasant viewing experiences. If you examine the occurrences of color in nature, you can find opportunities to create unusual and yet beautiful color pairings.

- *Context colors:* Some colors will always look bright, while others will always look muted. However, when you pair them in certain ways, context becomes a factor. A light gray will show up well on a black background but disappear on a white background. Bright orange can be easy or hard to read depending on whether it is in the foreground or background and what other colors are associated with it.

Are the elements complementary? Design is about using all of the elements together to create a comprehensive experience. If one piece is out of tune, the whole thing can fall apart. Color is one of the first places to look for harmony or disharmony. Some people have a natural eye for color connectivity, and others have difficulty matching a pair of socks. Behind the issue of color choices is the concept of color theory (the Helpful Hints box). If you examine the aspects of color theory as you select your colors, you will have improved color pairings.

Am I adequately using negative space? As Kim Golombisky and Rebecca Hagen note in the title of their design book, white space is not your enemy.[2] The authors argue that in many cases white space (or negative space) is an integral part of design. Amateur designers tend to fear empty space and thus cram every spot on the page full of material. Negative space can allow pieces to breathe. Text that has adequate white space around it is more readable, and photos can be easier to see when they aren't stuffed one on top of the other. If you don't have enough negative space on your page, your design will feel cramped and cluttered. Conversely, you can't have huge gaps of space between lines of text, so you will need to strike a balance between too much and not enough space on the page. Usability should remain your guide in this endeavor.

TYPE

Although type can serve as a visual element and an attention grabber, its primary aim is to convey information. Your font selections should help your users read the material easily and should match the tone of the content.

Font Selection

In picking fonts, you need to understand the underlying value of each kind of font. For example, a script font has an elegance and a delicate feel to it. However, it is difficult to read at a small size, and it can cause problems in large blocks of type.

Laura Franz, a design expert and a faculty member at the University of Massachusetts–Dartmouth, says good print fonts don't always make for good web fonts. Although the printed page deals well with most serifs, some smaller or more strident serifs can lead to readability problems on the screen.

When considering a body copy font, Franz suggests that you consider the following things:

- It should have a generous x-height.

- It should have a generous aperture.

- It should have generous letter spacing.

- It shouldn't have thin strokes that can get lost.

Many experts say sans serif fonts tend to work well on screen, but more robust serif fonts can also work well. The trick in understanding whether you should or shouldn't use a font comes down to reading it. If you can't read large blocks of the text without struggling, you should consider a different text font.

Font Size

Not all fonts are created equal when it comes to size. This is important to remember as you pick headline sizes and copy sizes. Your goal is to make the readers' experiences as user friendly as possible. If you pick both a good font and a good size for that font, you are moving in the right direction.

Traditional newspaper fonts tend to be anywhere from 8.5 to 10.5 points, with the understanding that 1 point is 1/72 of an inch. On the web, many body fonts are 12 or 13 points. Specialty publications vary their use of font size and font selection on the basis of audience needs or aesthetic choices.

A good way to determine if you have picked a good font is to read a large block of it on the medium in which you plan to produce it. If you can't read it without getting tired eyes or if the font doesn't look clear, try making it a point or two larger. If that doesn't help, reconsider your font choice.

In print, headlines are much larger than the body copy. The common rule for print headlines is: the more important the story, the larger the headline. In editing for the web, the point size of the headline will remain the same from story to story. The reason is twofold.

First, the headline has to say more because you are planning for search engine optimization. SEO doesn't care how big the font size is on your headlines. It only cares about what the headline says. To improve the optimization, you will write longer headlines.

HELPFUL HINTS
TYPE TERMS

Aperture: The open space within certain letters, such as the middle of "c" or "u."

Cap line

ABC

Cap line: The imaginary line where the tops of uppercase letters reach for a given font.

Baseline: The imaginary line where the base of your texts sits. From there, letters can grow up (such as with an "l") or down (such as with a "j").

bhkdd Ascender

Ascender: A vertical line of a letter that extends above the x-height. The word "height" has three ascenders in it.

Descender

Descender: The parts of some lowercase letters that extend below the baseline. The word "jelly" has two descenders and the word "giggly" has four. The letters "j" and "g" and "y" all fit this definition, even though the part extending below the line looks different in each case.

x-height: The distance between the baseline of the text and the tops of most lowercase letters. Traditionally, the letter "x" serves as the best indicator of the x-height, thus the name of this term.

taxidermy

x-line: The imaginary line marking the top of the x-height.

Serif

Serif: A small stroke added to the edges of letters, which can aid in readability in some media. This term also describes a font family that uses these lines.

Sans Serif   no serifs

Sans serif: A font that does not use small lines at the end of each letter. These have been valuable in traditional media headlines and body copy on the web.

Second, on the web, screaming headlines tend to repel readers. A giant, screaming headline on a website will look cheap and gimmicky. Well-written headlines of a modest size (perhaps two to three times the size of your body copy) will do the job.

Font Color/Contrast

Black text on a white background remains the standard for readability. It is not only what people have gotten used to over the years, but it is also a perfect study in contrast. Conversely, black on a navy blue background would result in minimal contrast and decrease the readability.

VIEW FROM A PRO
KYLE ELLIS

Courtesy of Kyle Ellis

An expert designer across multiple media platforms and a board member of the Society for News Design, Kyle Ellis credits his design acumen to his first job: weekend feature designer for the New York Post.

"The New York Post often gets criticized for its brash tone, but I think it does a tremendous job of reflecting the voice of its audience," he said. "That made it a really special place to cut my teeth as a young professional. I'm certain my time there made me a better designer — no matter how many devil horns I Photoshopped onto celebrity heads — because my art director instilled in me an attention to detail that has trickled down to every aspect of my work even today."

Ellis has served the design community in a variety of capacities. He spent time as the lead designer at the Las Vegas Sun and a digital designer for CNN, while also delivering sessions to industry conferences and mentoring design students at various universities through the United States.

In his current job, he is a product manager at American City Business Journals in Charlotte, North Carolina, where he works at the intersection of design/technology, business strategy and editorial content. His role is to come up with ideas that advance corporate business goals and then work with a variety of different teams, including editorial, design, engineering and revenue teams to make these goals a reality.

In each of his positions, he said he had worked to emphasize the importance of design as a key element in content provision.

"Designers — and especially news designers — aren't just artists or decorators," he said. "They are critical thinkers, fierce reader advocates, and ruthless editors. The most compelling and the most successful modern news organizations often have designers in top leadership roles and allow them to be involved in every aspect of the content-creation or product-creation process.

"As the world continues to be increasingly digital and increasingly visual, designers are critically important to ensuring the right content is distributed to the right people in the right way at the right time."

As editors and designers collaborate to construct pages for newspapers, magazines, newsletters, press releases or websites, Ellis said they should keep the audience's needs in mind and focus on storytelling.

"Strong editorial design should advance content and storytelling," he said. "The best designers are often fierce editors; they are ruthless about the decisions they make regarding the use of color, typography, photography/illustration, and how those elements play on the screen or on the page."

Ellis said that he often asks himself or his designers two basic questions in relation to the quality of the design: "Does the design make it easier for the reader to understand the story?" and "Does the design treatment reflect the tone of the content?"

Although the way in which people consume content has changed over time, the principles of design remain crucial for editors to understand, Ellis said.

"Whether you're talking about the interior design of a house or the front-page design of a newspaper, the fundamentals of what make something 'well designed' are almost universally the same: Balance, contrast, dominance, movement, proportion, repetition, unity . . . ," he said. "As technology continues to change the way we consume content, we will continue to need designers that deeply understand the implications of how that technology will shape the way we tell stories and the way we distribute those stories."

Contrast isn't the only thing to consider in choosing a font color. Although black on white reads well, white on black can be hard on the eyes. Even if your school colors are yellow and blue, that doesn't make them a good font/background pairing.

In selecting a font color other than black, consider the following things:

- Is this easy to read?
- Does it stand out well enough from the background?
- Could this be confusing to the readers?

PHOTOS, GRAPHICS AND OTHER VISUALS

Previous chapters deal with the specifics of these elements, so there won't be a lot of repetition here. Instead, this section will talk about how to use the images as part of your design.

Many of the rules for images apply universally among media outlets and platforms. The images must add value to the story. They must engage your readers. They must be of an appropriate size when considering the content of the photo. Graphics must include a headline, chatter and clear visual cues to help the reader understand the purpose of piece.

In terms of design, rules regarding the placement and usage of images also apply across these media and platforms. Each page requires a dominant element to anchor the overall design. The images should not make it difficult for the reader to continue reading the story. Images that impede the text are said to force readers to make a "**blind leap**" from one part of the text to the other in order to keep reading. When designing your page or spread, make sure the text remains one fluid piece.

However, some issues regarding technical needs and other aspects of design differ from platform to platform and should be considered.

Image Quality

In order to reproduce properly, photos and graphics need to be at a much higher resolution for traditional media than they do for the web. A glossy magazine requires 300 dots per inch (**dpi**) to give it a smooth and clear look. Newspapers can produce at that level as well, although, depending on the quality of the ink and newsprint, some presses will work better with 200-dpi images. On the web, the resolution on your monitor peaks at about 72 dpi, so saving files at larger sizes with higher resolutions makes little sense. If you save at higher resolutions, you just make the file bigger and thus force the computer to work harder and slower as it loads the file.

Pixels

In many fields, measures are clearly defined. A foot is 12 inches, a centimeter is 10 millimeters and so forth. However, computer monitors vary in terms of measurements, leading to some difficulty for web designers. Although traditional media tends to measure at dots per inch, web images are measured in pixels. A **pixel** is defined as the smallest part of an image that a monitor can control.

Within that definition, size is not mentioned because pixels don't have a size. The monitors upon which the images are displayed will be set to certain resolutions. The combination of the resolution and the monitor size will determine to what degree your images look better or worse.

Image Hierarchy

In print design, you can use multiple images to help tell your story, but a few factors limit your efforts. First, the printed page has space constraints. A page is only so big, so the more space you give to one photo, the less space you give to other things on that page. Second, and more important for this discussion, you must keep **image hierarchy** in mind. This term describes the way you should make secondary photos smaller than the primary image on the page. If the photos are the same size, they compete for your readers' attention and thus make it difficult for them to determine which photo is most important.

On the web, image carousels and slide shows do not force you to choose between primary and secondary elements. All of the photos can and should be the same size. You can change the type of shot from a long to a medium or from a medium to a close-up, but if you change the dimensions of the photos, each image that loads will alter the size of the frame and create a visual "hiccup." Keep the canvas of your shots the same size, even if you have to create a "letterbox" style border around them. However, on the web you don't have to worry about the hierarchy of the images.

HELPFUL HINTS
GESTALT PRINCIPLES

Gestalt is a set of principles in visual perception that attempts to help explain why the eye sees certain things the way it does. German psychologists in the 1920s developed this approach to explain how people saw disparate objects as a unified whole. Understanding how this works can benefit you as you create content that moves the readers' eyes in specific directions or in certain ways.

Below is the list of principles and how they work:

Similarity: This principle explains how people can view objects that are not together but similar as part of a larger image. This similarity can be used via shapes, colors or other items that demonstrate a repetition of pattern. The eye groups images that share common characteristics.

Notice how the triangles form both a bird's head and a sunburst halo around it. These items are nothing more than a series of smaller shapes, but when viewed as similar items, they are seen as a collective and tell a different visual story.

Jayce-s-Yesta Graphic Design Inspiration

Continuation: This principle describes the way in which the eye is drawn to move through an object or set of objects because of the way an object is structured. Lines, curves and other smooth flowing aspects of design can lead the eye to move from point to point seamlessly.

Although similarity suggests that the eye will view these dots as a constant line, continuation dictates that the eye will follow the curved line, even as the dots change color at the point of intersection. Lines that indicate motion and direction will help guide the eye through a design. Use objects that relate to this principle when you want to provide direction or movement.

Closure: When the eye sees two shapes that are placed close together and indicate a complete figure, the eye will "imagine" the connection across that open space. In other words, the eye will create closure.

These two images demonstrate the closure principle. In looking at the first picture, the eye can envision a triangle instead of only seeing three "Pac-Man"-style images. Even though the lines do not fully form the triangle, the eye sees enough of the image and thus closes the gap and creates the lines.

The same thing is true of the circle image, in that the eye can see the complete circle, despite the breaks along the perimeter of the shape. Instead of seeing several disparate curved lines, the eye completes the circle through the use of closure.

Proximity: When images are closely aligned, the eye tends to see them as a collective. The proximity principle states that the closer things are to one another, the more likely this will occur.

In this image, the eye will view the shapes as being ten separate squares because they are not ordered in any logical fashion, and they are far apart from one another.

Conversely, the squares in this image are likely to be viewed as part of a larger whole. Even though the nine squares are clearly delineated, the eye tends to see the grouping as one large square.

Figure and ground: The eye will distinguish the foreground image from the background upon which it rests. You have probably experienced this with a number of child's games in which you are asked to see one of two things, such as a picture of

(Continued)

(Continued)

Pixabay/ElisaRiva

an old woman or a picture of a young woman. In other cases, shapes are used to distinguish the demarcation between foreground and background.

This popular visual trick is based on the principle of figure and ground. When you look at the white space in this image, you see a vase or a chalice. When you study the black parts, you see two faces. By creating balance between foreground and background, you can create a visual presence on your site that allows the reader to better engage your visuals.

You might not use these principles each time you design, but it is important to understand how they work. In ensuring you make proper use of space, balance and symmetry according to the principles of gestalt, you will have a much more visually pleasing publication.

CREATING YOUR PAGES

Once you feel you have a handle on the principles involving the elements above and how they will play into your overall approach to design, you are ready to begin building your pages. Just as writing takes time to construct, edit, revise, polish and complete, design will also require patience and a willingness to tweak things. Your efforts will not be perfect on the first try.

Sketch Out the Basics

Before you sit down at the keyboard and start punching down photos and text blocks, grab a couple of sheets of paper and a pencil and sketch out the basics of your design.

In "White Space Is Not Your Enemy," Golombisky and Hagen argue that no perfect solution exists for any design project. The best way to figure out what works best is to create a rough sketch of the layout. These sketches don't need to be the "Mona Lisa." They can be simple doodles that help provide you with a sense of balance and proportion. They can also help you figure out what elements you have, which ones need to be placed in which spots, how big you need to make certain things and how the pieces will fit together.

Print is a linear medium, and you can direct people from spot to spot using things such as **jump lines** (e.g., "See 'FIRE' on page A3") or refers (e.g., a stand-alone photo with a caption that notes, "For the full story, see B1 in Sports"). The web, however, is a nonlinear medium, meaning that people have more choices in how they navigate a site and where they go. You have no guarantee that people will start at your home page when they land on your site. This means that you need to consider all of the places where they might first engage your site and where they might go from there.

When it comes to page design, you want to think about the elements the way you might think about bricks and mortar. Photos and graphics serve as bricks. They are solid elements that help anchor a page. You can change their size and their proportions, but they remain solid. In other words, you can't weave them in and out of spaces or split them in half.

Text serves as the mortar. It can flow around your visuals and help bring continuity to the page. You will need to use text in smaller columns, more fluid ways and to help the readers move down the page as they consume information. You can have the text weave around the images, or you can create a single block of text. However, it is more malleable than your visual elements.

Sketching out your ideas on the basis of the elements you have will allow you to see whether those ideas will create a good or bad set of pages. For example, if you decide to run a giant photo

HELPFUL HINTS
DESIGN DISASTERS TO AVOID

Below is a list of things you should avoid when you design your pages:

Dead Art

Visuals are important because they bring order to a page, anchor key stories and aid in hierarchy throughout the site. They also help tell stories, communicate emotion and give readers a chance to more fully experience the site. However, not all art is good for your layout.

Photos that don't do anything are boring and pointless (as you may recall from Chapter 9) and can lead to bad design as well. A giant picture of a building, a grassy field or an empty intersection does little to advance the story-telling or help anchor the page. Art should be alive with action and reaction. Art that fails to do this is known as **dead art**.

Connect with your photographers before they shoot something to make clear what you need and want in an image. If they return with only dead art, consider designing your site without it. You could also look for a suitable graphic or other visual to plug the hole. In any case, you need to avoid dead art whenever possible.

Cramped Pages

When designers are afraid their pages look too sparse, their first instinct is to jam them full of as many things as possible. This can lead to a busy background, overuse of photos and tight text. It can also lead to a really unpleasant experience for the readers.

Much like a fine wine, a page needs to breathe. Leave ample space for margins around your text. If you are dividing text into columns, make sure that you have enough space to separate the columns so that your readers don't view three columns as one big chunk of text.

When you piece your pages together, make sure you have adequate space between images. Also make sure that you leave space between text blocks and headlines and even in between lines of text. The goal is to ensure the information on your page is easy to consume. If everything is stuffed together, your readers will get a headache reading your site.

Unreadable Copy

Designers often feel the need to "jazz up" their text and their pages through the use of unusual fonts or text that wraps around the curves of an image. Nothing is wrong with flair and imagination, but content is king. Design is meant to augment and display content in an effective and clear fashion. Text that suffers because of design decisions does no one any good.

When approaching your copy, keep simplicity in mind. The simpler the font and the simpler the copy block, the easier it will be for your audience members to read the material. If the text is unreadable, you have failed as an editor.

at the top of every page, that's fine if you have good art. However, if you have no photo staff and your photos tend to be of buildings or clip art, you might want to rethink your approach.

Sketching out how the text will pour onto the page will also be helpful. If the text weaves through your visuals like a downhill slalom skier, you will likely annoy your readers. Conversely, a giant block of text that is too wide and displays with a jagged-looking right edge also won't make for a quality read. Understanding how to place your elements on the page will improve the likelihood that you will create a visually pleasing page that tells a coherent story.

Use Modular Design

Prior to the introduction of desktop publishing for printed material, text almost always ran down long narrow columns. Headlines overlapped or slid under parts of other stories. Text column lengths were uneven and often forced to fit. Photos and stories tended to be near each other, but packaging was difficult because of the way in which the pieces had to be put together by hand.

As desktop publishing programs became more common in newsrooms, designers received more freedom to lay out pages and use design as a storytelling tool. In that time period, the concept of modular design became more popular, and it remains the norm for traditional media today. As many web designers got their start in print, the conventions of modular design have carried over into online publishing.

The **modular design** approach requires designers to construct their elements in rectangular shapes. The text can be read in multiple columns, but those columns are all of even length. The photo serves as a rectangle, and the headline can help bridge across the photo and the text or serve as a piece that sits between the photo and the text. Here are a few simple examples:

Example of modular design that highlights a photo.

LIZ GRANBERG/ADVANCE-TITAN

Senior Stacie Jenkins performs on the balance beam during the Titans' close victory over Eau Claire on Saturday in Oshkosh. Jenkins took first place in the all-around competition earning her WIAC Gymnast of the Week honors.

Jenkins all-around effort vaults UWO to victory over Eau Claire

by Zachariah Cook

cookz14@uwosh.edu

Kolf Sports Center was the host for the gymnastics meet as UW Oshkosh came away with a narrow victory over fellow conference member UW-Eau Claire, 181.575 to 181.550 this past weekend.

Former UW Oshkosh gymnast, now head coach, Lauren (Mareno) Karnitz was encouraged by her team's performance at its home meet.

"It was great to see their confidence displayed through their gymnastics even when someone fell," Karnitz said. "I have so much pride in this school and faith in this program."

Senior All-American Stacie Jenkins won the all-around award with a score of 37.025, competing in four events. She can tell the morale of the team is positive as they continue to progress through their season.

"Our confidence is up from the win we just had," Jenkins said. "We need to show that to the judges in order to receive the scores we need."

Freshman Khrystyna Lychagina led the Titans in the win over team totals for beam with a second place score of 9.375 followed by senior teammates Jenkins (9.350) and Paula Delsart (9.275) to round out the top four.

Sophomore Abby Zubella added to Oshkosh's advantage in the floor exercise routines, winning the event with a score of 9.525.

With successful experience as a former competitor from her coach, Jenkins is eager to compete for the rest of the season.

"We have improved every season and I know we will continue to get better," Jenkins said. "Coach Karnitz is very determined to make us the best we can be and will push us to make it to Nationals as a team."

The Titans will travel to St. Paul, Minn. to partake in the Piper Invitational on Feb. 27 scheduled to begin at 1 p.m.

Advance-Titan, University of Wisconsin Oshkosh, "Jenkins all-around effort vaults UWO to victory over Eau Claire" by Zachariah Cook.

As you can see in this case, the design follows the standard photo-caption-headline-text format in terms of hierarchy. The pieces are all rectangular and create a solid block of space on the page.

In this case, you can see how the package incorporates multiple elements, each of which fits the rectangle style. The headline strips across the entire package, which includes the first story and the photo. The story on the left is one long column of text and is clearly a rectangle. The story below the photo is also rectangular as it runs across three columns of space. The "refer" box serves as a rectangle as well, offering options for people to see more news inside the paper.

Example of a modular design that highlights a heading.

BILL MOVES FORWARD

UWO union condemns attack on collective bargaining

by Ryne Eberle

eberlr60@uwosh.edu

The senate's surprise passage of the amended version of the governor's budget repair bill Wednesday night has sparked reactions from academic and classified staff at UW Oshkosh.

Paulette Feld, president of the American Federation of State, County and Municipal Employees 579, said Wednesday night's events overstepped boundaries.

"The reaction is that they've overreached and that they're taking advantage of rules and not following open meetings laws," she said. "They're creating a situation where they're going to get bigger protests and louder protests."

Feld also said this is an issue that won't go away even if the amended version is voted through on Thursday.

"It's not going to end tonight," she said. "This is something that will keep going."

Union employee Rob Deere said the passage is a violation and affects not only union workers, but entire economic classes.

"This is bigger than just union and non-union," he said. "It cuts out programs that help out the middle and lower class."

Like many union workers, Deere's father was in a union and it has always been a part of his life.

"It feels like a punch in the gut for me," Deere said. "My dad was in a union the whole time I was growing up. I feel like it's in my blood."

Since a union affiliation has been so important to Deere over the course of his life, he says it's important to fight for what he believes in.

"I think it's a time to stand up and fight back," he said. "For anyone who wasn't involved in politics before, it's a good time to get involved now."

Deere also said the increase in

PASSAGE, PAGE A3

CHRIS STEINERT/ADVANCE-TITAN

Protesters gather in downtown Oshkosh Thursday, March 3 to rally against Gov. Scott Walker's propsed budget repair bill.

Forum attendees worry about Oshkosh's future

by Anna Coenen

coenea38@uwosh.edu

Open forums about the budget repair bill were held at UW Oshkosh Tuesday as an opportunity for the campus community to be updated on the situation.

One of the four forums was focused on addressing students' concerns about how the bill will affect them.

Gov. Walker's proposed solution to the $14.8 million 2011-2013 biennial budget shortfall includes a 5.5 percent increase in tuition, which would have a direct effect on UW students.

The Oshkosh Student Association passed a resolution on Monday to address the proposed 2011-2013 biennial budget.

According to OSA resolution 10-020, the organization "supports that the entire University of Wisconsin System be granted

public authority status as a measure to cut costs, increase efficiency and educational quality and access" and stands against the proposal to grant public authority status to UW Madison alone.

Jeci Casperson, speaker of the OSA assembly, said that many students are concerned about whether granting UW Madison public status will negatively affect other UW schools.

"A lot of people say it as it was going to hurt the other 25 schools," Casperson said, "and some say it is an opportunity for their school to become the new flagship school."

OSA reps questioned whether sending a resolution would make an impact on the budget proposal, to which Petra Roter, vice chancellor for student affairs, said any opportunity to

voice concern should be taken.

Among those voicing their concern for the budget proposal are Oshkosh professors, many of whom have gone to Madison to participate in protests. Rocio Becerra, a geology student,said she thinks the absence of her instructors is appropriate.

"They're human," Becerra said. "Their jobs are at risk. Their income, their families."

Jessica Lauretic, a nursing major, said she relied on her professors as a source of information regarding the budget bill and how it might affect students like herself after graduation.

"This bill... has really made me realize how much harder my job is gonna be every day and how much I will be at risk when I graduate and get a job," Melinda Wulf, a nursing major, said.

STUDENTS, PAGE A2

More Inside...

- UW Oshkosh starts "Save My UW" Campaign to protest UW Madison split from system. See page A3.

- Staff editorial: nursing and education majors are among those impacted by budget repair bill. See page A5.

Advance-Titan, University of Wisconsin Oshkosh, "Bill moves forward: UWO union condemns attack on collective bargaining" by Ryne Eberle; "Forum attendees worry about Oshkosh's future" by Anna Coenen.

Counseling center introduces therapy dog

by Erin Clark

clarke10@uwosh.edu

This semester the Counseling Center at UW Oshkosh became the first university in the state to bring a therapy dog on to join its team.

Only seven other universities in the country have a therapy animal on staff. No other school in Wisconsin does, though Madison has animal assisted activities, which are very different from animal therapy.

Twice a week the boxer named Sherman is in the office and he, along with his trainer and owner Kim Charniak, a clinical social worker at the Counseling Center, meet with clients who struggle with anxiety, depression, grief, loss, trauma and social interaction.

"Students, faculty and staff have all responded very well to Sherman," Charniak said. "He is only in the office on Wednesdays and Fridays, but he has a full case load every day that he's here."

The idea of a therapy dog never occurred to Charniak until 2007 when she adopted Sherman. She adopted him from Green Acres Boxer Rescue, which is the only boxer rescue in the state. He was 18 months old, but still had to undergo puppy training.

After only a short time in puppy training and then obedience schools, Charniak was told by countless vets and trainers that Sherman had the characteristics of a therapy dog; he was very patient and highly intelligent.

"I began doing my research and found that a therapy dog could really benefit the University," Charniak said.

After doing extensive research on the subject, Charniak wrote a proposal for her boss Joe Abhold, the Counseling Center director. After reviewing the proposal, he passed it on to Vice-Chancellor of Student Affairs Petra Roter and Chancellor Richard Wells, who approved it.

"When Kim first brought the proposal to me, I thought it was a great idea," Abhold said. "I knew it was something students would love and respond well to. We are always looking for another way to help our students and this would serve that goal well."

Though Abhold said he never had any experience or knowledge of animal therapy before Sherman, he did research the topic after receiving the proposal so he could find the best way to run the program.

Though he has only been a therapy dog for a couple of months, Sherman has been preparing to be one for years. He had to go through three levels of obedience training, good canine citizen training and therapy dog training. He then had to undergo an assess-

THERAPY DOG, PAGE A2

EMILY JENS/ADVANCE-TITAN

UW Oshkosh Counseling Center therapy dog Sherman helps patients deal with conditions such as anxiety and depression.

Advance-Titan, University of Wisconsin Oshkosh, "Counseling center introduces therapy dog" by Erin Clark.

With a package that doesn't have a dominant visual element, you can use modular design to package the elements. The small photo of the dog is incorporated through the use of a headline. The package is two rectangles with a headline that connects them.

You will notice a great number of similarities between print and web design in terms of modular design. Most sites have a traditional banner, similar to the flag on the front of a printed page. The primary package on the page dominates a good chunk of space and usually includes a visual, a strong headline, a caption and some text. Sidebar elements, such as additional links to stories or photo and video galleries, are also presented in a modular format.

Although modular design isn't always used, it is a good, clean and simple way to organize your page and give readers a style with which they are familiar.

THE BIG THREE

Here are the three key things you should take away from this chapter:

1. **Design matters:** The ability to reach your readers effectively often comes down to how pleasing the content is to their eyes and how easily they can access the content they want. This is why design matters a great deal to you as an editor and should be considered on par with all other forms of content you use. If you ignore design or consider it nothing but "making things pretty," you will undermine your ability to reach your audience.

2. **Use elements appropriately to best serve your readers:** Just as you aren't writing for yourself as a reporter, you aren't designing for yourself as an editor. You need to understand your audience's needs and interests when you select visuals, apply colors and place elements on your pages. You should know your audience well enough to serve it appropriately through these choices. Focus on your readers' needs.

3. **Rely on basic design principles:** As Kyle Ellis noted, balance, simplicity, clarity and other basic design elements will anchor your work appropriately and make it valuable to your readers. Consider each principle in turn as you construct your pages and present them to your readers. This will make your work cleaner, clearer and more helpful for the audience.

KEY TERMS

blind leap 154

dead art 157

dpi 154

image hierarchy 154

jump line 156

modular design 158

pixel 154

DISCUSSION QUESTIONS

1. How important is the quality of design for you in terms of your ability to consume and enjoy content in multiple forms of media? How often do you notice design elements, such as type, modular design and color choices? Is it the best or worst uses of these items that draw your attention?

2. To what degree do you agree or disagree with the statement "Design is content and content is king" in terms of media layouts? Why do you feel this way?

3. Have you ever experienced media that used any of the key aspects of Gestalt outlined in this chapter? What do you remember about these experiences, and how interesting was the content as a result of the use of these principles?

WRITE NOW!

1. Select a print product and a website on the same topic and compare the design approaches they take to displaying the content. Include an analysis of color, image hierarchy and overall structure. What elements are congruent between the two sites, and which ones are platform-specific? What could be done to distinguish the two media outlets, and how could each better serve its readers?

2. Select a publication or website intended for children, one intended for teens, one intended for adults and one intended for senior citizens. Compare their use of fonts, color and layout on the basis of the principles outlined in the chapter. If you select websites, include the aspect of interactivity in your analysis.

3. Select several pieces of copy and visuals from any site or publication you enjoy and sketch out a traditional media product (newspaper layout, magazine spread, brochure etc.) using that material. If you have access to design software, refine your basic sketches as you create your piece digitally.

Visit **edge.sagepub.com/filakediting** to help you accomplish your coursework goals in an easy-to-use learning environment.

12 EDITING FOR NEWS

Editing traditionally rested in the realm of news, with the term "editor" relating primarily to the person who assigned stories, revised writing and published content. Old movies often portrayed the individual as a cigar-chomping tyrant who always seemed to know everything.

These days, editors no longer fit that mold, in terms of both the stereotype and the field. Editing has purpose and value in all forms of disseminated content, so editors are just as likely to be situated in a public relations firm or an advertising agency as they are in a newsroom. Over the next few chapters, we will walk through some of the various areas in which editing can occur.

In this chapter, we examine the traditional role of editors as news-based journalists. Much of what we have already discussed in the book will apply directly to editing for news, including issues of audience-centric thinking, management tasks and the various levels of editing. Rather than repeat this information here, this chapter will look at some of the areas specifically germane to the job of a news editor, including the selection of content, the various types of stories that constitute news coverage and the ways in which news editing differs from other areas we will discuss in later chapters.

IMPORTANT EDITING ISSUES RELATED TO NEWS

All editors aspire to keep their information accurate and their content clear. This thread runs through the various disciplines that see writing and editing as crucial to their mission. Within the area of news, several key elements emerge that editors must consider as both crucial and supplemental to the standard 5W's and 1H with which all editors deal. Most of these issues stem from news journalists' aspirations to be objective in their reporting and evenhanded in their writing. Consider these concerns for news editors:

Balance

News-based journalists should do their best to avoid taking sides in their reporting and writing. The idea behind news is to provide individuals with information from the key perspectives on any given story and let the readers decide for themselves which ones they favor. This means that news reporters seek to **balance** their coverage through the provision of facts and sources that will give their readers a well-rounded look at a topic. News editors should examine all stories for balance, looking to see if all sides receive adequate representation within a story and how the writer presents that representation within the story.

For example, in a story about a city council deciding to allow a company to build a factory along the banks of a river near a residential area, a reporter can easily see a couple of perspectives on the topic. Some city council representatives may favor the plan because it will provide jobs, while others may dislike it because of potential noise and pollution issues. A good editor would push that reporter to look for additional ways to balance this topic through the use of more sources, such as an environmental expert and an economics expert, to more fully show how seriously people should weigh each of these concerns. Another suggestion from a good editor would be for the reporter to dig into previous developments this company built to see how well things worked out for those communities. Finally, asking people in that area what they think about this would help round out the story.

The issue of balance is never just about getting side A and side B, but rather showing a complete picture of a story. Editors in news must constantly think about what elements are present, which ones are missing and how to provide the most multifaceted piece possible to the readers.

Fairness

The chapter on ethics touches on a lot of the choices editors face each day when it comes to producing content and advising writers. One key area that bears further examination here is the concept of fairness.

In using the same example noted in the section on balance, consider how best to write a story on the city council and its deliberations regarding the approval of a factory's construction. Balance is about getting all the sources and sides in the piece. Fairness is about who gets how much space or where each source is placed in the story. If the lead and the first four paragraphs of the story come from the council members who want the factory and factory officials who say it's a great idea, is this story fair to the people who see the factory as an environmental hazard and an eyesore? If you flip that around and give the prime real estate in the story to the environmentalists, is that fair to the people who see this as a financial boon to the area? As an editor, you have to weigh these issues and see how best to represent positions fairly in terms of story structure and source use.

Beyond those editing choices, you also have ethical concerns regarding fairness as you choose what to publish and how to publish it. Is it fair to cover one person's drunken driving arrest, but not someone else's? Is it fair to run a profile of one mayoral candidate on the front page, but run others on the inside of the paper or deeper in the website? Some people would argue that "it depends," while others would argue for a more structured system to deal with these concerns. The ethical paradigm to which you espouse will guide you as you consider the issue of fairness in publication.

Tone

An adage often attributed to Winston Churchill holds that tact is the ability to tell someone to go to hell in such a way that the person looks forward to the trip. In other words, it's usually not what you say but how you say it that matters. This concept captures the core of tone and why it matters to your readers.

Courtesy of Amy
Fiscus

Amy Fiscus serves as the national security editor for the New York Times, where she is responsible for the paper's coverage of the intelligence agencies, the justice department and the Federal Bureau of Investigation. As such, she oversees a variety of reporters who all report on some aspect of these agencies and what they are up to.

"My mandate is to ensure that we are covering the beats aggressively, both staying ahead on news developments and delivering enterprise that surprises and enlightens readers," she said. "At the Times, we expect to set the agenda on beats, particularly in Washington, and I am lucky enough to work with talented reporters who are capable of doing so and understand that that is the expectation from the masthead editors who run the newsroom."

Fiscus' job as an editor involves a great deal of planning and coordination responsibilities, as she works to coordinate the efforts of her reporters with the needs of her bosses in New York.

"My days are divided into a few chunks," she said. "We start with a morning meeting with New York to pitch our top stories of the day. By the time that call is done, some reporters have come in to the bureau, and I check in with them about what they're working on — progress on existing stories, new tips they're chasing, help they might need to land a story — and relay requests from New York."

To make sure everything runs smoothly, Fiscus said she often spends time with her reporters before they go after a story so that everyone is on the same page. This cuts down on the length of the editing process and leads to a cleaner overall piece of copy.

"I emphasize front-loading — talking about the story well before the reporter commits a single word to the screen," she said. "What's the news? How do your sources know these facts? What's the nut graf? Could we say this thought with more sweep or authority? What else do we need to include? How can we nail down that missing information? How will we organize the story? These conversations vary by reporter, but I work with mostly veteran journalists who have been involved in countless such discussions and anticipate what we need to do to land the story."

This front-loading approach does more than make the copy flow smoothly along the editorial chain, Fiscus said, noting that her ability to communicate fairly and effectively with her reporters benefits everyone involved, including the readers.

"It saves a lot of pain and produces a stronger story for readers," she said. "When the reporter and I talk early on, the stakes are a little lower because deadline is further away, and we can have a more open and honest conversation. The most productive reporter-editor relationships are based on trust and openness, where we feel comfortable sharing half-baked ideas with each other, which often spark discussion that leads to better stories than either of us could have come up with on our own."

The readers have always mattered in her line of work, but Fiscus said the technology available to journalists today make her better able to consider the needs of the audience.

"I think about audience more than I used to, now that we have instant metrics that tell us how many people are reading a story at the moment and how much time they are spending with it," Fiscus said. "I focus a lot more on writing conversational headlines than I once did, mostly just answering the question, is this something I would click on? Should this have more readers than it does?"

In the end, however, the core of her editing philosophy could apply to any journalist at any time.

"The secret to editing is this: Put the most interesting stuff at the top," she said. "(And) have fun. God, have fun. Don't do journalism if you're not."

Publications have expanded beyond the tenets of traditional newspaper newsrooms and adherence to strict Associated Press style. Websites, blogs, social media accounts and more push the boundaries of what is and what is not acceptable for readers, in most cases doing so out of a clear understanding of their audiences. Some people would be horrified at the use of the word "hell," while others have no problem with any manner of colorful cursing in everything from a columnist's tirade to a weather report. The same is true about the use of photographs from traffic accidents and leaked celebrity nude shots.

For example, a feature from the Indianapolis Motor Speedway's website discusses the biggest fans of the sport, including those who watch the race from the infield in a feature titled, "Fanfare: Stories of the Most Loyal Indianapolis 500 Fans."[1] A similar feature on fans who frequent the race's infield comes from Deadspin, a website that pitches itself as "Sports news without access, favor or discretion." Its headline states, "Hell is real and it's the infield of the Indy 500."[2] Not only do the headlines reflect differences in tone, but so do the authors' writing styles within the piece: The speedway's website provides historical stories of race fans in a prim and proper archivist's approach, but Deadspin's look includes a number of curse words and at least one photo of a man's naked butt.

What you decide to include or not include given your understanding of decency and taste will reflect the tone you choose for your media outlet. Your audience's expectations and desires will lead to your general sense of how to approach this editing standard.

Logic

In advertising and public relations, writers have the ability to advocate through the presentation of facts and sources to make their case. In addition, they have the ability to rely on puffery, which is the use of exaggerations regarding a product whose claims cannot be proved true or false. When a company says it has "the most amazing cure for hair loss" or that it sells "the most scrumptious peanut butter ever," it relies on **puffery**, as no one can quantify terms like "most amazing" or "most scrumptious."

News editors can't rely on such approaches as they produce content and instead must rely on logic in their publication. When reporters make claims about an event being "the largest" or a tax increase being "burdensome," quality news editors will push back and demand quantification and support. What makes the event the largest of its kind? Is it the size of the grounds where it was held? Is it the money it raised? Is it the number of people who attended? Also, what makes a tax increase burdensome, and who says it burdens them? What would qualify as a nonburdensome tax increase, and who establishes that as the appropriate level for taxes?

Good editors not only consider these holes worth plugging but the solid application of logic that helps codify objective content within the publication. If you work in a news field, you can't let puffery slide.

STORY ASSIGNMENTS

As a news editor, you will work with reporters to determine what kinds of stories the publication needs to cover and how best to cover them. Your approach to this task will vary on the basis of the size of your staff, the reach of your publication and the interests of your audience. With that in mind, here are a few basic types of stories you will see as a news editor as well as some of the benefits and drawbacks associated with them:

Events

The spectacle of public events often draws the interests of readers. The surveillance need that has roots deep in human evolution gives people a desire to know what is happening around them. This leads to a "gapers' block" near the scene of an accident on the freeway or a crowd of people who gather when two students start fighting in the cafeteria. Although every bit of breaking news or public display can qualify as an event, news outlets tend to cover three forms of planned public discourse: speeches, meetings and news conferences.

Speeches

A speech gives a person the chance to talk to a group of people for a given time period on a topic that matters to the speaker and the audience. Reporters find speeches easy to cover because the person at the front of the room is speaking at a relatively normal rate of speed with the purpose of effectively communicating a well-polished message. That said, these events contain an inherent bias because the speaker discusses the topic without any responses from another source who might offer an opposing perspective. In addition, the event is tailored to the group, so it can be more of an affirming message for the group's point of view instead of a broader discussion of the topic's pros and cons.

Meetings

Cities, counties and states often use meetings to pass ordinances, resolve disputes and seek public input. Other public and private bodies also host these kinds of events for similar purposes. Meeting coverage has been the stock-in-trade of local news outlets for years, with varying levels of interest from audience members. Some publications cover meetings because "We always cover meetings." Others avoid them in an attempt to go against the grain and push reporters to think differently about their work. Regardless of your publication's editorial philosophy, meetings happen, and a lot can happen at them, so pay some attention to them.

Encourage your reporters to scour each meeting's agenda in advance of the event to see if any items merit coverage for your audience. If they can't figure out from the agenda what a board or a council is doing, they have time to reach out to some sources and get some clarity. You should also encourage the reporters to look into any previous coverage the publication did on key items so they can incorporate that background into any story they write based on the upcoming event. Meetings can be a lot like fishing: You aren't sure if you'll catch a bite or not, and if you do, it's not entirely clear if it'll be a minnow or a whopper. This is where your reporters' expertise and understanding of their coverage areas will help you decide how to cover these events.

News Conferences

Of all the events you can consider for coverage, news conferences have the highest level of boom-or-bust potential. Organizations will host these events when they think something will interest a large number of media outlets. The conferences give them the opportunity to disseminate their well-polished messages to everyone in the field at once instead of fielding dozens of calls, texts and emails on the issue. Some news conferences are can't-miss events, such as one to announce the capture of a local murder suspect or one at which it is revealed that the longtime city manager plans to retire. Other news conferences have little interest to your readers and serve only for groups or organizations to promote themselves.

Localizations

Editors who seek to meet the needs of readers must answer a simple question for them repeatedly: "How and why does this matter to me?" The use of localization stories can provide readers with a narrow focus on a broader topic. When it comes to state, national or international stories, a good editor will look for potential story ideas that have local ties. This will help the reporters find ways to attach local importance to these larger issues in a meaningful way. One note of caution: Not every story deserves a **localization**, so don't fall into the trap of trying to make North Korea's nuclear disarmament an issue for a 300-person town in Nebraska. If the story matters locally, point it out. Otherwise, let it go.

Crime and Disasters

Stories like the "Son of Sam" murders kept New Yorkers and the rest of the country riveted to the news in the late 1970s, as did coverage of the Parkland school shooting and the hurricanes that devastated Puerto Rico and the southern United States in 2017. Even simply weird crime stories, such as the arrest of a man accused of repeatedly clogging a women's public toilet with 20-ounce soda bottles,[3] can capture the attention of readers.

Crimes and disasters tap into that surveillance need as well, with people wanting to know what's going on. In some areas, a single homicide can lead to around-the-clock coverage, while in other areas, deaths of this type barely merit a few paragraphs. Aside from audience interest, these types of stories tend to rely heavily on the FOCII elements to dictate coverage.

Personality Profiles

Reporters often find people on their beats who fascinate them, leading them to write compelling **personality profiles**. The goal of a profile like this is to help your readership learn about a person through an interesting and compelling storytelling effort. Famous people, like presidents and movie stars, often lead to quality profile pieces, but so do obscure individuals who live among us, like the oldest janitor at the courthouse or the lunch worker who always wears a "Casserole Happens" button on her uniform. You should encourage your reporters to find people of all kinds who would make for interesting personality profiles.

Investigative and In-Depth Stories

Some organizations are too small for writers to have a lot of time to dig deeply into stories, while others are large enough to dedicate entire teams to investigative work. Regardless of the size of your newsroom, you should encourage your writers to look for stories that need some in-depth

HELPFUL HINTS
BEAT REPORTING

To help reporters learn a lot about a topic that matters to the readers, editors often assign them to specialized areas of coverage called beats. Readers become familiar with the bylines of specific reporters who know a **beat** well and who can provide them with important information consistently on that topic. Here is a nonexhaustive list of some beats you could assign to your reporters, on the basis of the interests of your readers and the area in which your media outlet would operate:

- Agriculture
- Business
- City government
- County government
- State government
- Crime
- Fire
- Courts

- K-12 education
- Higher education/university education
- High school sports
- College/university sports
- Science and environment
- Arts and entertainment
- Culture
- Food
- Health and fitness
- Faith and spirituality
- Features
- Labor
- Transportation

work and that can lead to important revelations. Reporters can rely on the Freedom of Information Act to seek federal records and "sunshine laws" to gather public documents at the state level. The goal here is to examine the inner workings of governmental operations and those of other public bodies. The benefit of this kind of story is that it can reveal long-term misdeeds, such as the sexual abuse scandal the Boston Globe uncovered. Investigative stories can also provide a deeper look at common issues or interests, such as what happens to the money in your student meal plan account if you don't use it all. The drawbacks to these stories include the heavy investment your staff will need to make in digging through records, transcripts and interviews to tell it. Even more, an investigative effort carries with it no guarantees that a story will emerge from the documents. In some cases, it's a lot of work for nothing.

CONTENT CONSIDERATION

As a news editor, you will need to decide how to "play" your content. In traditional media outlets, that consideration can include how much space to give a story, how close to the front of the publication the story will go and what visual elements will accompany the piece. In digital media outlets, it can include how much linking should go with the story, what other elements should go with it and how much social media promotion to use with the piece. If you work in a newsroom that maintains a presence on multiple platforms, this could include where you want to publish which pieces of the story, how to break the story and other considerations similar to those listed above. Here are a few topics to consider when it comes to how best to position and disseminate your content:

Placement

The issue of where something should go will force you to prioritize the importance of your content. As much as reporters always think their stories are the most important ones, you need to determine which pieces matter most to your readers and position them in the publication accordingly. Breaking news stories, big investigative pieces and other stories that touch on most of the FOCII interest elements will demand space at the front of the newspaper, on the cover of the magazine and on the home page of the website. Some pieces can push their way out front on the basis of other considerations, such as valuable graphics, compelling photos or a need to highlight an ongoing series of stories.

When it comes to traditional media outlets, placement considerations will also dictate how large a headline should be, how much space a story can receive and if images will have color options. Digital media platforms don't have these concerns, but stories that lack links from the front page of the site can get lost or ignored. When you decide how best to position your content, you should consider these and other issues related to reaching your readers.

Size

As discussed elsewhere in this book, the idea of size versus value should play a heavy role in determining how much space you dedicate to any storytelling element. Traditional media will force you to balance the relative importance of pieces against one another, given that space on this platform is finite. If you only have one page worth of space, you can't give each of the three stories you have a half of that page. You need to decide if the pieces have equal importance and thus should each get one-third of that space or if something is worth half of the page with the other two stories receiving portions of the remaining half. Space issues will also require editors to determine if a photo or graphic should accompany the story or how many images should package with the text on a printed page.

On digital platforms, you don't have the same problem when it comes to space, as your writers can type until their fingers fall off and they won't run out of real estate for their stories. However, you have to consider the issue of your readers' attention span and how that plays a role in story size. Experts in internet media argue that because of the diminished attention span of digital media users, writers need to cut their copy in half to keep the readers connected to the story until the end. Just because the writers write it, it doesn't follow that the readers will read it.

Platform

When you work across multiple platforms, including print, web and social media, you need to consider how and where to publish your content. In some cases, a single tweet will do the job, as in the case of alerting people about a traffic crash or announcing a game's final score. In other cases, the dynamics of the layout will demand you to produce the content only on a printed page or via an interactive web game.

During the earliest days of media convergence, when broadcast, print and online operations first merged to provide content across all platforms, journalists often resisted the idea of publishing content online first. Broadcast and print journalists saw announcing important stories via digital media as "scooping themselves" and giving competitors a chance to catch up on a story before the next newscast or newspaper. However, with the heavy shift to mobile and digital media, you don't need to worry about that issue as much anymore and instead should consider which platform does the best job of reaching your readers with the best version of your content.

HYPERLINKING

Linking isn't only available to news sites, but it is a valuable element of your storytelling as a news journalist. Editors who embrace this concept can use interactivity to its fullest potential and serve their audience well. In talking about **hyperlinking**, we need to discuss how links work, the ways in which you can use them and some of the rules to keep in mind when you link.

Basics of Hyperlinking

Editors can use hyperlinking, or linking as it is often known, to direct readers to additional information both on and off their website. When a reader clicks on a link, it transports that reader to the website that is attached to that link. It gives readers the opportunity to navigate the web as they see fit to gain more information. From an editing standpoint, links allow you to help a reader better understand a story without having to construct all the material yourself.

For example, if you were editing a story regarding the city council's approval of a tax increment financing (TIF) district, you could add a number of links to improve the story. When you first mention the TIF, you could link to an online glossary of business terms that explains how a TIF district works. Additionally, you could add a sidebar with a series of links to previous stories dealing with TIFs in the area or prior stories on this particular TIF. You could also link to data regarding how TIFs work, letters to the editor regarding this plan and the city council meeting minutes that contain information about this vote.

You can't determine to what degree readers will use all or any of these items. Some readers know what a TIF is and so they will skip the definition link. Other readers will click on the definition and then spend time surfing through that website. If this TIF story is a big deal, readers who already followed topic will probably skip the links to previous stories. People who are new to town and curious might be interested in all the background from those pieces. Even if many of these links go unused, you have provided your readers with as many opportunities as possible to be informed.

Link Types

In the TIF example, we discussed two main types of links: internal and external. Internal links keep people on your site. In the example above, the previous stories your site has hosted are internal links. You can link to those stories and people can read them, but your readers are not going away from your site.

External links send your readers to other websites. For example, if you have a story about the Humane Society and you want to include information about how people can donate money to the group, you can link to the society's website. External links are valuable because they help you tell a story but do not require you to do a lot of work. When you use an external link, you run the risk of not having your readers return to your site. If the links are better than the story, you might never get your audience back.

HELPFUL HINTS
THINKING ABOUT LINKING

Links can be a valuable part of a website, but only if an editor applies sound logic when using them. Slathering a site with links to show how interactive you are isn't a good idea. Instead, think about what it is that you want to communicate with the material that is on the other side of the click-through. Below are a few good reasons why you should use links.

Historical perspective and background: In the pre-internet days of print archives, each newsroom had a library of previous stories known as "the morgue." This room was where the news agencies kept copies of their published or "dead" stories for future use. Librarians were hired to clip out articles and place them in small folders according to the topics involved in the stories or the people named in them. When journalists needed background for a story, the librarians in the morgue would help them find these folders of brittle, yellowed newspaper clippings. Broadcast newsrooms also had tape libraries, where staff members would log and categorize film and video footage. This material was kept on hand in case it was needed for a future story, such as a 50th anniversary of a major event or the death of a public figure.

The web allows us to avoid the paper cuts and dusty tapes when we build our stories. Even more, it allows us to provide our readers with large sets of background material from previous articles. Digital files of timelines, photos, graphics and more can be linked to the current stories. Best of all, the material is already created and waiting to be used.

Clarity: Much like dictionaries and encyclopedias, some websites are built to define words or clarify concepts. As an editor, you should take advantage of those sites to better inform your readers. Just because a source or a reporter knows what something means, it doesn't necessarily follow that your readers will know what it means. Linking to terms in fields of business, medicine and government can provide clarity for your readers. When sources introduce topics or ideas that go beyond what the average reader should be expected to know, find links to sites that will help them understand these things better.

Interactivity: The web is a sharing medium, so treating it like a one-way conduit of information is counterproductive. The more opportunities you can provide your readers to share information and interact with you, the better received your site will be. These readers can then present you with additional information, ranging from factual corrections to additional news tips. In creating a conversation between you and your readers, you can benefit from increased interactivity and gain knowledge from these people.

Basic Rules for Linking

Links provide great opportunities for you to integrate interactivity and additional information into your site. This approach can be particularly helpful when you are putting together a story. Here are a few hints and tips that will help you decide how to use links to your advantage:

Have a Purpose for the Link

Just because you can link to something doesn't mean you should. Just like anything else, the more you do something, the more desensitized to it people become. If you pour links all over every inch of your copy, your audience members will be less inclined to click on those links. Make sure you see value in the links that you provide.

Make Sure Your Links Are Clear and Focused

When you highlight a few words in the middle of the story to create a link, it should be obvious where that link will take readers if they click on it. For example, if a story includes the line "The mayor released a statement on the new crime statistics," and "statement" is clickable, your readers will assume that they can click on the link and be directed to a copy of the statement, either online or as a downloadable PDF file. If you instead link to the mayor's home page or some other city website, you will mislead your readers. People will click on links if they have a sense of where they lead.

Establish a Style for Your Links

If your organization doesn't have one, try to work with some of your colleagues to create a style for links. The style is meant to establish consistency for your readers and a pattern for you and your colleagues. When looking at establishing a link style, consider some of the following questions:

- Should links be set off from the main story, written in a full sentence with a full explanation?

- Should links be a few words wherever they're needed?

- Should links all be on a sidebar, out of the way of the reader?

- How many links should be included in any one story?

- Do we need to differentiate between advertising-driven links and news links? If so, how?

- How do we handle internal versus external links?

Link to Strong Sites

You don't want to link randomly to things on the internet without making sure these sites are legitimate sources of information. Just because someone posted a piece of information somewhere online doesn't mean that you want to be associated with it. If you have good material from a good source, use it. If you can't verify the source or if the source isn't reputable, avoid linking to it.

THE BIG THREE

Here are the three key things you should take away from this chapter:

1. **News editing requires more than the basics:** Micro- and macroediting matter a great deal to editing for news, but you have additional concerns when working in this area of the field. Balance, fairness, tone and logic all matter as you attempt to remain objective in conveying content to your readers. You need to assure your audience members that you have presented them with the most thorough and well-rounded set of facts and information possible. Perfectly structured copy that fails to do this is worthless.

2. **Choose coverage wisely:** You have a variety of story types and beats from which to choose when you assemble your coverage and create your assignments. What you choose to cover and how you want your reporters to cover it will make a big difference in the quality of your publication. Don't cover meetings because "We always cover meetings." Instead, think about what your readers will want and how best to deliver it to them.

3. **Consider your platform options:** You have the ability to break news digitally, follow it up with video clips and then plan a giant spread for the printed publication. You also have the ability to do none of those things and stick to a social media stream to keep your readers informed. One of the tenets of this book is to use the right tool for the right job, so always consider your platform options when you publish content.

KEY TERMS

balance 163
beat 167
hyperlinking 169

localization 166
personality profile 167
puffery 165

sunshine laws 168

DISCUSSION QUESTIONS

1. How well do you think news outlets do at abiding by the key elements listed at the top of the chapter: balance, fairness, tone and logic? Do you see differences between certain types of news media in relation to these topics? Do the media outlets you use do a particularly good job of abiding by any one of those elements?

2. How often do you click on the links writers use to support their positions in pieces they wrote? Why do you or don't you check on the material that the writer has linked within the story?

3. Digital writers now must write on many more topics and cut the overall amount of words they write in half, given shorter attention spans of readers. Do you think this shorter approach to writing has value, or is it a case of providing only surface-level content? How do you think writers can do more with less to improve information providing while limiting their word counts?

WRITE NOW!

1. Compare and contrast the printed version of a media outlet's content with its online content. Is this content all the same, or does either version contain content not available in the other? Is the repetition you found valuable to reaching additional audiences, or is it a case of simply being lazy in your estimation? Use examples as you outline your thoughts in a short essay.

2. Select a story from an online publication that does very little hyperlinking and paste it into a digital file that allows you to link material, such as a personal blog or a class website. Then, pick through the piece and augment it with links that provide additional value and depth. Try to add a link that represents each of the types of links listed in the

chapter, but don't force the issue. Then, write a short essay on what you did and why you think it improved the piece.

3. Using your school or university as your intended audience, select between 8 and 10 potential beats you believe would have specific value to your readers. Look to balance the number of beats according to the overall importance of the beat, a wide array of interests among your readers and a sense of how you could best allocate reporting resources. Then, sketch out at least two or three stories you would expect a writer to do if he or she were assigned to this beat.

Visit **edge.sagepub.com/filakediting** to help you accomplish your coursework goals in an easy-to-use learning environment.

13 SOCIAL MEDIA

LEARNING OBJECTIVES

After completing this chapter, you should be able to:

- Understand how social media can connect you with your audience.

- Assess ways to draw, develop and cultivate a social media audience.

- Evaluate a tweet for accuracy, clarity and appropriateness.

- Compare and contrast social media and traditional media with regard to use, trust and value.

- Understand ways in which social media disasters can harm your organization and how you can avoid them.

The concept of mass media has always been a one-to-many model in which a primary source of news, such as a newspaper or television station, disseminates information to a homogeneous group of people within the reach of that medium. Audience members had few choices in the early part of the previous century. One or two newspapers often served a single area, and three or four major television networks blanketed markets within a region.

With the advent of digital technologies, more options became readily available. Cable and satellite television provided additional channels and niche-based choices, and the internet provided access to news from across the country and around the world.

Despite these changes, journalists remained in charge of content and how it was disseminated. Traditional media powers added websites to their media empires, and although some web-only sites, such as the Drudge Report and the Huffington Post, became prominent, the web did not see a great democratization of content. Journalists still produced media, and audience members still consumed it.

However, as social media tools began to emerge, editors saw their grip on content loosened and their gatekeeping function diminished. Editors have the ability to create, format and present information as they always have, but social media gives audience members more say over what will be read. Websites aggregate news stories and allow readers to determine what is important or interesting. Some sites and internet applications give readers the ability to vote for or against a story's significance, thus changing its prominence among the readers' peers. All of this is done without the editor's consent or input.

As an editor, you need to understand what makes social media work, what tools are available to you and how you can use them to your advantage. Editors remain important in this digital realm, but they have gone from gatekeepers to tour guides. Instead of determining what will and will not be published, editors now provide direction, focus and options for their readers.

This chapter will help explain what social media is, how it works and what you need to know about it as an editor. It will also include a look at how you can use social media to meet the needs of your audience and ways to develop policies that govern the use of social media in your organization.

SOCIAL MEDIA DEFINED

Social media refers to websites, tools and other digital approaches to information sharing among and within social groups. Social media are more user-friendly, scalable and adaptable to the whims of users than are traditional media.

For example, when Twitter was introduced in the mid-2000s, the service was geared toward the sharing of personal information with close friends or family members. To help facilitate this, the Twitter prompt used to inspire tweets was "What are you doing?" As Twitter became a more powerful marketing and networking tool, the company changed the prompt in November 2009 to "What's happening?" In addition, Twitter allowed interfaces from third-party applications to make sorting, searching and following tweets easier. It also augmented its listing and service functions to recognize certain characters, such as hashtags.

Social media can take a number of forms. Blogs and wikis mimic traditional formats like newspapers and encyclopedias; podcasts and video streaming share the characteristics of radio and television. Twitter serves as a digital "word-of-mouth" approach through sharing and retweeting. The magnitude of options can be daunting, but you should worry less about the tools you use and more about how effective those tools are at informing, engaging and entertaining your audience.

What helps define social media in terms of reach is that the material is shared from many people to many other people. Authority is built on the basis of trust, and individuals bestow that trust on one another. People who continue to maintain that trust will remain valuable to other members of their social media networks. Other sources of authority will replace those people who don't keep up their end of the bargain.

The best part of social media can also be the worst part of social media. It lacks definition, which means that more people can become involved and rules are often established on the fly. This is great for people who want to help shape and mold an audience, but it is tough for editors who are trying to determine what to produce and how to market it. Anyone can participate in social media, which democratizes media and allows a wider array of voices to emerge.

Social media can also change direction quickly, forcing editors to examine what they are doing and how they are doing it. As an editor, you need to keep an eye on which trends are helpful and popular and which have become old and stale. You need not follow every whim of social media, but you should not be averse to experimentation either. Stick with the core values of journalism and apply them to your social media approach, and you will see positive gains in terms of readership, audience participation and credibility.

WHY IS SOCIAL MEDIA VALUABLE?

Social media outlets have a great benefit to media professionals in all fields, as both tools to share information and ways to receive feedback from audience members. Social media gives you direct access to people who have an interest in your content, your products or your causes. In addition, the door swings both ways, allowing readers to offer reporters news tips, give PR practitioners feedback on events and show advertisers what they think of recent campaigns. Here are some of the things that make social media valuable to your audience members and thus important to you:

Access Almost Anywhere

The ability to keep in touch with potentially interested audience members at any point in space and time makes social media extremely valuable to all journalistic organizations. The ubiquity of social media means that reporters, public relations practitioners and advertising firms can keep in touch with those people on a variety of devices. The constant contact between the senders and the receivers means that habits will develop for both parties in terms of constantly sharing information.

Snowballing Audiences

In contrast to a one-to-many model, social media expands the potential number of sources of content in a many-to-many model. This means that content can be sent from a variety of sources at multiple points in time, thus improving the likelihood that people will see a message. The ability to share and reshare information can lead to the viral spread of content, much in the same way an illness can spread through a college residence hall. One person reaches a few others, and those few share the illness (or the information) with a few others each and it will continue to spread.

Transferred Trust

As noted elsewhere in the book, credibility matters a great deal to you as an editor. One of the benefits of social media is that you don't have to earn the trust of every person who sees your content. The trust will transfer from source to source as the message continues to spread over a network. In other words, if Sue trusts group A, she is likely to share information about that organization via her social media platforms. If Jack follows Sue, he probably trusts her judgment and will thus trust the information she shared. Therefore, he will likely trust whatever she shared from group A, and he might then share it with his followers. This viral pattern outlined earlier continues, with more and more people sharing information and supporting it with their own reputations.

BUILDING A SOCIAL MEDIA AUDIENCE

In the 20th century, traditional media outlets tended to be monolithic and dominant within a geographic area. Cities tended to have one or two major newspapers and three television stations. Media outlets had little trouble in conceptualizing of an audience as well as reaching the audience members effectively.

Today, it seems like the media outlets outnumber the media users. Although it is much easier to create a media outlet and reach a larger number of people, the number of voices calling out to users can leave them lost in a sea of noise. Social media requires a lot of work on your part to reach, retain and develop an audience. Here are some key tips on how best to do this from the experts at IMPACT, an award-winning inbound marketing firm[1]:

Choose Your Platform(s) Wisely

The clichéd line "If a tree falls in the woods and no one is there to hear it, does it make a sound?" applies here pretty well. Before you open an account on every possible social media platform out there, you should determine which ones your readers use and how involved they are on them. Then, you want to develop an approach to share your content in a way that meshes with their needs and wants. It doesn't make any sense to dump content everywhere in hopes your readers will eventually get it. Instead, select the platforms wisely and proceed with using them logically.

Connect Frequently With Users

Your audiences want to hear from you as much as you want to hear from them. This means that you want to let them know you're real and that you're paying attention. It never hurts to provide background information about yourself on the platforms you use or to begin dialogue with frequent users. Stay connected to people and let them know you are listening.

Make Your Content Worthwhile

Social media followers might flock to you quickly if you provide something of interest, but they can leave you just as fast. The thing that will help you develop a strong, constant audience over time is the quality of your content. If you are meeting their needs in a way they appreciate, your readers will stick around. If not, they'll look elsewhere for what they seek. IMPACT pros suggest the "70/20/10 rule," which means that 70 percent of your content should provide a direct benefit

HELPFUL HINTS
TIPS FOR TWEETING

Twitter is a microblogging phenomenon that moved from an interpersonal tool to a strong marketing and news-breaking media platform. As Twitter has continued to grow and change, the rules on how and what to post, or "tweet," have evolved as well. Although a constant stream of notifications regarding a person's breakfast, lunch and dinner plans was once the norm on Twitter, more sophisticated users, including news organizations and companies, have found ways to use tweets more effectively.

If you are responsible for sending tweets that represent your organization, here are a few helpful tips to keep in mind:

Know the Rules

As an editor, you might be responsible for tweeting as you see fit, or a dozen people might need to approve something before you send it. In some media operations, the social media policy requires you to include specific hashtags to connect your work to a larger discussion. In other areas of the field, specific brand-based terms need to be present in each tweet. If you know the rules

regarding tweets, you save yourself a lot trouble. You should know who is allowed to tweet, when tweets can be sent, who must review them first and what kinds of things can never be tweeted. If your organization doesn't have a Twitter policy, it would be good for you to help build one.

Tweet to Be Read

When **short message service (SMS)** first became available, Twitter was often used from cell phones with 12-digit keypads. This forced people who used text messaging to hunt and peck through several letters per key to type their message. This approach also led to a lot of abbreviations (OMG: oh my God; IMHO: in my humble opinion; IDK: I don't know) and the use of numbers in the place of words (2M2H: too much to handle). Now, with full QWERTY keyboards on phones and websites that allow you to tweet from a computer, typing isn't as difficult.

You get only 280 characters to make a point, but that doesn't mean you should cut corners and limit readability. If you can't fit your full thought into that tweet, look for ways to exchange longer words for shorter ones. You

(Continued)

(Continued)

can use abbreviations that others would know, but keep grammar and simplicity at the forefront of your mind.

For example, if you were an editor at a Milwaukee news outlet when a freak snowstorm caused problems at the airport and on area highways, you would tweet about it. If you write, "MKEPD, SHDPT, TSA confirm 3rw crash d/t 4I snow & MKE apt to close @ appx. 5pm; I94, 41, 45 +1h TT d/t weather crashes," you have used 109 characters that tell your readers nothing. Instead, push some of these items into a story on your website and make the tweet clearer: "Authorities say Milwaukee airport has 3 runway crashes due to snow & will close by 5pm; highways slowed by crashes too." This gives you about the same number of characters but is much clearer.

Tweet for Your Audience

Your job as an editor is to make sure your audience members get the information they need to know. You know that rule, but you might have trouble abiding by it when tweeting.

When individuals use Twitter as a personal medium, the rules are a bit different regarding tweets. If they saw a celebrity, had lunch with a friend or ran into a particularly bad traffic jam on the ride home, they can fire off a tweet about it, and most of their followers will be fine with it.

People who follow your media outlet's tweets want information that matters to them, not your personal problems. If a staff meeting runs long, a boss is being demanding or something else is going poorly in the office, keep that off the Twitter feed. You need to maintain not only a level of professionalism, but also a sense as to what the feed is supposed to accomplish.

In addition, making a glib comment about a traffic crash ("Pile up on I-95 keeps piling up.") or a news event involving a celebrity ("Lindsey Lohan lands in rehab . . . Lindsey Lohan lands in rehab . . . This is a recording.") can make your organization look bad. One of your followers could be caught in that traffic crash and seriously injured. Another follower might have spent time battling alcohol or drug addiction, and that person might know how hard it is to stay clean and sober. You need to keep in mind that your audience has specific needs. Your sense of humor might not be their sense of humor. Work to put forth information that is audience-centric, and you will have a good group of loyal followers.

Be Careful With the Tweets of Others

Good journalists vet information prior to reporting it as their own, and that traditional value should translate clearly to Twitter. You wouldn't allow a reporter to publish a story based solely on a rumor. You wouldn't disseminate a press statement without verifying the key elements included in it. This is common sense to anyone dealing with media. However, many people are willing to publish secondhand information with a click and a "retweet" and not even think twice about doing so.

The internet has a way of letting all sorts of rumors, half-truths and innuendo fly everywhere, so before you retweet something and give it your stamp of approval, check it out. If you don't fact-check before retweeting content, you will add to the confusion and upset your readers when they find out you passed on inaccurate content. If you take the time to make sure things are right, your readers will thank you.

Respond Properly

Twitter has several direct contact functions, including direct messaging and @ messaging. Your readers may avail themselves of these options to reach you, the same way they would with an email or a telephone call. As an editor, if you are responsible for the Twitter feed, you need to respond to these people. Ignoring a voicemail message or failing to respond to an email is bad form, but failing to respond to a tweet can lead to a viral hostile reaction. People who use social media have no problem complaining about your lack of attention, and they have an audience. Even a simple response that acknowledges you received their message can help.

Give Credit

Media outlets have long used material from other sources to improve their content. A press release from a public relations firm can provide the impetus for an editor to assign a staff-written piece on the topic. Newspapers that can't confirm certain facts independently will cite other media outlets as the sources of key pieces of information. Websites link to original articles when they post commentary or use large sections of someone else's source material. When using Twitter, the same rules apply. It's good form to provide the original source with credit, and this approach allows your readers to see where you got your information.

Post Information Judiciously

When you post tweets, a steady flow of information is much better than a giant slab of it. For example, if you are working for a news outlet, such as a TV station or a newspaper, that produces a large quantity of information once or twice per day, you will have a lot to tweet about all at once. Instead of dumping all of that information into the Twitter feed when you get it all, consider a controlled-release approach, in which you send out one or two tweets every half hour or so. If the news is breaking or the information is crucial, you can tweet as often as you need to keep the audience informed. For marketing organizations or promotional groups, you can make large announcements when you need to on Twitter, but you can also provide scheduled, topical posts as well. If you have standing features that you promote on certain days or times, you can keep your audience engaged without cluttering their feed with random information.

to your audience, 20 percent of your content is "shared" from other sources, and only 10 percent should straight-up promote you or your organization. The better the quality, the stronger the audience, so stick with fewer great posts as opposed to a bunch of bad ones.

SOCIAL NETWORKING SITES

These sites are a mishmash of news, information, entertainment and connections. If you think of them as a job-fair-meets-cocktail-party environment, you have the right idea.

The topic and scope vary from site to site. Social networking sites like Facebook are meant more for interactions among people in an entertaining and relaxed social atmosphere. The sites include the ability to share personal news, play games and reconnect with distant family members and old schoolmates. A site like LinkedIn has a work-oriented purpose. People use this site for job networking, business connections and professional advice from other people in their field.

Editors can use these sites to drive traffic to their websites if they understand the social networks these sites serve. Business editors provide a site like LinkedIn with a link to a story about job hunting. Entertainment editors can post links to music stars' profiles on Facebook fan pages for those stars. The people who use these social networking sites might never otherwise look to your website for information, but when you reach out to them, you can entice them to try your site.

When you post information to these sites, you need to be engaging, informative and succinct. You want to use these posts to prompt people to click through to your site and get the full story.

In addition, the posts must meet a certain level of rigor, as spelling, grammar and style all matter. You also want to make sure that you conducted enough research to post intelligently on the site. Make sure you have the facts straight when you post to Facebook. Make sure the links work so that people can click through. Make sure you follow the rules of the site for posting information. Failing on your site can be a damaging blow to your organization's credibility, but failing on a social networking site can be exponentially worse. Each time you post a message at one of these sites, you represent your organization. You need to make sure you represent it well.

SOCIAL NEWS SITES

Social news sites allow individuals to submit links to items they think would interest the sites' audiences. Site users can create profiles, and other members of the site can follow those users' postings. When a user posts new material, the people who follow that user receive a notification of that update. The material on the site is subject to user reviews, as the users vote on the value and importance of the stories.

For example, Reddit gives users the ability to read content on a wide variety of topics, such as education, humor, and politics. Within each of those areas, users can create "**subreddits**" that focus on more specific and narrower topics. Readers can post content and then "vote up" or "vote down" each individual link or post. The most popular pieces on the site can rise to the top of the list until something else gains prominence on that subreddit.

In addition to individuals, marketing companies, traditional media outlets and other organizations have used these sites as a way to market information to niche audiences, expand the reach of regional news coverage and share information.

VIEW FROM A PRO
KELLI BLOOMQUIST

Courtesy of Kelli Bloomquist

Over a 22-year career in media, Kelli Bloomquist has used almost every medium available to reach an audience. She owns a 139-year-old community newspaper and runs a media organization that does public relations pitches for clients. She has also created and run a digital mass communications program at Iowa Central Community College that focuses solely on digital and social media in the fields of journalism and public relations.

In addition, she has worked for radio stations KICD AM/FM and KLLT in Iowa. Throughout it all, she said she carried certain skills with her from one stop to the next.

"No matter what platform you're using or form of media, solid writing and understanding your audience are hands down the most important and transferable skills," Bloomquist said.

Quality editing skills such as tightening and clarifying copy reside at the core of all aspects of media, but specifically social media, where the stakes can be higher and the rules can feel more nebulous. Bloomquist said too many organizations misunderstand how best to use social media to serve their readers, and therefore undercut their connections with readers.

"Too many organizations feel that everything and anything is allowable on social media, but that's the furthest thing from the truth," she said. "Posting everything and anything ruins your branded voice and creates confusion amongst your audience as to what you stand for and the value you will provide to them. Professional organizations need to look at their audience and look at what that audiences' expectations for them are."

Bloomquist said editors need to ask what readers expect of the media outlet, whether that organization works in news, PR, advertising or another area. The goal for good social media is to meet the expectations of the audience members in a way that properly resonates with them.

"I think a great representation of this is Wendy's and Netflix social media presence," Bloomquist said. "Wendy's looked at their audience, their demographic data, and changed their social media voice to one that is funny and that pokes fun or 'burns' others. It works for them. In fact, it's gone over gangbusters! But when Netflix tried the same approach last Christmas, they fell flat on their face and their audience saw them as rude and bullying instead of as funny. They lost social media followers and subscribers."

How to determine what rules to follow or what voice to use can become difficult for editors who need to establish policies for their organizations. Bloomquist said her organizations have tried to put together a physical policy guide, but the changes to social media happen too quickly for that to be effective. However, she said that doesn't mean anything goes when it comes to social media.

"One of my biggest policies is to look at social content and consider whether or not that content is necessary and will it do harm," she said. "I ask these questions every time we report on what could be considered a sticky or controversial situation. Too many times I've seen video and photos posted to social media solely for the value of shares and likes and retweets, but otherwise the content isn't serving a purpose. What is the value of this photo? What am I trying to achieve with this video? Shock and awe has been used too much and has aided in feeding people's news biases. I don't want my brand and what I've worked so hard for to be grouped in with that mess."

To keep her brand clean and her approach clear, Bloomquist said she encourages media professionals to pick through the data social media can provide and seek ways to best cater to the audience.

"We live in a world that allows us to have so much data at our fingertips that not utilizing it is foolish," she said. "Every audience is different. I know that for my newspaper, my audience engages if we talk about local kids doing things in the community and cops and courts content. But a radio station that I work with gets the most engagement not from news content but from asking their audience questions about themselves. A large tourism company that I work with gets the most engagement from their audience when they post historical photos and content relating to their brand. None are the same but all of these data points were found through looking at audience demographics found through A/B testing and analytics as well as talking with each audience."

Above all else, Bloomquist said she encourages media professionals to think about the value of their work when they post to social media and to emphasize that value in their communication with readers and viewers.

"In a world that is consumed by social media and a never-ending news cycle, why should your reader stop scrolling and read your piece of content?" she asked. "Don't spin it and make it into something that it's not, but why in the midst of thousands of other posts, tweets, snaps, should they stop for you?

"Tight writing and editing about a topic that your readership is interested in is always going to be a reason to stop scrolling and read, sometimes even start to finish. If an article or even a social media post isn't well written, it doesn't matter because readers have other opportunities and other platforms to go to for it. . . . Stop and think about how you're going to make your readership care."

WEB COMMENTS

Reaction always has been a part of the media and has taken many forms. Newspapers dedicate portions of their opinion sections for letters to the editor, and radio stations have call-in shows to allow people to discuss issues of importance. Today's editors have those options and more.

Online comments serve as instantaneous reactions to stories. Instead of having to type out a letter or wait for a switchboard operator, readers can post their thoughts and feelings immediately after viewing a piece on your website. The comments are attached to the end of that piece, which allows other audience members to read and react to previous comments. This can lead to a conversation among readers, much like an old-fashioned town hall meeting. It can also lead to a rambling tirade of personal attacks, as tempers grow short and people feel cloaked in anonymity.

A good editor can sense when comments have reached a tipping point from constructive and spirited debate to name-calling and bullying. Your organization has (or should have) established rules regarding your role in shaping the discussion in the comments section. Some websites have a restrictive policy on netiquette, and others allow a "no-holds-barred" approach to their comment boards. As an editor, you will likely have some say over what can be posted and how you will deal with people who break the rules. You will want to give fair warning to people who appear to be abusive before you remove their posts or ban them.

Even if you aren't there to shape the conversation, you should read the comments under the stories you post. In some cases, people will alert you to mistakes you made. In other cases, people will tip you to additional material you might have missed or other stories that could be valuable. Although you need to verify this information, it can serve as a good starting point for additional news coverage.

DISADVANTAGES OF SOCIAL MEDIA

Social media often seems easy and fun at first glance. It allows you to reach people in new ways. It gives you a broader reach for your stories, videos and photos. It helps people get in contact with you after they've used the material on your site.

For every positive, a negative exists, and social media is no exception. Below are a few of the things that can go wrong when using social media.

Failure Goes Viral

The best thing for a good story is a large and interested audience. The worst thing for a horrible mistake is a large and interested audience. The concept of social media cuts both ways, and it's never good when it cuts against you. In 2018, the cryptocurrency startup Waltonchain embarrassed itself on Twitter while conducting a promotional campaign for Valentine's Day. The company gave away small amounts of WTC to about 200 random Twitter followers, but after it announced the winners, an employee accidentally bragged from the company's own Twitter account that he or she won a prize.[2] This led to accusations that the giveaway was a scam, and Waltonchain's price plummeted as investors sold off their ownings.[3]

In some cases, something as small as a typo can cause a major catastrophe. Sephora, a beauty and makeup company, failed to copyedit a hashtag before sending a message out to its followers. The company used the tag #CountdownToBeauty to promote the opening of its first Australian store. However, the person who sent the tweet didn't catch a missing "o" in "Countdown," thus leading to a vulgar message.[4]

Heavy Workload

Internet experts say one of the biggest mistakes organizations make regarding social media is underestimating the amount of time it takes to do it right. Social media moves your organization out of a local area and into a global market, forcing you to compete with more voices, pay attention to more customers and create more material. A 9-to-5 operation can morph into a 24/7 job and more. The time it takes to respond to constant tweets, monitor conversation boards, post new content, link to additional sites, review competing media outlets and more is often beyond what one person (or a few people) in an organization can do. Readers demand reciprocity and immediacy. Trying to balance what your audience craves with what you have the ability to produce is a tough job.

New Playing Field

The democratizing effect of the web has been great in decentralizing media. For years, without a Federal Communications Commission–approved license or access to a printing press, people were unable to produce messages for a massive audience. The web allows anyone with an idea and internet access to build a site dedicated to any topic they choose and gives them a chance to reach millions of readers. For media companies that once served as gatekeepers and abided by certain rules, this concept can be disturbing.

As an online editor, you will be dealing with more feedback, more media outlets and more problems than most of your traditional editing counterparts. If you take the time out to answer every challenge, respond to every comment, rebut every assertion and question every motive, you will end up chasing your tail far too often. You don't need to respond to everything posted on your site.

Identity Management

Social media research states that the organizations that do the best with social media are those that have a strong sense of what they are and what they do. This branding or image maintenance leads to improved relations with audience members and a better sense of purpose. It also leads to a better internal understanding of what are and what are not acceptable social media practices.

Because much of the social media landscape is uncharted, many organizations lack proper identity management and fail to have policies that are proactive. Instead, they find themselves reacting after something occurs that they didn't foresee and didn't like.

The ability to set ground rules, establish policies and determine the purpose of social media for an organization is key to improving the environment both inside and outside of your organization. If your organization doesn't have these rules or can't define its identity well, problems will occur. As an editor, it is your responsibility to help set the stage for a discussion on this topic.

Measuring Feedback

For as long as there has been journalism, there has been the stereotype that journalists hate math. If you dislike math, you will be at a disadvantage because to fully understand social media's value, journalists need to engage in some routine data analysis.

For example, if you use a set of parameters to write your headlines, you should check to see if those headlines garner attention from your readers. If the audience isn't finding those stories or clicking on those headlines, it would behoove you to look at some data from competing websites. If they are receiving more traffic than you are, start asking some of the following questions:

- What is it that they are doing that is different from what we are doing?

- Could I try using different words in my headlines to make them more appealing?

- Does my approach to the material not mesh well with how search engines look for things?

- Are my headlines too vague? Too specific?

You will also want to see which social media venues get you the most site traffic. Is your audience responding more to email pushes or your Twitter feed? Does posting on your organization's Facebook page get people to pay attention, or does posting on other people's Facebook pages work better?

In order to get social media's full effect, you need to understand how it works, when and how to use it and which channels work best for you. To see how well you are doing in this regard, you need to make sure you're looking at data. That might not be something you think you're good at, and it might be time consuming, but it's the best way to make sure you are doing your job right.

THE BIG THREE

Here are the three key things you should take away from this chapter:

1. **Be careful on social media:** It doesn't take much to destroy everything you've worked for on social media. Failure goes viral in a hurry, people will leave you as quickly as they arrived and it's really hard to hide from media trolls. This is why you want to take care with each post, tweet and message you release into the digital realm.

2. **Social media is hard work:** Social media requires you to produce content for multiple platforms at a relentless pace. As an editor, you are responsible not only for what you publish but for how your writers conduct themselves on these platforms, what rules will best serve your organization on social media and many other similar concerns. This can take a lot of time and energy, so be ready to work hard if you embrace social media as a key way to reach your audience.

3. **Trust is everything:** Trust is not a boomerang: If you throw it away, it won't come back. It doesn't take much to get people to follow your organization on social media, and it can take even less for them to abandon you if things aren't to their liking. As an editor you will want to spend an adequate amount of time developing a social media strategy that allows you to demonstrate your value to your readers and providing them with reasons to trust you.

KEY TERMS

short message service (SMS) 177   social media 175   subreddit 179

DISCUSSION QUESTIONS

1. The chapter dictates that "trust is everything." How true do you find that to be when it comes to your use of social media? Has anyone ever "burned" you on social media? How severely did that undermine your trust in the sender?

2. How important do you think identity management is on social media? Does this vary on the basis of your area of media writing? Why or why not?

3. A number of athletes and celebrities have seen tweets they wrote many years earlier come back to haunt them. Regular citizens have also seen previous social media posts harm them. Do you think it's fair to hold people accountable for things they said or posted several years earlier that went undetected at the time? Do you think there should be a "statute of limitations" in terms of things people wrote or posted on social media?

WRITE NOW!

1. Select a media outlet you enjoy that frequently posts content on a social media platform. Analyze the outlet's posting of content as it relates to the 70/20/10 rule discussed in the chapter. How well does it do in fitting this model? If it fits the model, do you think it is successful in meeting its audience or not? If it doesn't fit the model, where is it placing more emphasis than the model dictates it should? Can you see a good reason for the outlet's approach? Write a short essay that answers these questions.

2. Find a topic that news reporters and public relations or marketing practitioners are discussing on social media. Compare and contrast the approaches these journalists take on the topic. How are they similar in their approach? How are they different? If you were the editor for either side, how would you refine that side's approach to better serve its audience? Outline your answers in a short essay.

3. Find at least five horribly written posts or tweets from any area of media writing. Explain what you think is wrong with them and then rewrite them. Finally, explain how your version is better than the original.

Visit **edge.sagepub.com/filakediting** to help you accomplish your coursework goals in an easy-to-use learning environment.

14 EDITING FOR PUBLIC RELATIONS

Public relations mixes the information-provision elements of news writing with the advocacy and salesmanship of advertising to reach a wide array of audiences. The abilities to adapt to various publication formats and to tell stories in a compelling and engaging way reside at the heart of public relations.

This form of communication has several elements that all good practitioners should embrace. Some of these concepts might seem counterintuitive or overly simplistic, given what most people erroneously believe to be the purpose of PR. However, practitioners need to communicate valuable content to multiple publics in a clear, concise and meaningful way that benefits both the readers and the organization from which the information originates.

As an editor, much of your job will be balancing the need to promote with the need to inform as well as looking to help writers find a voice that speaks on behalf of an organization. In addition, you will need to use the core tenets of persuasive communication to guide writers as they attempt to capture readers' attention and compel the audience members to act.

This chapter will review some basic aspects of public relations and outline the ways in which editors can help writers stimulate, engage and advocate on behalf of clients. We will also explore the specific elements that remain standard in public relations communication and the ways in which writers need to shift their approach to communicating on the basis of the needs of their platforms.

WHAT IS PR?

Public relations serves as a conduit between organizations that want to reach specific audiences with important information and audiences that will benefit from that information. To make this happen, practitioners must write in a clear and organized fashion that advocates for the client without overdoing it. The way to make this happen will vary from organization to organization and from audience to audience, which can be frustrating for newer PR writers. Another frustrating element for newer PR writers is the lack of a generally accepted definition of the field. To help define PR, here are a few terms that appear in many definitions for this form of communication:

Deliberate

Practitioners take specific and intentional action as they engage an audience. They plan their communication approach with the goal of a clear and specific outcome, such as the election of a candidate, an increased awareness of a crisis or a public announcement regarding something an organization wants to share. These and other deliberate actions are goal-oriented and meant to reach a specific end.

Prepared

Research is a crucial aspect of all forms of media, but it often is overlooked when some individuals discuss public relations. For all the criticisms PR faces regarding the use of hype and spin, the truth is that this form of writing requires just as much preparation as any other communication that enters the public sphere. News releases require facts and figures to support their claims. Speeches need heavy editing and a great deal of revision. Spokespeople need a good amount of preparation before they discuss a topic with news reporters. Good PR is prepared PR.

Well-Performed

The PR practitioner is judged on the quality of the product the public sees, whether that product is an event or a news release. This may seem unfair, but for all the great press statements an organization makes or all the great campaigns an agency creates, it is usually the one thing that goes wrong that will live in infamy. A well-structured campaign could contain a horrible error or double entendre that has people laughing at your firm or your client. In addition, the media can draw unwanted attention to this error, making you a laughingstock among your peers. This makes editing even more crucial when it comes to PR, as the public can judge only what it sees, not all the effort behind what you produced.

Mutually Beneficial

In news, editors seek to balance side A and side B to ensure fairness in presenting information to the public. Although public relations practitioners serve as advocates for their clients, a sense of fairness and balance remains at the core of their work. PR must be mutually beneficial, as it strengthens long-term relationships between the clients and the audience. If the communication benefits only the organization paying for PR, the public will become distrustful of that group and its messages. Communication that serves only the audience could undermine the organization's goals, thus leading to diminished returns for the group. Editors need to shape their copy to ensure that both sides will see positive gains.

Transparent

This is often the most counterintuitive of all elements associated with public relations because it requires an organization to let the public see everything the group is doing right and doing wrong. **Transparency** essentially says, "Here is everything we know: The good, the bad and the ugly. Have at it." This would seem to make little sense, as this approach would seem to undermine people's faith in you and your organization. However, editors who emphasize transparency will likely see much stronger relationships between themselves and their audience.

The more you hide something, the worse it gets, because people will eventually find out the truth. Once they do, they will see the lengths to which you went to keep them from knowing something and thus distrust you even more than if you were just initially honest. Much like you do when you have to undergo painful experiences in other parts of your life, it is always best to bite the bullet. The more quickly you admit to a problem, the more quickly you can show people how you are solving it.

Responsive

Editors serve as a public face of the organization, or at least a connection between the public and the group. This requires them to work as a two-way conduit of information, sending it out on one hand and dealing with feedback on the other. In public relations, receiving feedback is a crucial part of the communication loop, so editors need to not only work with the information they receive from the public, but also respond to it in a timely fashion. In analyzing what people tell them about their work, editors in PR can use the information to determine what works and what doesn't as they continue to shape their messages over the course of a campaign.

MICROEDITING IN PR

Chapters 5 and 6 dealt at length with the various types of editing errors that can creep into copy in any area of the discipline. Instead of rehashing those here, let's take a look at the PR-specific areas of concern that can create problems for writers and places where editors can really improve copy:

Jargon

Practitioners want to reach readers in the clearest and most effective way possible. One thing that gets in the way of that is a heavy reliance on "insider language" that places a premium on knowing specific types of lingo. Writers often cover their work in **jargon** for one of two reasons:

- They are experts in a field and assume that everyone else shares their understanding of terminology within that area.

- They aren't experts and thus fear looking stupid if they try to move away from technical terms that they can't translate to the readers.

Regardless of the reason, writers will use jargon that makes it difficult for certain audiences to understand and thus limit their effectiveness in reaching those readers. This is where a good editor with a strong sense of audience centricity can drastically improve the writing.

First, understand that the use of technical terms can benefit readers, as long as they know those terms and understand them as the writer uses them. The editor should determine the degree to which the terms match the educational level of the readership for which the content is intended. For example, a blog for expert knitters can easily use the term "worsted-weight yarn" with no concerns, as most people reading it would easily understand it. However, an article on milk for a general-interest audience would want to explain the difference between pasteurized, homogenized and raw milk, as well as what terms like "rBST" and "rBGH" mean.

Second, a good editor can help a writer better explain jargon in a clearer way through some simple conversation about the terms as they relate to the audience. In public relations, jargon can not only leave readers confused, but can give them the sense that the authors want to deceive them. This is often where the accusation of "spin" comes into play, because readers distrust writers who confuse them while trying to persuade them.

Finally, editors who force writers to shed jargon and focus on meaning will help the writers better understand the concepts themselves. In many cases, writers have difficulty explaining things they intuitively know, even something as simple as why a sentence is grammatically correct or why something "sounds wrong." Editors who push writers to slow down and find a way to explain the underlying aspects of a term or concept can help those writers become more effective in relaying it to the audience.

Hype

Promotional writers often suffer from excessive hyperbole, whether the author is an opinion columnist, a public relations professional or a marketing expert. The reason **hype** infests writers' copy comes down to their inability to effectively explain specific benefits of their organization or differences between their issues and those of others. Thus, instead of finding a way to clarify these elements appropriately, the writers will slather on adjectives and adverbs that puff up the awesome nature of their good, service or idea, in hopes this will get readers to buy whatever it is the writers are selling.

The problem with this approach is that readers have become desensitized over the years to hype, thanks in large part to its heavy use. People hear how something is "the best" or "the most amazing" over and over to the point that they tune the message out. This is where research on the part of the writers and copy shaping on the part of the editors can break through the hype and provide the readers with value.

Start with a basic idea that everyone thinks their product, service or idea is amazing. A good editor will ask the writer, "What specifically makes your item better than or different from other similar items?" This approach will help you help your writer focus on certain elements that need promotion in the writer's copy. If the writer can't come up with an answer, send him or her to do some research on the topic with the goal of finding ways to differentiate this item from the rest of the field. If the writer provides you with specific things that make this item worthwhile, have him or her select one or two primary aspects that will create the best overall pitch to readers. After that, you both can flesh out those specifics in detail-oriented ways that will demonstrate value to the readers of the piece.

Numeric Avalanches

On the other end of the spectrum from hype sits the numerical avalanches of data that will bore people to tears. Research is a crucial aspect of public relations, but you can't just bury your readers under a pile of numbers. Consider the following example:

Bad Example

In 1998, the state's unemployment rate moved from 2.1 to 4.2 percent, an increase of 100 percent, even though the state's hiring index grew from 8.2 to 10.2 percent. By 2018, however, the unemployment rate had fallen back to 2.1 percent, a 75-percent cut after the rate hit 8.4 percent during the 2008 recession. The state's hiring index did not move from 10.2 percent in all that time.

Somewhere between reading about the years, the percentages, the percentage increases and more, the readers likely tuned out. The point of any kind of writing is to tell the readers what they need to know in a simple and clear way, emphasizing why it matters to them. When the numbers invade the copy, this becomes nearly impossible.

Better Example

The state's unemployment rate now mirrors the 2.1 percent figure of 20 years ago, state officials said Tuesday, noting the state's hiring index has remained stable throughout that period. This low rate means that most people are finding work and that employers haven't cut back their hiring rates throughout this time.

If people really feel the need to get into the weeds on this and dig into the numbers, consider a chart or graph to break those numbers out. You can always include this with your piece.

Insensitivity

Dennis Wilcox and Bryan Reber note in their book "Public Relations Writing and Media Techniques" that bias, stereotypes and politically incorrect language often can creep into PR copy, thus insulting readers and limiting the writer's effectiveness.[1] The authors note that a good way to keep insensitivity out of your writing is to avoid thinking that all members of a group are the same and to keep up with preferred terms when discussing people in terms of race, gender, sexual orientation and ethnicity.

In some cases, insensitivity emerges when people speak off the cuff and fail to think about the impact of their actions. In May 2018, Sen. John McCain pressed fellow senators to vote against Gina Haspel's confirmation as the head of the CIA. In response, White House press aide Kelly

Courtesy of Elizabeth Connor

Elizabeth Connor is the managing editor for AIDSFree, a USAID-funded program that implements HIV education, prevention and treatment efforts in Africa. During her career, she has worked in multiple media disciplines, dating back to her high school days, when she wrote for the "teen" section of the local Scripps-Howard afternoon daily.

Connor worked as a newspaper journalist for the Miami News and the Fort Lauderdale News/Sun-Sentinel, a public relations practitioner, an executive director for a health administration nonprofit and a manager for a Big Six accounting firm. Through those experiences, she said she developed a passion for writing and a great appreciation for editing.

"It's not that you need editing skills even if you're not going to work at a newspaper," she said. "You need editing skills, period. The successful people in my company — and virtually all companies I've worked for — are those who can express a thought, and quickly. Every day, I am grateful for the skills and values I picked up in my journalism education so many decades ago."

Her ability to express a thought quickly and clearly benefits her greatly in her current position, Connor said. In working with a wide array of writers from varying backgrounds and countries, she said the need to communicate clearly and help her coworkers understand specific needs is vital.

"Many of the writers are very highly educated and have a first language other than English," Connor said. "It's not the first time I've worked with non-native English speakers, but it is the most intensive experience of the type. It's fascinating. Having to explain English to someone who is not a native speaker has forced me to learn syntax and grammar on a very basic level."

Another basic-level element that remains crucial in Connor's work is the ability to help writers organize their thoughts in descending order of importance.

"I worked on a Defense Department contract where they called it 'Bottom Line Up Front,' or BLUF, and acted like the Defense Department invented the idea," she said. "Just a few weeks ago, the second-in-command of my current company sent around a clip on the inverted pyramid, exhorting anyone who wrote — i.e., everyone — to absorb its tenets. . . .I struggle all the time to find writers who can read a document and find the lede. They just can't. People who can structure a document well are in short supply; they will forever have a job."

As she continues to work with writers, Connor said she has made editing a collaborative effort so that her writers can continue to grow and develop their skills while still effectively reaching their readers.

"I had an editor once tell me that 'editing is a conversation,' and I agree," she said. "An editor makes suggestions on someone's creative output. It's a delicate back and forth, and the more skill and care you bring to that relationship, the better."

Sadler said of McCain, who was battling brain cancer, "It doesn't matter. He's dying anyway." The White House did not deny the statement, and Sadler did not immediately apologize for her glib reference to McCain's illness.[2] In June of that year, she left her post at the White House.

Obviously, editors can only do so much to limit those types of gaffes, but when it comes to writing, editors should treat each piece of copy like a minefield of potential problems. In addition to looking for fact errors, typos and other obvious writing failures, you should comb through terminology and phraseology to see if anything written has the potential to insult your readership. You can't make every reader happy, but you should do your best to catch the truly catastrophic statements that will only serve to make you look ill mannered and uncaring.

EDITING TO ACCENTUATE THE KEY ELEMENTS OF PERSUASIVE WRITING

As we discussed elsewhere in the book, writers often construct copy from their own perspective, thus limiting its applicability to the audience in many ways. Good editors will look at what is there that could apply to readers and accentuate it properly. They will also determine what is missing and help the writers reshape the copy to fill those holes.

In public relations writing, editors have to help writers not only communicate with readers through the provision of facts and figures, but also persuade readers to think in the way the writers do. To help you do this as an editor, consider the three key elements of persuasive writing listed below and see how you can successfully help writers accentuate them in their copy:

Stimulation

News reporters receive dozens of requests for coverage every day. Members of the public receive hundreds of emails each day as well, many of which come from public relations professionals or marketing firms that want them to do something, read something or buy into something. Many of these get deleted or destroyed without so much as a glance. The few that do get a look-see have only a few seconds to grab the attention of the reader before they suffer a similar fate.

The most important thing you can do in any form of persuasive writing is to stimulate an interest within an audience member and compel that person to continue reading. If the writer failed to do this or left an item that could stimulate readers buried deep within the piece of copy, it's up to the editor to help fix this problem. Here are some ways in which editors can reshape the focus of copy to stimulate readers:

Rely on Self-Interest

Writers often forget that they need to focus on the audience's needs and interests and thus don't accentuate elements of a story that speak to the readers' self-interest. As an editor, you should remind writers that readers will always want to know, "What's in this for me personally?" If the writer has difficulty determining why a reader would care about the story, it might stand to reason that the reader shouldn't care about it. However, in many cases, the answer is in there, and it's up to you and the writer to find it.

Focus on personal interests, such as things that will benefit the reader's life, the lives of the reader's family members or the reader's community. Look for the piece of the story that showcases a specific element that has a direct tie to that reader in a meaningful and useful way. Move that aspect of the piece up to the top and highlight it as a crucial reason for the reader to pay attention to this story.

Personalize Content for Readers

People like to feel special, so sending them a generic and impersonal news release or pitch will turn them off and make them give up on you. A form letter, a release that lacks a direct local impact or anything that just screams, "I don't know you and I don't care about you," will only serve to have your work tossed aside. Instead of giving everyone the exact same information, personalize the content whenever possible.

As an editor, you should look for key areas in your writers' work to insert elements that make the readers feel like they aren't a dime a dozen. This could be making references to cities or businesses in their area as opposed to simply making a generic reference to "nearby cities or businesses." It could also be demonstrating that you have read content in their publication. For example, if you work for a nature conservancy and you want a local newspaper to write about an event you planned, you could address the information to the science and nature writer on staff and even mention something like, "I read your last article on the migratory pattern of geese, a subject that really matters to us here. . . ." Although this takes more time and effort, it is also more likely to yield positive results than cranking out hundreds of copies of a "Dear Editor" press statement.

Use Interest Elements

The FOCII interest elements located in the first chapter will help you a lot here, in that you can rely on information that naturally intrigues people to stimulate your readers. Fame, oddity, conflict, immediacy and impact all work well to entice readers and encourage them to read beyond the first few lines of your work.

Fame and oddity often work nicely to show how something is special or different, such as if your event will host a star athlete or showcase a rare item. Conflict, such as team sports and political disagreements, can draw readers to your copy, just like when little kids would yell, "Fight! Fight!" on the playground when two third-graders would start duking it out during recess. Immediacy always gives people a sense that they need to act right away and impact provides that sense of self-interest mentioned above. If your writers have trouble figuring out a way to stimulate readers, have them go back to the FOCII and determine which elements matter the most to their work.

Explanation

Once you get someone's attention, you have to keep it. Writers can often draw a reader into a piece, but once they get past the "Look at me!" portion of the story, they don't know what to do. Editors understand that helping the writer explain more about an idea, a product or a service can help the reader better understand the inherent value of the topic at hand. Here are some ways to help your writers accentuate the value of their pieces through proper explanation:

Statistics and Sources

"Says who?" is a fair question that readers often ask in reading persuasive copy, as they want to know how seriously they should take the writer's opinions. The ability to support an opinion with documents and data will help your writer substantially in explaining why a topic matters and why the readers should consider the writer's opinion on it.

In the first read, look for spots where the writer failed to support key suppositions or arguments and ask for additional information to strengthen that part of the piece. This will help you figure out if your writer knows the material and just underplayed the support or if the writer is clueless and needs to do more research. Also, poke at the quality of the sources your writers include in their work. Make sure the content will stand up to rigorous testing from readers and any counterarguments that could emerge.

Examples and Endorsements

All forms of media writing advocate the "Show, don't tell" philosophy because it allows the readers to better understand the information you want to share with them. Writers often see themselves as experts and thus bypass the "showing" part of the process, relying instead on their own experiences and ideas. As an editor, you can help your writers better connect with readers through the inclusion of examples and endorsements. In some cases, these "real people" or "true story" elements are called exemplars, which is just a fancy way of saying, "Here is something that really happened that better explains my point."

Examples of people who have benefited from your program or endorsements from celebrities can provide your work with not only stimulating content, but also some explanatory support. If the writer has a good example of a situation that typifies the point the story needs to make, push that example to the top of the piece and use it to stimulate the readers:

Bad Example

The Smithton Animal Shelter needs more people to adopt pets this month, as overcrowding can lead to illness or the euthanasia of animals.

Boring and nonspecific openings like this can often hide a great story a writer can tell. In most cases like this, an emotional appeal based on an example of someone who has benefitted from the organization works best:

Better Example

Andy Fisher remembers the first time he saved a life, and how that life saved his.

"I was in remission just before my 12th birthday," Fisher said, referring to his battle with leukemia. "We went to the Smithton Animal Shelter to play with the puppies as a treat. Sparky came right up to us and started yapping like crazy. He then sneezed."

The worker at the shelter came to retrieve Sparky, Fisher said, noting they worried about his diminished immune system. The beagle-bulldog mix couldn't shake a constant illness and was now scheduled to be put down.

"I cried," he said. "I begged my mom to take him home with us. You don't just throw away a life because it isn't perfect. I told her I'd never give up on Sparky."

Six years and one recurrence of the leukemia later, Sparky and Fisher remain best friends.

"When I was going through that next round of treatment, I wanted to quit, but Sparky wouldn't let me," Fisher said. "He was always there, reminding me of how important a life can be."

This week is the anniversary of Sparky's adoption, and the Smithton Animal Shelter is hosting the "Save a Life" campaign, where adoption fees will be waived and people are encouraged to find their own "Sparky story."

In this case, the opening is much longer, but it has a great example that draws the readers into the piece much more strongly than the simple lead. This is where an editor has to be willing to let a story unfold more, and a writer has to be willing to look for an example that will engage readers.

Simplification

Explanations often become overly complicated for no good reason. The writers get too deep into the weeds on an idea and get lost in there, leaving the readers wondering what exactly it is they should get out of the piece. As an editor, a good motto to follow is that explanation is about simplification. As noted earlier, removing jargon and cutting down piles of numbers can do this in many cases. However, in a lot of cases, working with a writer to get to the point is simply about getting the writer out of "media professional mode."

HELPFUL HINTS

KEY ELEMENTS TO INCLUDE FOR NEWS RELEASES

The formatting of a news release will vary from organization to organization and from platform to platform. However, some key elements remain consistent and essential for all contact between public relations practitioners and their publics. Robert S. "Pritch" Pritchard, who advises the Lindsey + Asp public relations agency at the University of Oklahoma after a quarter-century as a public affairs officer in the U.S. Navy, has outlined these specific items[3] for his students as they ply their craft:

Slug: This should contain essential facts about the person responsible for the news release, including the person's name, title and contact information. In standard press releases, the **slug** is single spaced and appears near the top right corner of the page. In digital formats, the information may be left justified and listed near the top. Regardless of placement, this information is crucial to engage media writers who want to find further information about this topic.

Embargo information: In most cases, releases will note that the information is available "for immediate release," meaning that the reporters can do whatever they want with this information as soon as they get it. However, in some cases, content needs to be held back from the public until a certain point in time. An example of this might be a state of the state address, where the governor's office makes the speech text available to reporters in advance, but doesn't want it published until the governor delivers it. If an **embargo** is necessary, the specific time and date in which the information can become publish should go here. If not, simply clarifying that the information can be released immediately is helpful at this point.

Headline: This part of the release can be capitalized, bolded or in some other way presented to distinguish it from the body copy of the piece. Much like headlines in print and traditional web stories, the noun-verb-object structure should constitute the core of this element and should accentuate something valuable to the readers that will stimulate their interest.

Dateline: To help the lead sentence focus more on the "who did what to whom/what" aspect of the piece, the **dateline** provides the "when" and "where" elements at the front of the lead. It usually lists the name of the city and state as well as the full date in parentheses. This element also helps readers determine the freshness of the information.

Boilerplate: The last paragraph of the release usually contains **boilerplate** information that provides the reporters with background on the organization responsible for the piece. It often contains a brief history of the group or the general purpose and size of the organization. It is standardized and used on all releases to end the piece and provide a sense of closure.

End-of-story symbols: Many printed releases provide a clear close using the old printer's mark ---30--- or a set of three hashtags (###) at the end of the content.

Try this approach: Ask the writer to simply explain the complex topic as if the two of you were sitting together at lunch or hanging out at a friend's house. Most writers will relax and focus on the easiest parts of the idea or the simple elements of the concept. They will then just tell you something without trying to couch it in jargon. That simplified version of the story can serve as their basis for their written work. Another effective trick to simplification is to have the writers start off sentences with "This matters because. . ." or "This means that. . ." to help them focus on the underlying value of what they want to say. You can easily remove those "training wheels" when you edit, leaving behind only the simple ideas that make sense to the readers.

Advocacy

Once you've gained your readers' attention and supported your position, you need to tell them what to do. Writers often forget to do this because they see the action as self-evident, but experienced media professionals know that it pays to nail down every detail and leave nothing to chance. Good editors will go the extra step to tell the readers what they should do and why they should do it. Consider these "extra steps" that will seal the deal as far as advocacy is concerned:

Provide a Path to Act

The easier you can make it for people to act on what you told them, the more likely they will be to act. It sounds simple, and it is, but most people fail to do everything they can to give their readers a simple path toward the action they want the readers to take. In each news release, pitch or other piece of copy you edit as a PR professional, look for any areas where additional information can create a stronger and easier path toward action.

When you evaluate a press release that promotes an event, look for specific elements that promote action: Does the release contain time, date and place information? Does it include any costs associated with attending the event or directions to the event? Does it include helpful hints as to when to arrive or where to park? Does it provide additional help for people who might have limited mobility or other specific needs? If you find that these things are missing, have the writer go back and add them as needed. Consider similar ideas for fundraising proposals to CEOs or story pitches to editors. You want these people to do something, so tell them how to do it and make it easy on them.

Demonstrate Clear Benefits

In addition to telling the readers how to do something, reinforce the reasons why they should do it. As mentioned earlier, self-interest will draw the readers into the piece and keep them engaged. It will also give them a reason to take action, as long as you can clearly demonstrate the benefits they can accrue once they act.

Writers often think that the benefits of any action are common sense, so they don't need reinforcement. However, if it were "common" sense, everyone would have it, so don't assume people know that whatever the writer has described will benefit them. Either have the writer clearly add the "act now and you will receive" paragraph that highlights the benefits of taking action or add it yourself.

Offer Support or Get Out of the Way

The fine line between advocacy and being pushy exists mostly in the minds of the readers, which is why understanding your readership makes a big difference in all media fields. If the audience members feel pressured to act, the "fight-or-flight instinct" might kick in and they will back away from your pitch. A lot of this relates to the overall tone of the piece, which we discussed elsewhere in the book. The more intense the push to act, the stronger the backlash from cautious readers. Besides, nobody really likes being told what to do, even if it is good for them. Parents who want kids to clean their room, eat their vegetables or be home at a certain time can attest to this.

The goal here is to empower action through support, explanation and engagement. At this point, if the writer starts acting like a yappy dog, the readers will become annoyed and they will walk away. As an editor, your job is to fine-tune the tone of the piece to advocate action without crossing the line.

THE BIG THREE

Here are the three key things you should take away from this chapter:

1. **Public relations is information plus persuasion:** To do quality PR work, you need to pair in-depth research with a convincing message as you ask your readers to engage in some form of behavior. Editors in this area need to determine what the message should say as well as the best way to communicate it to the readers. This requires them to make sure the information in the message provides a foundation for the advocacy that will follow.

2. **Address the needs of the readers in a personalized way:** Media organizations and members of the

public receive hundreds of "asks" every day, which can make them feel mentally fatigued and numb to all of them. The best way to break through this and get your "ask" in front of them is to personalize your message to them and then show them how your message matters specifically to them. This can be as simple as editing individual releases that include personal touches or as involved as using data to determine how certain people want to hear about your topic. It will take more time and effort, but you more likely will succeed in getting your readers' attention.

3. **Stimulate, explain and advocate:** This approach to promotional and persuasive writing will help you gain the attention of your readers, support your claims and nudge your readers into action. As an editor, you should make sure your writers include all three of these elements in every piece of copy they create. If any of these items are missing or weak, have the writer go back and make the appropriate fixes.

KEY TERMS

boilerplate 193
dateline 193
embargo 193

hype 188
jargon 187
slug 193

transparency 186

DISCUSSION QUESTIONS

1. Of the words traditionally associated with PR that are listed at the beginning of this chapter, which ones do you see as the most important to doing well in the field as a practitioner? Which ones are less valuable?

2. How important do you believe transparency to be in the field of public relations? Does the idea of showing everyone all of the good and bad things you deal with in your area make sense to you? Why or why not?

3. What are your feelings about hype as a way to convince people of the value of your organization, product or idea? How much hype is justified, in the form of puffery, and how much is way over the top?

WRITE NOW!

1. Select a press release from an organization that interests you and analyze it in terms of stimulation, explanation and advocacy. How well does the writer do in each of these areas? Which area is the strongest and which is the weakest? How could this be improved? Explain your thoughts in a short essay.

2. Select a topic that interests you and then write a one- to two-page press release on that topic. Make sure you include the key elements of the release, such as the slug, the embargo and more. Then, exchange your release with a classmate and edit each other's work both for the microediting elements listed throughout this book and for the ability it has to stimulate, explain and advocate. Rework the release on the basis of your partner's edits and turn in both versions to your instructor.

3. Find an example of insensitivity that emerged from a public relations official or a public official who has PR responsibilities. Examine what happened and how the situation resolved itself. What could this person have done to prevent this situation? What did you think of how well or poorly the situation was resolved? Outline your thoughts in a short essay.

Visit **edge.sagepub.com/filakediting** to help you accomplish your coursework goals in an easy-to-use learning environment.

15 EDITING AND MARKETING

The job of marketing, from an editing perspective, can encapsulate multiple areas and interests. You can edit as a marketing professional who works with clients in an attempt to help them best reach audiences that matter to them. In other cases, your own media organization might task you with improving the overall brand identity of your employer, increasing traffic to the company's website or making people more aware of who you are and what you do as an entity.

In the digital era, marketing continues to evolve in terms of how best to reach readers, what platforms matter most and which search engine optimization techniques work best. This chapter can't capture everything associated with marketing and the media, but it can help you conceptualize of the idea behind marketing. This chapter also will explain how content editing matters in this area and ways in which you can apply specific editing techniques to reach your audience. The goal here will be to touch on key topics with hints and tips that transcend any particular trend.

MARKETING BASICS

Your goal in marketing, whether you work for your own organization or as an editor for hire, is to present a clear and constant image to your audience. When done well, marketing shapes the overall understanding people have of your purpose and your essence. To do this, you will need to present content that helps define the brand of the organization through the use of multiple campaigns that reach your audience.

Brands

The goal of any organization is to define itself positively in the eyes of the public and differentiate itself from other organizations within its field. To do this, organizations seek to establish an identity that allows audiences to recall their products, goods or services in a specific way, relying on key terms or unique identifiers. This entire process will lead to the organization's **brand**. The brand encompasses everything from the organization's name and logo to its activities and relationships.

In most cases, editors will not establish a brand, but rather enhance it, support it or rework it. The brand accounts for the long-term, hard-fought identity of an organization. Unless market forces, such as a shift in an audience's needs or an extremely negative incident, demand it to happen, an organization will rarely alter its brand.

Campaigns

An organization relies on its brand to shape shorter term efforts to reach audience members on specific topics. These forms of outreach, known as campaigns, allow the organization to reinforce the brand while marketing specific elements of it to niche areas of its overall reach. The **campaign** works as a short-term attempt to raise awareness of a particular element or promotion within the organization's brand. This approach allows more direct targeting of ideas and audience subsets while still maintaining a broader sense of organizational identity.

Editors will likely be responsible for campaign work within an organization or as part of an agency that works for outside entities. In some cases, the editors will monitor a specific campaign, overseeing the content that is disseminated as well as the reactions to it. In other cases, the editors will work like a news copy desk, sharpening language and providing suggestions for clarity. No matter your level of involvement as an editor, understanding the premise of copy writing will benefit you.

EDITING FOR COPY WRITING

As we discussed earlier in the book, you need to understand how something is supposed to work at the big-picture level before you start digging into the micro-level editing. Much of what makes copy writing successful in the marketing area broadly applies to all forms of media writing, so much of what you have learned to this point will apply to this field.

However, author Jonathan Chan built a nice three-step approach for "telling a compelling brand story" that does a great job of boiling down some key aspects of copywriting.[1] On the basis of his three key points, here are some strategies that will help you edit effectively in this realm:

Know the Specific Needs of Your Audience

Much of what we have discussed to this point mirrors this edict, in that you need to fully understand who your readers are and what they expect from you. The FOCII interest elements come into play here, as does the idea of telling people what they need to know and why they should care about a given topic. Those standards remain important in this area of the media.

Chan makes a key additional point that is crucial for editors, namely, selecting a specific and narrowly focused need for the audience and emphasizing that within the copy. Writers often decide to throw as much information about as many topics as possible into a piece for fear of missing something. Editors can improve the copy when they strip away the extraneous angles and items, thus allowing the main point of the piece to shine. If you know what your readers really need, you will know which specific need requires your attention, and then you can edit accordingly.

The "Highlight Reel" Approach

In a similar vein, Chan argues that expert communication skills will allow writers to best reach the readers. In discussing Harry's, a shaving company that markets online, Chan referred to this as knowing how to provide a "highlight reel" of information to the readers. In other words, avoid the extended, chronological boring story and get to the things that have value to the audience.

In this aspect of the editing process, you need to make sure the writers emphasize the benefits and features of the good, service or idea you want to promote. These elements work in tandem to help readers better understand what you can provide to them and why it matters.

A feature is an aspect of the item you want to promote that helps distinguish it from competitors. For example, a feature of a car might be a 1.8-liter, four-cylinder engine, while a feature of a truck might be four-wheel drive. A feature of a phone might be a screen made from transparent aluminum or a 60-terabyte hard drive. In many cases, you can amplify these features by comparing them with those of competing products, saying the hard drive is the largest among competing phones or the engine is the most fuel efficient within this class of car.

A benefit explains why a feature matters to the users. Four-wheel drive may be interesting to people, but they might not fully understand why they should like it. The same could be true with a transparent aluminum screen on a phone. These seem like cool things, but nothing about them explains their value. Specifically, four-wheel drive will make it easier to drive in the snow, and a transparent aluminum screen won't crack, like glass ones do, when dropped.

Editors must make sure these elements are clear within the body of the marketing material. A feature without a benefit will leave a reader feeling perplexed as to the value of the feature. A benefit without a feature will come across like puffery or hype.

Create a Community That Shares and Cares

A community tends to share a vocabulary that resonates within the group. To help shape this vocabulary in a way that reinforces the brand, many organizations have word banks or brand dictionaries. These allow a common vernacular to emerge within the community, one that clearly connects the users and the organization. If your group or organization doesn't have something like this, you should consider developing one so that every writer is on the same page when it comes to promotional work and interacting with readers.

MARKETING YOUR OWN ORGANIZATION DIGITALLY

As mentioned earlier, some of your goals as an editor might include marketing work for your own organization, be it a PR agency, a news publication or any other media outlet. How best to reach your readers will depend greatly on your organizational goals and your platform. Given that one component that cuts across most of media companies is the digital element, this part of the chapter will examine digital marketing, both in terms of websites and social media operations.

Website Marketing Goals

Marketing seeks to establish goals with regard to an organization's value and achievements. Setting up your approach to marketing this way will keep you focused and allow you to better measure your results. Among possible marketing goals you may consider are the following:

Increase New Visitors

If you can't lure new visitors, you're in trouble. At best, site traffic will be stagnant; at worst, it will decline over time as various forces nibble away at your numbers. How many new visitors to target is open to conjecture, but you typically should aim high while keeping this goal reasonable.

First, you should have a handle on who is in your target audience, on the basis of the strategies outlined throughout the book. With the target audience identified, figure the total number of potential visitors. Of those, how many can you already claim for your site? What remains is the pool of people who can become visitors to your site. You may not get every member of your target audience to click to your site, but you want most of them to do so.

As you lure more people from that pool, the number of visitors to your site increases, resulting in a number of benefits. For one, as your content reaches a larger audience, more people are better informed, better educated and better entertained — long-standing goals of journalism. For another, increased traffic means you can deliver more eyeballs to your advertisers, the bottom-line factor in generating ad revenue from any media platform.

However, as we've discussed in earlier chapters, the numbers alone are not the end-all in effective journalism or effective marketing. Experts agree that the right mix of visitors and their engagement in the site have the potential to churn better results in a marketing plan than just sheer numbers.

Improve Visitor Return Rate

Getting visitors to your site once is great. Getting them to return is tougher to achieve but equally important. First-time visitors must find what they came looking for or must find something valuable they weren't looking for. If they don't, they won't come back. If they don't come back, your traffic gain is temporary and illusory. It's as simple as that. Your goal here is to make your site "sticky," a term that refers to how long visitors "stick around" and how many of them return because you gave them a useful, memorable experience.

Retain Current Visitors

Even as you work to reach new visitors and increase your overall traffic, you must make an effort to hold on to current visitors in order to avoid a revolving door, where one leaves as a new one enters. When your site meets visitors' needs, delivers what it promises and provides them with an

HELPFUL HINTS
A LOOK AT ANALYTICS

Understanding who shows up at your site, what they see and how long they stay is vital to shaping your approach to marketing your content. Sites such as Google Analytics offer the following data, most of which include the dates when the action occurred:

- Total number of visits

- Number of pageviews

- Number of pages per visit

- Bounce rates, which tell the number of single-page visits

- Average time on site

- New visitors versus return visitors

- Browser used

- Connection speed used

- Sources of traffic (direct, referring sites or search engines)

- Keywords used

- Which pages were viewed, including average times on pages

- Measurement of "goals pages," which include such pages as "Thank you for registering," receipts, flight itinerary and download completed

Interpreting these data takes some practice, but it's possible for a relative web novice to come away with informative numbers concerning visitor engagement on their sites.

experience uniquely tailored to them, you gain their loyalty. It becomes a matter of their trusting you. They don't just come to your site; they return to your site.

Customer loyalty can be linked to conversion rates, that is, the percentage of visitors to your site who complete a desired action. The easier you make navigating through your site and the longer you can keep a visitor at your site, the higher the conversion rate tends to be.

Improve Visitor Engagement Rate

Successful sites engage their audiences. Visitors come to these sites to do more than just look around and leave. They read. They comment on content. They discuss issues with one another. They respond to surveys or polls. The list goes on, but the key thing about each action is that it engages.

This component of your marketing mix involves a variety of opportunities you provide visitors once they arrive at your site. Not all visitors are interested in the same content, but giving each some engaging content is essential.

How many stories do they read? How long do they spend with each? Do they comment on stories? Do they suggest story ideas? Do they respond to reader surveys? Do they "like" your site? Do they click to follow you on Facebook or Twitter? Do they click to on-site archived content or to off-site related links? These questions all deal with reader engagement and help convert a one-time visitor to a regular reader.

Improve the Visitor Experience

That visitors get something valuable from your site, that they enjoy their experience, is a significant achievement, directly related to their engagement.

Some tips to improve visitor experience include the following:

- Know your readers and what makes them tick so you can deliver content they want.

- Make page design professional and inviting, a look that reflects the quality of its content.

- Make navigating through the site easy.

- Use clear, concise page titles.

- Display contact information, and give visitors options for contact, including email address, surface mail address and phone number.

- Provide internal links to help visitors find what they want.

- Regularly visit your site to click interactive media, navigation buttons and links to make sure they work.

- Check the usability of your site with popular browsers.

- Keep regular visitors informed through email and social media contacts.

- Roll out new content for preview by regular users.

- Be willing to admit mistakes.

- Ensure that content is the best and freshest your staff can provide.

You also glean quite a bit about visitors' experience from the evidence of their behavior on site, the kind of data that web analytics generate.

VIEW FROM A PRO
EVE PEYTON

Photo by Kyle Encar

Eve Peyton serves as the editorial director for the department of marketing and communications at Loyola University New Orleans, where she works on the branding of the university. In this role, Peyton said she has used a wide array of tools that she picked up throughout her editing career.

"The main skills that have benefitted me in all of my jobs are skills I learned at the J-school: the ability to write clearly, to turn in clean copy, and to rigorously fact-check all information," she said. "Whether you're reporting on the cops and courts beat or trying to solicit donations from generous benefactors, you need to make sure people's names are spelled correctly or you lose your audience."

Peyton began working as an editor while in graduate school, where she did editing for an alumni newsletter. After that, she spent time as a marketing assistant and then an advertising, exhibits and direct-mail manager at the University of Missouri Press.

She then moved to New Orleans, taking on editing jobs for New Orleans Homes & Lifestyles, Louisiana Life and Gulf Coast Wine + Dine. She has also worked as a freelance editor on more than five books in that time. Throughout all of this, she performed microediting tasks as well as larger edits for the bigger picture.

"In an ideal world, nothing in my department goes to the printer until I have had a chance to make sure the commas are in the right places, everyone used the correct form of 'your' vs. 'you're,' and all names and phone numbers are correct," she said. "For the magazines, I do both micro- and macro editing. I try to work with writers to strengthen their stories — getting more sources, making the leads more compelling, fleshing out certain aspects that I feel aren't adequately reported — but on occasion, I will take the liberty of moving paragraphs in a story around to improve the flow without asking the writer to do it."

As an editor, Peyton said the job can feel thankless, as people tend to only see the things she misses as opposed to all the things she caught. However, she said the collaborative process and the quality stories she helps tell make the effort worthwhile.

"Having a strong relationship with your writers is crucial because they can tell you when they think you're overstepping and you can tell them when you really think you're right and here's why," Peyton said. "It requires trust and honesty, but it almost always results in a better, clearer, more effective story. I've had more than one writer tell me that I'm 'just neurotic enough' to be a great editor, and I take that as the highest professional compliment."

As a marketing professional, Peyton said she not only has to keep an audience-centric focus, but she has to constantly keep an eye on how the audience continues to evolve.

"The audience is, of course, central to everything we do, but even the definition of 'audience' is a constant discussion," she said. "A big part of the redesign of the alumni magazine was changing our perspective from being just for the alumni and potential donors to being for the entire campus community, including prospective students. We used a survey from the Council for the Advancement and Support of Education to gauge alumni opinions on what topics they wanted to see more and less of in the alumni magazine. It was tremendously helpful in guiding us as we redesigned the magazine."

In performing this type of outreach, Peyton said the university's marketing still remains faithful to its Catholic, Jesuit roots.

"Sometimes, we think more about our mission than our audience — stories about social justice or protest movements that might be controversial to a certain audience are still highlighted because social justice is central to our mission as a university," she said.

As she transitioned through multiple editing jobs in her career, Peyton said her ability to adapt and grow kept her employed and happy.

"The best thing I learned in J-school was that you have to know a little bit about everything," she said. "The more you can broaden your skillset and be flexible — I learned back-end website design on the fly; I have switched between Chicago and AP styles several times over the course of my career — the better-positioned you'll be to weather changes and shakeups in the workplace. Also, listen to your editor. He or she is almost certainly right."

SEARCH ENGINE OPTIMIZATION

Search engine optimization involves various specific activities that increase the visibility of your website to search engines. You or your web team can perform many of the optimization steps, or you might contract with one of hundreds of online services to do so. Regardless of how you do it, you must optimize your website if you hope to compete successfully in the vast web marketplace.

Although we touched on this topic in other chapters, to fully understand how best to optimize your content in hopes of improving marketing opportunities, you have to understand how SEO works. Here are the basic things search engines do and why these things matter to you.

They Crawl the Web

Search engines have automated programs that crawl the web to find information. These "bots" look for webpages, images, videos, files and more. When they find these items, the "bots" analyze the data within each element they locate and store the results to create a sense of where that element is and how it could be located if a user needed it.

They Index the Documents

The search engines take those data points they find and create basically a giant file cabinet full of information for future use. In its most basic form, the index serves like this book's index, as it catalogs and categorizes information on the basis of key words people might look up. It then attaches a specific "where" on the web for the word itself, so it can go get the information when someone searches for it.

They Process User Searches

When someone types a certain set of words into a search, the engine goes into its information banks and finds content that matches those words. It then returns the results that matter to the user from its collection of information.

They Rank Results

The search engine not only returns the information but it ranks the information on the basis of what it thinks would be most helpful and valuable to the user. This ranking approach should help users get the best overall results first, with less valuable results showing up much later in the search.

What search engine optimization essentially tries to do is find a way to improve your site's ranking so it shows up higher in the results than your competitors. Most people won't go more than a page or two deep into any search engine results, so the more you can do to optimize your site, the better the chances you have of being seen.

HOW TO OPTIMIZE YOUR SITE

Optimizing a website can seem daunting for editors, many of whom might say, "But I'm not an IT person!" A search of the internet can also return a lot of optimization tips that seem like a mix between snake oil sales and attempts to game a system. The goal of an editor, obviously, is to be neither a weasel or a tech nerd, but rather to make it easier for interested readers to find the content their staff worked hard to create.

With that in mind, Moz co-founder and SparkToro CEO Rand Fishkin sketched out some basic things you can do to improve your SEO rankings[2] without resorting to becoming a carnival huckster:

Use Crawlable and Accessible URLs

To make life easy on search engines and their "bots," you need to make sure the content is easy enough for the bots to understand what is there and how best to index the content. Fishkin said this can be done by creating pathways that are intuitive for the readers and interconnected for the search engines. Pages that lack pathways to them will leave both groups unable to access them and thus limit your traffic.

Do Keyword Research

You intuitively know what you do and what you have to offer the readers, but that doesn't mean the search engines will be able to figure it out. To help them, you should look into what **keywords** and phrases people who search the web use to find things that are akin to what you do. For example, if you work for a homeless shelter in Springfield that provides family health care, you should outline the words that typify your mission. Look for other words that might be akin to those terms as well to see if you can broaden your overall reach.

Conduct SERP Investigation

One of the easiest ways to figure out if your view on what you are all about mirrors what search engines think is to conduct some searches. Fishkin says looking at the search engine results page, or **SERP**, will help you see what the engine thinks of your terms. Conduct a few searches on those keywords you think make your site important and then examine what some of the searches of those terms return. Once you figure out what it is that brings people to you as opposed to other sites that are not like you, you can analyze what works and what doesn't. In addition, you can figure out what other words show up consistently with your terms to see if you should include those keywords as part of your site.

Use Title Tags and Meta Descriptions That Matter

An important part of SEO involves adding or revising **meta tags**, H1 tags, H2 tags and **alt tags** for images using the essential keywords you've located. One goal is to establish an appropriate keyword density on your site, aiming for a 3 to 5 percent target, according to many SEO pros. Content in header tags as well as bold, italic, anchor text and other formatting options increases the weight this text carries. You don't want to cram keywords into every single aspect of your site, as search engines have begun to penalize people who look like they're trying to game the system. However, being aware of words that fit best with your site and playing toward them in your tags will improve your SEO rankings.

SOCIAL MEDIA MARKETING

As we discussed in Chapter 13, social media can provide you with the ability to reach readers, inform audiences and generally build credibility among interested parties. The many-to-many model provides you with an exponential outreach opportunity that other forms of media lack, so taking advantage of this in all areas of this discipline is important. When it comes to marketing, social media can be a mixed bag and a dangerous minefield, especially if you don't conform to the platform's social norms or you run afoul of a group of angry users.

Rather than running through everything you could encounter in social media again, here are some important ways you can market your content as an editor on social media while minimizing the risks associated with this form of communication:

Have a Reason for Publishing

Before you post content to a social media site or send out a tweet, ask yourself why you think this would be important for your readership. Is this likely to reach your readers in a timely fashion for your purpose? Will it provide them with something important in a meaningful way? Will this do more than get people to look at whatever you published and then turn away quickly? Does this material engage the readers? If your answer to any of those questions starts with, "No, but. . ." don't post the content. Once you figure out how to affirmatively answer those questions, you are ready to post.

Use a Sniper's Mentality

Instead of firing off dozens of posts, tweets and other missives, use the mentality of a sniper when you use social media. You should take aim at your target, remove all distractions and then fire once with the goal of hitting the bull's-eye. When audience members become inundated with a barrage of content, they tend to shut out everything a source provides to them, regardless of the content's value. Your goal is to hit the center of the target each time you provide content to your readers, so look for that single, perfect shot each time and take it only when you feel confident that your work is ready for public consumption.

Avoid the Stupid

If you can't find perfection each time you use social media, at the very least, you should avoid making the kinds of mistakes that will bathe you in the scorn of the Twitterverse. Traditional media professionals have warned beginners against making foolish errors with a missive like, "Imagine how it would feel if your grandmother read this." That kind of admonition could keep people from typing sarcastic or vulgar "filler" headlines or using inappropriate language in the newspaper. When it comes to social media, however, the risks associated with dumb mistakes are exponentially worse and far more damaging.

Each time you type something on social media, particularly with the intention of marketing or branding your organization, imagine it becomes the one thing everyone on Earth knows about you. Also, imagine you will never be able to shake it off, no matter what else you do for the rest of your life. With that kind of reality check, you should easily be able to avoid 99 percent of the problems associated with bad social media use.

Learn From Others

After the kind of "downer" listed in the last point, you might feel paralyzed when it comes to trying social media, as the risks can seem way too high for whatever rewards you might receive. That said, if you look before you leap, you can find some great examples of what others have done via social media and see how you can adapt their successes for your own ends.

Find organizations like yours that have a successful presence on social media and see how they target their audiences. Look at the tools they use and how they use them effectively. Once you get a sense of what works, see how you can do similar things for your readers. In addition, look at some organizations like yours that have a disastrous presence on social media and see what makes these places bad on these platforms. It often becomes easier to see ways to avoid failure than discovering techniques that allow you to mimic success.

Be Patient

You will not rocket to stardom immediately upon entering the field of social media marketing. The ability to create a loyal and valuable following will take some time, as you move from a handful of readers to a slightly larger handful of readers. Once you demonstrate value to your readers on a consistent basis, you will see incremental growth in your audience, and that audience will continue to consume your content as long as you provide it.

THE BIG THREE

Here are the three key things you should take away from this chapter:

1. **Marketing develops and showcases your identity:** The creation of a brand and the use of campaigns to codify and advance that brand will help show the world what your organization is all about. This is why you must have a good sense of your purpose, your tone and your value when you begin marketing to your audiences. If you don't know what makes you valuable or unique, you won't be able to tell your readers why they should care about you.

2. **If people can't find you, your efforts won't matter:** Much of what you do in social media and on the web will involve efforts to attract readers. To improve your likelihood of doing this, you must find ways to improve your search engine optimization and your social media outreach. If you understand where your readers exist and what terms matter most to search engines, you can improve the likelihood that you'll connect with audiences that matter to you.

3. **Be patient:** Even though the internet can deliver content quickly and easily, it will take you some time to build a solid marketing presence. Don't go for the quick and easy tricks to grab unsuspecting readers who have no real interest in your content. The true measure of marketing goes beyond the number of clicks or the volume of traffic. It is truly in how well you serve your target audience.

KEY TERMS

alt tags 203
brand 196

campaign 197
keywords 203

meta tags 203
SERP 203

DISCUSSION QUESTIONS

1. What is the value of the data provided through web analytics? What can they tell you and why do they matter to you as an editor and a marketer?

2. To what degree do you think everyone involved in a media organization should engage in promotional work? Should this be the purview of just a specific department, or should everyone in the organization be expected to chip in?

3. Is it better to gain a large number of followers who do little to engage your organization or to gain a small number of followers who are actively engaged with your organization? Why do you think this is the case?

WRITE NOW!

1. Select a topic that interests you and do a search engine results page (SERP) investigation on the basis of several key words you associate with that topic. Note the nonsponsored and advertising links that it returns on the first page or two. Then, look for additional words you see as connected to that topic, which could broaden or focus your search. Conduct the search and compare the results. How well do the keywords you selected bring back content that meets your needs and focuses on your topic of choice? Write a short essay on your experience.

2. Review a website of your choice and see how well it meets Jonathan Chan's three points for telling a brand story. Examine each point and provide examples of how the site meets this need or fails to meet it. What does it do well and what could it do better? Explain your thoughts in a short essay.

3. Select a social media marketer you think does its job well, on the basis of your experiences and the items outlined in this chapter. What social media platforms does this marketer use, and which aspects of social media marketing outlined near the end of the chapter does it do well? Then, propose a topic, a group, an idea or an organization for which you would like to engage in social media marketing and sketch out a plan for your campaign. Mimic the elements of the successful aspects of the marketer you examined for this assignment.

Visit **edge.sagepub.com/filakediting** to help you accomplish your coursework goals in an easy-to-use learning environment.

GLOSSARY

5W's and 1H: The staple crop of an inverted-pyramid lead: the "who," "what," "when," "why," "where" and "how" of the story a writer wishes to tell.

Absolute privilege: A legal standard that allows officials to make statements in their official roles without fear of libel.

Action box: A simple graphic that provides information that allows readers to act on the information provided within the story, such as the time of an event or the location of a store.

Active voice: A form of sentence structure that places the subject in a position in which it is performing the action of the verb. The noun-verb-object structure denotes active voice. (Bill hit the ball.)

Actual malice: A standard of fault in libel cases that requires the plaintiff to show that the publisher of the content acted with a reckless disregard for the truth. This is the standard used for public figures in libel suits, and is more difficult to prove than negligence.

Adjective: A word that describes a noun or pronoun.

Adverb clause: A collection of words that is used to modify verbs, adjectives and other adverbs.

Alt tags: A collection of words that serves as an alternative to an image on a website. They are often useful in improving search engine optimization.

Anonymous source: A person used within a story whose identity is not known to the journalists publishing the content.

Appositive phrase: A collection of words that renames a noun right next to it. Example: "The bird, a large, red-tailed hawk, pounced on the field mouse."

Audience centricity: An approach to journalism that focuses on the interests and needs of the audience while conveying content to readers and viewers. Journalists who apply this standard ask, "What do people want to know and how would they prefer to learn it?"

Balance: A standard of editing within news that seeks to provide equal information from all sides of an issue discussed within a story.

Bar chart: A graphic representation of numbers using horizontal or vertical bars, used to help readers compare or judge quantities.

Beat: An area of specific news coverage.

Biography box: A simple graphic that provides some basic information about a person featured within a story.

Blind leap: The positioning of an image, a graphic or another display item in design that blocks the reader's eye from continuing to consume text within a column. This is a problem that emerges from poor design.

Boilerplate: The portion of a news release that provides the reporters with background on the organization responsible for the piece. This traditionally appears at the end of the release.

Brand: A collection of identifying characteristics that come to mind when consumers think of an organization or its goods and services.

Breakfast test: A standard of publication that asks if people in the audience would be able to eat breakfast while consuming the content presented to them.

Bubble chart: A graphic that uses circular representations of numbers to help readers compare or judge quantities.

Campaign: A series of promotional pieces, including but not limited to advertisements, public relations copy and marketing efforts that promote a product or service.

Caption: Also known as a cutline, this text accompanies a still image to explain what is happening within the photo as well as some context to explain why the image has storytelling value.

Categorical imperative: An ethical standard that requires individuals to determine right and wrong before acting and then accept those standards in others as well.

Chatter: A sentence or two included under the headline of a graphic that explains what the graphic is about and why it has value.

Circumlocution: A collection of words that could be replaced with a clearer, shorter set of words or single word. These are often vague or fail to make a direct point.

Cliché: An overused statement that lacks imagination.

Close-up shot: Also known as a detail shot, this photographic approach zooms in on a small bit of action. It is useful for otherwise undetectable action, such as fingers typing on a keyboard or a doctor stitching a wound.

Collective noun: A word that identifies a group of individuals acting as a single entity. Example: "The jury found Smith guilty." (A jury contains multiple people, but in this case acts as one unit.)

Column inches: A print publication term that refers to the space content occupies, calculated as the number of columns times the depth in inches.

Communications Decency Act: A piece of federal legislation enacted in 1996 in an attempt to regulate pornography online. Section 230 of this act provides the owners of websites with legal protection against libelous comments posted there by people who don't work for the sites, such as commenters.

Conflict: One of the five key interest elements. This element emphasizes situations in which two or more people or groups are competing for a mutually exclusive goal.

Conjunctive adverb: A word that connects part of one sentence to another to show ordering, opposing ideas and other relationships. Examples include however, indeed, therefore and thus.

Contrast: A visual editing approach that shifts the shading of certain elements within the frame in perspective to other elements within it.

Coordinate adjectives: Also known as paired adjectives. These words precede and modify the noun while carrying equal weight. Example: "Zoe is a polite, caring girl." ("Polite" and "caring" modify "girl," and neither is more important than the other in modifying it.)

Coordinating conjunction: A word that connects words, phrases and clauses of equal status within a sentence. The seven words that do this are for, and, nor, but, or, yet and so.

Copyright: The exclusive legal right of people who create content to use the content or allow others to use it.

Creative Commons: A licensing option for intellectual property that allows content creators to dictate how others can use that content without forcing the users to obtain express permission from the creators.

Cropping: An editing approach that removes extraneous material from the outer edges of a still image. This allows the key element of the shot to become more prominent.

Curator: A leadership style in which the person in charge uses the position to create overall betterment for the audience he or she serves. This leadership style denotes a lack of ownership but a general pride in the material being displayed.

Data visualization: An interactive graphic that uses rich data and graphic arts to make difficult content easier to understand.

Dateline: The portion of a news release that explains when the release was created and where the event discussed in it is occurring.

Dead art: Photos that lack people, action or reaction. Photos of buildings or books are examples of dead art.

Deck: A secondary headline element that goes beneath the main head and elaborates or augments it.

Demographics: Measurable aspects of a group you hope to reach. Demographics commonly include age, gender, race, education and relationship status.

Dependent clause: A collection of words that does not express a complete thought and thus is not a complete sentence.

dpi: Stands for "dots per inch" and represents the resolution of an image.

Editorial discretion: The rights of editors to oversee content publication and decide upon what will and will not be published as well as how and when it will be disseminated.

Editorial illustrations: A visual storytelling technique that uses raw images and content manipulation to tell a story in a complex fashion.

Embargo: The portion of a news release that requests or requires that the reporters do not publish the information before a certain day or time.

Environmental portrait: A posed photograph of an individual that is used to accentuate the purpose of the story.

Ethics: Guiding principles that shape the actions of individuals as part of a social contract.

Euphemism: A word or phrase that softens language in an attempt to be less direct or harsh.

Fair comment: A legal standard that allows journalists to provide their opinions on topics of public interest in the form of columns and reviews without fear of libel, as long as it was not done with the specific intent to harm an individual.

Fair use: The right of media professionals to use copyrighted material without the permission of the copyright holder for educational and information processes.

Fake news: A term that emerged in the mid-2010s to describe content that is purposefully false in the hope of drawing audience members through partisan ideology or shocking headlines. It is also used to describe content individuals dislike in an attempt to discredit the material.

False light: The publication of material in such a way as to inaccurately depict an individual, thus causing harm to that person.

Fame: One of the five key interest elements. This element emphasizes the overall importance of the individual involved in the content. Subjects who fit into this interest area can be important over an extended period of time or be living out their "15 minutes of fame."

Fast-facts box: A simple graphic that provides basic information to readers in a quick and clear fashion. A short breakdown of a budget or information that answers "What?" "So what?" and "Now what?" would be examples of this.

Federal Communications Commission: An independent federal agency that regulates communication via broadcast, satellite and cable within the United States and its territories.

Fever chart: A graphic that demonstrates quantity changes over time. This is also known as a line chart.

First Amendment: The first of 10 amendments outlined in the Bill of Rights. It guarantees freedom of speech, freedom of the press, freedom to peaceably assemble, freedom to petition the government for redress of grievances and freedom of religion.

Flow: The smoothness of movement among elements of a story.

FOCII: A memory device helpful in remembering the five interest elements: fame, oddity, conflict, immediacy and impact.

Font: The style in which letters and numbers are presented. Also known as a typeface.

Gatekeeping: A process of news filtering that helps determine what information the general public gets to see. David Manning White's study on an editor he dubbed "Mr. Gates" helped popularize the term "content-selection process." Editors are occasionally referred to as "gatekeepers," meaning they choose what information is published and what information is not.

Geographic information: An audience characteristic media practitioners rely on to target audience members on the basis of their physical location.

Gerund phrase: A collection of words that includes a verb and other modifiers and complements. Example: "Swimming across the lake is too hard for Jimmy." ("Swimming across the lake" includes the verb "swimming" and the prepositional phrase "across the lake.")

Golden mean: An ethical standard that attempts to find the most good for all people involved in an ethical dilemma.

Hammer: A headline treatment that displays a few words in large bold type.

Headers: Tags used to create headlines, decks and subheadings for webpages.

Hole: A place within a story where a writer raises an issue of interest, but doesn't provide readers with enough information to satisfy that interest. Example: "Bill Smith was the second man to win the tournament." The hole emerges when the reader asks, "Who was the first man to win it?"

Hype: A shorter version of the word "hyperbole."

Hyperbole: A statement that is so ridiculously overblown that it could not be reasonably believable.

Hyperlinking: A web-based element that allows readers to access data on another web page by clicking on a word or phrase that has been attached to the link.

Identification: An element of a libel claim that requires the person claiming to be libeled to be clearly identifiable in the potentially libelous material.

Image hierarchy: The positioning of photos, graphics or other display elements into an ordering that indicates overall importance.

Immediacy: One of the five key interest elements. This element emphasizes the timely nature of content, with the newest information being seen as the most important.

Impact: One of the five key interest elements. This element emphasizes the degree to which the information will affect the audience members. It can be measured quantitatively and qualitatively.

Independent clause: A collection of words that works as a complete sentence and expresses a complete thought.

Infinitive phrase: A collection of words that use the infinitive form of the verb plus at least one modifier or complement.

Instructive graphic: An interactive visual that demonstrates action in a step-by-step approach.

Interest elements: Informational aspects of content that are used to draw audience members to content.

Intrusion: A standard of invasion of privacy that prevents journalists from entering private areas to gather material for publication.

Inverted pyramid: A format of journalistic writing in which information is provided in descending order of importance. The higher a fact is in the copy, the more valuable the writer thinks it is.

Jargon: Terminology that is specific to a field that people outside of that field have difficulty understanding.

Jump line: A traditional media term that denotes to a reader that more content exists on another page. (At the bottom of an incomplete front-page story, the notation "FIRE, see PAGE 3" is an example of a jump line.)

Kerning: The addition or reduction of space between specific letters and numbers.

Keywords: Terms that define or relate to your content that allow search engines to find it.

Kicker: A headline treatment that uses a short phrase or a few words to lead into the main headline.

Leading: The spacing between lines of type. Tight leading means that little space exists between the lines, while loose leading means that additional space exists between the lines.

Libel: A false published statement that damages a person's reputation.

Localization: A writing approach in which a journalist covers a broader issue from a local angle. A story that explores how the Affordable Care Act will affect doctors within a newspaper's audience is an example of this form of story.

Long shot: Also called a wide shot, this type of video approach is used to showcase a lot of action within a frame to provide the viewers with a sense of place or activity.

Medium shot: A photographic approach that provides a smaller slice of a larger event. It is used to capture interaction between two people or the actions of a single individual.

Meta tags: A collection of words that appear in a web page's code to provide search engines with additional information regarding the content on the page.

Microediting: A term to describe corrections focused on punctuation, grammar, spelling and other small copy errors.

Misappropriation: A standard of invasion of privacy stating that people have a right to determine when their likenesses, voices and other items associated with them can be used to promote something.

Modular design: A layout approach that presents text and images in rectangular blocks to provide cleaner overall structure.

Mug and chatter box: A simple graphic that provides a head shot of an individual and a quote from that person regarding a topic of interest to readers. It can augment a story or stand alone.

Mug shot: A photograph of an individual from the middle of the chest to the top of the head.

Narrative graphic: An interactive visual that provides readers with a story about an event, idea or topic.

Negligence: A standard of fault in libel cases that requires the plaintiff to show only that the publisher of the content did not make reasonable efforts to prevent the libelous activity. This is a standard used for private individuals in libel suits, and it is easier to prove than actual malice.

Nominalization: The creation of a noun from an adjective.

Nonrestrictive clause: A collection of words that adds extra information to a sentence but is not crucial to fully understand the sentence. This is also known as a nonessential clause. Example: "My wife, who ate blueberries for breakfast, lives in Omro."

Notebook emptying: A poor journalistic practice in which every piece of information a writer gathered is wedged into a piece of copy.

Noun phrase: A group of words that serves as a subject or an object in a sentence.

Oddity: One of the five key interest elements. This element emphasizes rare feats, strange occurrences and "news of the weird."

Off the record: An agreement between a source and a journalist to conduct an interview in which the source will not be identified within the story.

Ollman test: A four-part test used to differentiate fact from opinion in cases of libel. It is named after the 1984 court case Ollman v. Evans.

Online Copyright Infringement Liability Limitation Act (OCILLA): A federal law used to protect internet providers and website managers from copyright lawsuits based on content posted on their sites or via their organizations by outside parties.

Opt-in: A marketing technique that allows interested consumers to notify an organization that they wish to receive additional information via email or social media.

Owner: A leadership style in which the person in charge uses the position as one of power and control. This leadership style does not concern itself with the person being liked but rather the overall outcomes that best fit the leader's expectations.

Pace: The speed at which a reader can move through a story on the basis of how it is structured. This speed is also influenced by the use of punctuation and the length of sentences in the piece.

Participial phrase: A collection of words that begins with a verb and includes at least one modifier or complement.

Passive voice: A form of sentence structure that places the subject of the sentence in a position in which it is receiving the action of the verb. (The ball was hit by Bill.)

Personality profile: A feature story that explores the life of an individual through in-depth reporting and observation.

Pie chart: A graphic that uses segments of a circle to demonstrate numerical portions of a larger whole.

Pixel: A digital measurement that represents the smallest physical element of an image on a screen.

Pluralism: An ethical standard stating that more than one ethical value exists at any point and that those values compete for dominance in the decision-making process.

Point: A measurement equal to 1/72 of an inch often used to indicate text size.

Prepositional phrase: A collection of words that includes a word of placement as well as a descriptive noun related to it. Example: "Ralph left his keys on the table." ("On" is the preposition, "table" is the object of the preposition and the whole thing, "on the table," is the prepositional phrase.)

Process diagram: A graphic used to demonstrate action in a step-by-step approach.

Pronoun: A word that replaces or refers to a noun.

Pronoun agreement: The requirement that nouns and their pronouns be parallel in terms of number.

Psychographics: A set of characteristics audience members hold, including, but not limited to, personality traits, values, interests and attitudes.

Publication: An element of a libel claim that requires the potentially libelous content to be sent to someone other than the person claiming to be libeled.

Public disclosure: An aspect of invasion of privacy in which a person is accused of publishing information about a regular person that is private without his or her permission and that offends sensibilities.

Puffery: A term often associated with advertising in which media professionals can "puff up" the value of a product without relying on facts or in a way that cannot be objectively disproved. This is akin to hyperbole and is often viewed as legally protected speech.

Qualified privilege: A legal standard that allows journalists to quote officials acting in their official capacity without fear of libel.

Redundancy: Words within a sentence that are unneeded and repetitive.

Sans serif: A font family that lacks small strokes on the edges of letters and numbers. It means "without serifs."

Satire: A legal standard that allows writers to publish commentary that uses humor and ridicule to draw attention to topics of public interest without fear of libel, as long as a reasonable person could not believe the content to be true.

Scoop: An exclusive story garnered by a journalist at one media outlet that is published before other outlets in the field.

Search engine optimization: The process of formatting content on a website to improve its overall position on the list of returned results.

Serif: A small stroke found on the edges of letters and numbers in some typefaces. This is also used to describe typefaces that contain letters and numbers with these strokes.

SERP: Abbreviation for "search engine results page."

Servant leader: A leadership style in which the person in charge works for the people under him or her. This leadership style involves heavy collaboration from subordinates and the provision of support to them.

Sharpening: A visual editing process that creates contrast between pixels in the image to pull out details within a frame.

Short message service (SMS): Also known as simple messaging service, this is another term for text messaging, referring to the way in which users can send short digital messages to one another via mobile devices.

Simulative graphic: An interactive visual that allows users to experience something in a hands-on fashion via the web.

Slug: The portion of a news release that includes essential facts about the person responsible for the release, such as the person's name, title and contact information.

Social media: Digital information-sharing tools and approaches that allow people to gain information on the basis of their interests from a variety of sources in a many-to-many media model.

Stock art: Images that represent concepts but that aren't directly attached to the story in any meaningful way.

Subject-verb agreement: The requirement that singular nouns receive singular verbs and plural nouns receive plural verbs.

Subordinating conjunction: A word that precedes a subordinate clause.

Subreddit: A digital area dedicated to a specific topic of interest on the social media site Reddit.

Sunshine laws: State laws that provide access to documents and information crafted by public officials. These are also known as "open-records laws" and are intended to keep public officials honest and provide transparency in governmental dealings.

Surveillance need: An element of a communication theory that describes how human beings have an inherent desire to know what is going on around them.

Teammate: A leadership style in which the person in charge works with everyone else in the organization on an equal footing. This leadership style tends to emerge in people who work in a "flat" organization.

Timeline: A graphic that demonstrates events over a chronological period.

Title tag: A web coding process that determines how much information will appear at the top of the browser's window bar.

Toning: A visual editing approach that shifts the darkness or brightness of an image.

Tracking: The addition or reduction of space between letters and numbers in blocks of text.

Transparency: A public relations approach that allows everyone within your audience to see what happened in a situation and why it happened.

Unnamed source: A person used within a story who is known to the reporter and/or the editor but whose identity was not divulged to the public.

Utilitarianism: An ethical standard that attempts to create the largest overall benefit through the minimization of harm or the maximization of gain, regardless of the impact on specific individuals involved in the dilemma.

NOTES

Chapter 1

1. Jeffrey Gottfried and Elisa Shearer (2017, Sept. 7). "Americans' Online News Use Is Closing in on TV News Use." Accessed at: http://www.pewresearch.org/fact-tank/2017/09/07/americans-online-news-use-vs-tv-news-use/.

2. Associated Press and NORC (2017). "New Understanding: What Makes People Trust and Rely on News." Accessed at: http://www.mediainsight.org/Pages/a-new-understanding-what-makes-people-trust-and-rely-on-news.aspx.

3. Robinson Meyer (2018, Mar. 8). "The Grim Conclusions of the Largest-Ever Study of Fake News." The Atlantic. Accessed at: https://www.theatlantic.com/technology/archive/2018/03/largest-study-ever-fake-news-mit-twitter/555104/?utm_source=atlfb.

4. Kevin McSpadden (2015, May 14). "You Now Have a Shorter Attention Span Than a Goldfish." Time. Accessed at: http://time.com/3858309/attention-spans-goldfish/.

5. David Manning White (1950). "The 'Gate Keeper': A Case Study in the Selection of News." Journalism Quarterly, 27, 383–391.

6. Cathy McNamara Fitzgerald (2013, Aug. 27). "Readership Surveys: 10 Good Reasons Why." Accessed at: http://associationmediaandpublishing.org/sidebar/Readership-Surveys-10-Good-Reasons-Why?&Sort=.

7. Mu Lin (2014, May 29). "Web Analytics for Newsroom and Classroom: Essential Metrics Journalists Should Know and Use." MulinBlog. Accessed at: http://www.mulinblog.com/web-analytics-for-newsroom-and-classroom-essential-metrics-journalists-should-know-and-use/.

8. Vincent F. Filak, (2015). "Dynamics of Media Writing." Thousand Oaks, CA: Sage.

9. "World's Largest Ball of Paint." Accessed at: https://www.roadsideamerica.com/story/9792.

Chapter 3

1. Parker, R. (n.d.). "Valentine v. Chrestensen (1942)." Accessed at: https://mtsu.edu/first-amendment/article/212/valentine-v-chrestensen.

2. Parker, R. (n.d.). "Central Hudson Gas and Electric Corp. v. Public Service Commission (1980)." Accessed at: https://mtsu.edu/first-amendment/article/198/central-hudson-gas-and-electric-corp-v-public-service-commission.

3. LoMonte, F. (2013, Feb. 11). "Stop the Courts From Weakening Student Journalism." Chronicle of Higher Education. Accessed at: https://www.chronicle.com/article/Stop-the-Courts-From-Weakening/137221.

4. Craig, B. (2008, Dec. 9). "Korean Cleaners Sue The Pants Off Infinite Energy Gas Company." Accessed at: https://www.lawyersandsettlements.com/articles/consumer_financial_fraud/pardue-lawyer-interview-11630.html.

5. Crisco, A. (2016, March 24). "Atlanta Attorney Cleared in Defamation Suit." Courtroom View Network. Accessed at: http://blog.cvn.com/atlanta-attorney-cleared-in-defamation-suit.

6. Wiser, M. (2014, May 16). "Supreme Court Rules Against Rick Bertrand in Defamation Suit." The Gazette. Accessed at: http://www.thegazette.com/subject/news/public-safety/courts/state/supreme-court-rules-against-rick-bertrand-in-defamation-suit-20140516.

7. Cornell Law School, Legal Information Institute (n.d.). Hustler Magazine, Inc. v. Falwell. Accessed at: https://www.law.cornell.edu/supremecourt/text/485/46.

8. Schultz, E. (2005). "Michael Moore: A Biography." ECW Press.

Chapter 4

1. Knight Foundation (2018, Jan. 15). "10 Reasons Why American Trust in the Media Is at an All-Time Low." Accessed at: https://medium.com/trust-media-and-democracy/10-reasons-why-americans-dont-trust-the-media-d0630c125b9e.

2. Shephard, S. (2017, Oct. 18). "Poll: 46 Percent Think Media Make Up Stories About Trump." Politico. Accessed at: https://www.politico.com/story/2017/10/18/trump-media-fake-news-poll-243884.

3. Patterson, P. & Wilkins, L. (2013). "Media Ethics: Issues and Cases." 8th ed. New York: McGraw-Hill Education.

4. Mellon, S. (2017, Jan. 6). "Can Terry Bradshaw Spell 'Cat'? The History of an Insult." Pittsburgh Post-Gazette. Accessed at: https://newsinteractive.post-gazette.com/thedigs/2017/01/06/can-terry-bradshaw-spell-cat-the-history-of-an-insult/.

5. Reid, J. (2011, March 13). "Jalen Rose's Comments on Race in ESPN Documentary Are Misguided." The Washington Post. Accessed at: https://www.washingtonpost.com/sports/jalen-roses-comments-on-race-in-espn-documentary-are-misguided/2011/03/12/ABFHbLS_story.html?utm_term=.925c46b31bec.

6. "Debating the Rules and Ethics of Digital Photojournalism." (2015, Feb. 17). The New York Times. Accessed at: https://lens.blogs.nytimes.com/2015/02/17/world-press-photo-manipulation-ethics-of-digital-photojournalism/.

7. Kennerly, D. (2009, Sept. 17). "Essay: Chop and Crop." The New York Times. Accessed at: https://lens.blogs.nytimes.com/2009/09/17/essay-9/.

8. Bronx Documentary Center. "Altered Images." Accessed at: http://www.alteredimagesbdc.org/oj-simpson/.

9. Palmer, T. (2018, Feb. 25.) "Commentary: A New York Times Picture Is Worth a Thousand Lies." Albany Times-Union. Accessed at: https://www.timesunion.com/opinion/article/Commentary-A-New-York-Times-picture-worth-a-12706740.php.

Chapter 6

1. Flesch, Rudolph. (1949). "The Art of Readable Writing." New York: Harper.

Chapter 10

1. Jennifer George-Palilonis (2013). "The Multimedia Journalist." New York: Oxford University Press.

Chapter 11

1. Jennfier Kyrnin (2007). "About.com Guide to Web Design: Build and Maintain a Dynamic, User-Friendly Web Site Using HTML, CSS and Javascript." Adams Media.

2. Kim Golombiski and Rebecca Hagen (2016). "White Space Is Not Your Enemy: A Beginner's Guide to Communicating Visually Through Graphic, Web & Multimedia Design" (3rd ed.). Boca Raton, FL: AK Peters/CRC Press.

Chapter 12

1. Spencer Frady (2010, May 29). "Fanfare: Stories of the Most Loyal Indianapolis 500 Fans." Indianapolis Motor Speedway. Accessed at: https://www.indianapolismotorspeedway.com/news-multimedia/news/2010/05/29/fanfare-stories-of-the-most-loyal-indianapolis-500-fans?startrow=2484.

2. Jake Malooley (2018, May 29). "Hell Is Real and It's the Infield of the Indy 500." Deadspin. Accessed at: https://deadspin.com/hell-is-real-and-its-the-infield-of-the-indy-500-1826375331.

3. "Sheboygan Police Arrest Suspected Toilet Clogger" (2018, May 29). WBAY.com. Accessed at: http://www.wbay.com/content/news/Sheboygan-Police-arrest-suspected-toilet-clogger-483990511.html.

Chapter 13

1. Justine Timoteo (2017, January 16). "How to Build a Social Media Following in 2017." Accessed at: https://www.impact-bnd.com/blog/grow-social-media-following; Karisa Egan (2016, September 19). "Are You Posting Too Much on Social Media?" Accessed at: https://www.impactbnd.com/blog/are-you-posting-too-much-on-social-media.

2. "Cryptocurrency Waltonchain Rewards Employee in User Give Away And Outs Itself on Twitter" (2018, March 1). Accessed at: https://thenextweb.com/hardfork/2018/03/01/cryptocurrency-waltonchain-twitter-fake/.

3. Andrew Munroe (2018, March 1). "Waltonchain Price Plummets as Twitter Mishap Shows Faked Giveaway." Accessed at: https://www.finder.com.au/waltonchain-price-plummets-as-twitter-mishap-shows-faked-giveaway.

4. Geoff Weiss (2014, Dec. 5). "Sephora Mistakenly Rolls Out Vulgar Hashtag." Entrepreneur. Accessed at: http://www.entrepreneur.com/article/240530.

Chapter 14

1. Dennis L. Wilcox and Bryan H. Reber (2016). "Public Relations Writing and Media Techniques." 8th ed. Boston: Pearson.

2. Philip Rucker (2018, May 10). "White House Official Derides Mccain Over Haspel Opposition: 'He's Dying Anyway.'" Washington Post. Accessed at: https://www.washingtonpost.com/politics/white-house-official-derides-mccain-over-haspel-opposition-hes-dying-anyway/2018/05/10/b8aa4422-54a2-11e8-a551-5b648abe29ef_story.html?utm_term=.486148977b7b.

3. Vincent F. Filak (2019). "Dynamics of Media Writing: Adapt and Connect." 2nd ed. Thousand Oaks, CA: Sage.

Chapter 15

1. Jonathan Chan (2017, Jan. 4). "3-Step Guide for Telling a Compelling Brand Story." Huffington Post. Accessed at: https://www.huffingtonpost.com/entry/3-step-guide-for-telling_b_13956386.html.

2. Rand Fishkin (2017, Dec. 27). "How to Rank in 2018: The SEO Checklist." Accessed at: https://moz.com/blog/rank-in-2018-seo-checklist.

INDEX